150 years of

True Crime Stories

from the *News of The World*

150 years of

True Crime Stories

from the *News of The World*

JEAN RITCHIE

Michael O'Mara Books Limited

First published in 1993 by
Michael O'Mara Books Limited
9 Lion Yard
Tremadoc Road
London SW4 7NQ

A CIP catalogue record for this book is available from
the British Library

ISBN 1–85479–911–8

Designed and typeset by Florencetype Ltd,
Kewstoke, Avon
Printed in England by Cox & Wyman, Reading

Contents

Acknowledgments

The author and publishers would like to thank the following people for helping in the preparation of this book: Pat Chapman, Sue Carroll, Tony Harris, Peter Picton, Martin Malin, Conrad Hafenrichter, Mark Lomas, John Young, David Rigby, Gary Jones, Andre Dupre, Melanie Aspey, Eamonn Dyas, the *News of the World* Archive and all the staff at the *News of the World* Reference Library.

Picture Acknowledgments

Unless otherwise stated the pictures in this book are reproduced with the kind permission of the *News of the World*: Keystone (Hulton Picture Company): plate 6, below; plate 11, above. The Press Association: plate 2, below; plate 7, above; plate 13, above.

1. 'Extraordinary Occurrence . . . Much Sensation'

In the flickering gas light from Davies' coal wharf in Lambeth a labourer, one of a gang working a night shift loading barges with sacks of coal, caught a glimpse of something struggling in the murky waters of the Thames. He called to his mates, and they peered out into the gloom.

'It's a woman! And she's alive!' one of them yelled. They shouted to the figure in the water but the woman, weighed down by her long skirts and petticoats, was unable to reply. The labourers watched as she was twice dragged under by the current, but twice surfaced, still struggling. Two of the men pushed one of the barges out into the river and, with a great deal of difficulty, they were able to haul the exhausted girl on board and get her back to the bank.

The girl, a very pretty seventeen-year-old servant girl called Emma Munton, was half dead. She had been drugged, brutally raped, and pushed into the river to die. It was only her own determination to cling to life – and the chance observation of a coal labourer – that rescued her from a watery grave. She was pulled ashore at one o'clock in the morning of Friday, 21 September 1843. Nine days later the story of Emma's narrow escape made the front page of a newspaper that had never been published before: the *News of the World*.

The savage rape of the servant girl was the first crime story ever covered in the paper, a newspaper which, over the next 150 years, would make the coverage of crime its greatest speciality. Her story had all the ingredients that have, ever since, fascinated the paper's millions of readers. The reporting style may have been different, the look of the newspaper, with very small type and no photographs, may have been very different; but the details of the appalling attack on an innocent girl started the tradition that the paper has held ever since.

'Extraordinary occurrence – much sensation was created in Lambeth under the following circumstances,' said the headline over Emma's story. Emma, who was described in the report as 'very handsome', had been working as a servant to a wealthy middle-class family. She had been drugged, raped and thrown into the Thames by a young doctor whose surgery she had visited to buy medicine for her mistress's child.

The *News of the World* was born on 1 October 1843, into a world that Charles Dickens was describing in his novels. The young Queen Victoria, just twenty-three years old, had been on the throne for five years, the country was in the grip of the industrial revolution and ordinary working people had to endure harsh conditions. But the growth in education meant that more of them could read and write, and the *News of the World* came into existence to give them something to read. From its very first issue, the paper knew that crime is a fascinating and important subject. The importance of crime – and particularly murder – stories to the paper and its readers has never changed.

Every big crime committed in Britain (and many

abroad) is covered in detail by the *News of the World*. The paper has had scoops, it has handed murderers over to the police, it has extracted confessions from killers, it has received letters from criminals condemned to hang, it has had phone calls from killers on the run. On one notable occasion it was the *News of the World* that handed over a hanged murderer's clothing to Madame Tussaud's museum where it can be seen to this day on the waxwork model of its owner, acid-bath killer John George Haigh. Within the last couple of years it has saved a wife from being the victim of her husband's hitman.

Looking back at the crime covered in the first issue, it is the similarities, and not the differences, between the paper then and the paper now which stand out. Crime has not changed a great deal, it seems. The *News of the World* in the 1840s based its circulation on sales in London, and so it covered many details of the courts sitting in London, with a round-up of news stories, including crimes, from 'the country', meaning anywhere outside the capital. It had a more parochial, local-paper feel to it. But the major crimes were all there, covered in the same kind of detail, though without the attention-grabbing headlines, that we are familiar with today.

In that very first issue of the paper there was a bizarre kidnapping story from Liverpool. A tall, good-looking, wealthy black man, who was married to the daughter of an English peer, had recently arrived in the city and was staying, with his servants and a doctor, at the Adelphi Hotel. The doctor was needed because the man, from the East Indies, had recently been declared insane and was in Liverpool for 'a change of air'. One night he disappeared wearing his nightclothes but with a large sum of money on him. The *News of the World* report guessed that he had been kidnapped and was being held by thieves who would keep him until the money ran out.

Manchester – Supposed Murder was another headline:

'Some lads, being out early with their dogs and passing Messrs Tweedale's mill at Broadley, one and a half miles from Rochdale on the Bacup road, they observed an apron, a handkerchief and a pair of clogs by the waterside and something in the middle of the dam, like a human head, floating a little above the water', was the first paragraph of the story.

When the body was fished out it was that of a local mill girl, eighteen years old, and she had obviously, from the extensive details given in the report, been beaten to death before being thrown into the river. The report quaintly stated that she was 'supposed to be enceinte but from medical examination the contrary was found to be fact'. In other words, she'd told people she was pregnant, but she wasn't.

This was enough in itself to give the man described as 'her sweetheart' a motive, perhaps; but the report carried details of his alibi – he could prove he was at home in bed when she met her fate.

The report ended: 'It is currently stated and fully believed that the unfortunate girl has met with foul play from some hand at present unknown, as the wounds upon her face and neck could scarcely have been inflicted by herself.'

From Huddersfield came a report of a 'Diabolical Attempt at Incendiarism', when arsonists tried to set fire to a flour mill. From Sunderland came a spate of smuggling cases, with local sailors bringing tobacco and rum ashore. The Customs and Excise officer who foiled one attempt was watching a French ship leave port, accompanied by a local tugboat. Through his telescope he saw that, when the French vessel dropped her line to the tug, the tug went close alongside. Something else, as well as the line, was dropped into the tug; when it docked the Customs men were waiting for it and found a crate of rum bottles.

From the cathedral city of Wells, in Somerset, came a fascinating report of the arrest of a notorious highwayman, Gipsy Jack – probably the last highwayman to be tried in Britain as his crimes had been committed sixteen years earlier. He had evaded capture at the time, and was popularly believed to be dead or to have been transported to penal servitude in Australia for crimes committed elsewhere in the country. But a young London policeman, who had been born and brought up in Somerset, spotted him at Smithfield meat market and recognized him from posters he had seen in his youth. He followed him to a village in Leicestershire but did not arrest him because he was not sure whether or not Gipsy Jack had already been imprisoned for his crimes. But when the policeman reported back to his superior officer, the ex-highwayman was arrested and taken to Wells where he was remanded to stand trial at the next Assizes.

The London court reports were less dramatic, but just as entertaining. Many of them read like extracts from any local-paper coverage of magistrates courts today: there was a policeman assaulted by two Irishmen during a pub disturbance, there was a pub landlord and one of his customers coming to blows over a small disagreement, there was a more serious pub fight in which a 'pugilist' or boxer carried out a 'brutal and serious' assault on a publican.

There was a youth remanded for stealing, an unemployed man who had been caught stealing butter, and another youth fined £5 for threatening behaviour towards his parents after they suggested that he was old enough to move out and earn his own living.

A seventy-six-year-old widow was embezzled out of £500 – a small fortune in 1843 – by a manager employed to run her business after the death of her son two years earlier. A 'perfectly sober' cartman was remanded in custody for killing a girl under the wheels of his distillery cart. He had shouted a warning to her as she tried to cross the road in front of him as his horses pulled the cart round a corner. The cart swung wide, the girl became confused and did not know in which direction to run, and was knocked down. The cartman stopped immediately and tried to help her, but she died.

Fraud was as common then as it is now. A man was remanded for trial at a higher court for running a phoney charity, and claiming to be the nephew of the Lord Mayor of London, in order to obtain clothes on credit from tailors. And at Marlborough Street magistrates court a 'masculine-featured Scotchwoman' was charged with attempting to obtain goods under fraudulent pretences. She claimed to be 'Lady Elizabeth Charlotte Berkeley Craven', and had duped an unfortunate young groom into believing she was going to marry him. He believed they would honeymoon in Paris, and then set up home in Corfu, where they would have three carriages with their coats of arms emblazoned on the side. Although he believed she was rich and titled he handed over his watch and £5 to her. She was arrested attempting to buy clothes for her 'fiancé' on credit.

Domestic violence, caused by drunkenness, was probably even more common than the court reports suggest, with most of it going unreported – as it still does today. There were two cases in the first issue of the *News of the World*, both resulting from men attacking their wives while they were the worse for drink.

One, a man called John Sweet from Brentford, was sentenced to 'hard labour at the House of Correction for one calendar month' for attacking a policeman who tried to save his wife from violence. The paper reported that 'the prisoner looked aghast at his sentence which appeared to give great satisfaction to a crowded court'.

He obviously felt it was a tough sentence. But when you read the chronicle of evidence against him, he got off lightly. His wife apparently dragged him, drunken and protesting, from the bed of a prostitute in the early hours of Saturday morning. As he went home with her he threatened her loudly, and she called to a policeman that she felt her life was in danger. The policeman followed the warring couple towards their home, and arrested Sweet when he saw him hit his wife. Sweet then turned his violence on the policeman, punching him to the ground and kicking him 'brutally in the groin'. Eventually Sweet broke away, rushed into his own house and came out with a 4ft-long crowbar with which he started to attack the constable. Screams from neighbours brought more police who managed to arrest and subdue Sweet.

Some of the cases were not the sort we would ever see in modern newspapers. A vicar and his son were charged with stealing a coffin and 'its remains', presumably to sell the body for medical research. But as the son had absconded to France the case had to be adjourned. Tragically, a young girl was brought before the court with her baby, charged with attempting suicide. She had been found on Blackfriars Bridge, threatening to throw herself off. Suicide was a crime in those days, but the court dealt with her leniently. She had apparently been thrown out of St Mary's workhouse, Newington, London.

'More task work was set her than she could possibly perform, and for this she was deprived of her meals, and altogether she was so miserable there that she thought any life, or no life, preferable,' the court was told. The magistrate told the police to take her back to the same workhouse and explain what had happened to her. At least she was not fined or sent to jail – though whether or not she was able to cope with all the work they made her do at St Mary's, we will never know.

Another case – one which made front-page news on 1 October 1843 – is one that would not happen today. A Woman Poisoned by Endeavouring to Procure a Miscarriage was the headline, and the report told of the arrest of a twenty-four-year-old oil-shop proprietor, William Haines, after the death of his wife. He appeared in court 'frantic with grief'.

She had apparently been taking 'sulphate of potass' which had been recommended in a cheap medical publication as a way to bring on a miscarriage. The couple already had one child but could not afford another. Although the defence was that the woman took the potion herself, therefore her husband could not be guilty of killing her, the magistrates ordered him to be remanded for trial because it was an offence 'of serious description' to attempt to procure an abortion. Haines was tried for murder four weeks later, and was acquitted. He was then tried again, two months later, for attempting to procure an abortion, and was sentenced to two years' hard labour.

There were some success stories, too, among the crime reports in the first edition of the *News of the World*. The Case of the Girl Murphy was the headline over a touching story about a young girl who had been rescued from a life of prostitution.

About three weeks since, a Mrs Murphy, residing in Princes Street Vauxhall, applied to Mr Clive, the sitting magistrate, stating that her daughter, a girl about 13 years of age, had been decoyed by a woman to Plymouth. The magistrate kindly gave the woman 10s [50p] to assist her in her journey to Plymouth, and on the second day from the application Mr and Mrs Murphy came to the magistrate with the gratifying intelligence that they had found their daughter at Plymouth and, although discovered in one of the vilest houses in the town, she had successfully repulsed all the efforts of her decoyer and other parties, although the struggle almost cost her her life as she was perishing from hunger when found by her father. The publication of a statement embracing the above facts has, we understand, had the effect of bringing a host of friends around them and the girl has the fairest chance of doing well in the world.

That is how the first issue of the *News of the World* introduced its readers to the fascinating world of courts and crime. The dressing may have changed, but the recipe has remained more or less the same for the following 150 years. In this book we look at a selection of the major crimes of the last century and a half, all of them taken from the files of Britain's biggest circulation newspaper, the *News of the World.*

2. Poison and Passion

When the old lady began to feel sick it was only natural that her doting nephew, a qualified doctor with whom she was staying for a few days, should give her some pills to make her better. But Aunt Bentley was a tough old girl, she didn't really approve of all this new-fangled medicine, she preferred to let nature take its course. So the next morning, when her nephew William came to see how she was, he noticed the pills untouched on the dressing-table. He seemed strangely upset that the old lady hadn't taken them, and not at all pleased to hear that she was feeling better. To calm him down, Aunt Bentley promised to take them that evening.

Not wishing to offend him again, that night Aunt Bentley opened her bedroom window and threw out the pills, and then settled down for a good night's sleep. But she was woken early by the cries of the servant girl whose job it was to feed the chickens, kept in a run just below Aunt Bentley's bedroom. Several of the birds were dead – and there was no trace of the tablets that the old lady had thrown out.

Aunt Bentley had had a very narrow escape. She could have become yet another victim of Dr William Palmer who killed at least fourteen people and ranks as one of the greatest serial killers in British criminal history. His trial in 1856 was one of the most celebrated in Victorian England. One court at the Old Bailey had to be rebuilt to accommodate all the lawyers and expert witnesses. Queues started at 5am for places in the public gallery and a rollcall of the side galleries – where influential people sat – read like a page from *Debrett's Peerage*: the Duke of Wellington, the Marquis of Anglesey, the Earl of Derby, the Earl of Denbigh and plenty of other 'eminent persons', as the *News of the World* described them.

Palmer was on trial for murdering by poisoning one of his closest friends. But the charge was only the tip of the iceberg: the rollcall of those he killed included his wife, his uncle, his mother-in-law and several of his own children, as well as friends and acquaintances. If he had managed to cheat the hangman on the charge of killing his friend, the prosecution was prepared to go ahead with a charge of murdering his wife, Annie.

Palmer himself, who enjoyed all the attention he was getting, was convinced he would get off – he even placed a £100 bet with a friend who visited him in jail that he would be out in time for the 1856 Derby.

The full details of Palmer's murderous career will never be known: he took them to the gallows with him. But his first victim was probably a man called Abley who Palmer killed when he was only a twenty-one-year-old apprentice. He gave Abley, an illiterate shoemaker, a glass of brandy containing strychnine, which killed his unfortunate victim the same day. No suspicion was aroused and Palmer's motives are not clear; one theory is that he was having an affair with Abley's wife, another is that he was simply experimenting out of fascination with poison.

William Palmer, who was born in 1824, came from a

wealthy Staffordshire family. He was thirteen when his father died, leaving Palmer's mother, Sarah, very comfortably off, and a massive £70,000 fortune to Palmer's oldest brother Joseph. William himself inherited £9000 (the equivalent of £540,000 today) on his twenty-first birthday.

Young William was an able but lazy pupil at school; even before he left, at the age of seventeen, he had developed a taste for the two things that were to be his downfall: horseracing and women. He was apprenticed initially to a chemist's firm in Liverpool, in those days a standard pre-training for young men who wanted to be doctors. Drugs and medicines were sold by the doctors who prescribed them, and one of Palmer's duties was to make up the pills and potions. He did not last long in the job, however, being caught stealing money from letters addressed to the firm, to fund his betting habits.

He took another apprenticeship, this time in Hayward, Cheshire. He stayed in this job for five years, but only because it took his employer, a rather unworldly elderly doctor, a long time to find out what he was up to.

Palmer loved girls, and found a ready supply of maids and serving girls who were seduced by his quick line in chat and the fact that he came from a class above them; he promised them all marriage and a happy future, but gave them only misery – and babies. In an age before sophisticated contraception, Palmer faced the problem of a succession of unplanned pregnancies. He started a private and illegal practice in abortion, originally to get rid of his own problems, but then he expanded to provide a good source of ready cash for his betting.

Astonishingly, even with his illegal medical practice to help him, he fathered fourteen illegitimate children in five years. The fates of all these children, and their mothers, is not known; it could be that Palmer had already embarked on his main career, as a poisoner, as he certainly, later on, included his own illegitimate children in his list of victims.

When the doctor who employed him found out about the abortion clinic Palmer was sacked for 'grossly abusing his master's hospitality'. His family's good connections were used to get him another job, this time at Stafford Infirmary, where he started his training as a doctor. It was while working there that he conducted his trial run on Abley; after that, anyone who stood in Palmer's way was likely solicitously to be offered drinks and pills prepared for them by his own fair hand.

It was only after his eventual arrest, ten years later, that Palmer's earlier crimes were uncovered, and the chronicle of his poisonings was built up. An amazing number of people who came into contact with him were taken ill and died; it was impossible, afterwards, to exhume all the bodies and nobody knows for certain whether any of them were, genuinely, accidental deaths or whether Palmer murdered all of them. What is certain is that he wasn't a man from whom to accept a drink.

After Abley his next victim was one of his own illegitimate children; he asked for the child to visit him, and shortly afterwards it was stricken with convulsions and died. By this time Palmer, who had used his inheritance to pay off his mounting gambling debts, was courting his wife, Annie, who was the illegitimate daughter of a colonel in the Indian army. She was not a beautiful young woman, but she came with a large dowry and Palmer was desperate for money.

He was an ardent suitor. When he left Staffordshire for St Bartholomew's Hospital in London, to finish his studies and get a certificate allowing him to practise as a doctor, he wrote to her:

Dearest Annie,

I snatch a moment to write to your dear, dear little self. I need scarcely say that the principal inducement I have to work is the desire of getting my studies finished, so as to be able to press your dear little form in my arms.

With best love, I am, my dearest Annie, ever yours,
William.

It may not be long and passionate, as love letters go, but it was enough to persuade the plain and homely Annie that she had found her ideal husband: a loving man with a bright career – as a doctor – ahead of him. The proliferation of illegitimate children around him was obviously an embarrassment to Palmer, and at this stage the numbers of them were rapidly whittled down by the 'medicines' he prescribed.

So, tragically, were Annie's own children. After Palmer qualified, he came back to his home town of Rugeley in Staffordshire, married, and put a brass plate outside his door announcing that he was a doctor. Four of his and his wife's babies died in the first few months of their lives, always with convulsions, or, at least, that's what it said on the death certificate. Only one of Palmer's legitimate children survived, a boy called Willie who was seven at the time of his father's execution. Palmer appeared to dote on Willie but in his diary, found after his death, there are ominous references to Willie being ill – perhaps he just had a stronger constitution than his brothers and sisters. Palmer's diary recorded the illnesses of his victims with cryptic remarks and strange underlinings, his own secret hit-list code.

Children, to him, were an unnecessary expense and he had other things to spend his money on; although he should have been able to make a good living, he was obsessed with gambling and was frequently away from town, attending race meetings and building up colossal debts. His practice in Rugeley could have been a thriving one, as the only other doctor in the town was a Dr Bamford who was in his eighties and not in the best of health.

His mother, Sarah Palmer, apparently adored her wayward son, but even she was not prepared to subsidise his extravagances indefinitely. On more than one occasion he was reduced to forging her signature in order to obtain credit.

One easy way to get rid of debts, Palmer decided, was to eliminate the men to whom he owed them. The first to go was a man named Bladon who was invited to stay with the Palmer family in 1850. Soon after arriving he was taken ill. Palmer was treating him, and when it was obvious that death was near, he called in the elderly, and slightly senile, Dr Bamford. Mrs Bladon arrived but was given no time on her own with her husband before he died. Bladon's friends were suspicious of Palmer and urged Mrs Bladon to go to the police. But Palmer turned his charm on her and she accepted his explanation of her husband's death, describing the deadly doctor as a 'wonderful friend'.

Having successfully eliminated one person to whom

he owed money, Palmer then poisoned a man called Bly. Before his death Bly managed to tell his wife that Palmer owed him £800; when she tried to collect the debt after her husband's funeral Palmer calmly turned the tables and told her that he was the creditor, and asked her for the £800 (the equivalent of £48,000 today) he claimed Bly owed him. Mrs Bly eventually had to write the money off as a bad debt.

Palmer now turned his attention to his family and his wife's family. One of his uncles on his mother's side, a man as partial to drink and debauchery as Palmer himself, was challenged to a brandy drinking match. Palmer poured the brandy out, measure for measure; the only difference was that Uncle Beau's glass contained strychnine, and within three days he was dead.

Aunt Bentley was next in line for the Palmer treatment. As we have previously heard, while staying with William and his wife she began to feel ill but did not take the pills her doting nephew gave her. When she saw their effect on the poor old chickens, she fled to the safety of her own home. It was only after Palmer's arrest that she realized what a narrow escape she had had.

His mother-in-law only survived for two weeks in the Palmer houshold. She was a wealthy woman and, on her death, a substantial sum of money passed to her daughter; under the law at the time, a married woman's property belonged to her husband, so William Palmer came into a tidy little sum to help with his debts.

It was probably all too easy for him. He certainly never made any effort to control his wild spending at the race track and get his life on a more even keel; in 1853 he wagered £10,000 on the Oaks, a fortune which, in today's terms, would be the equivalent of £600,000. The horse lost.

Life at home was far from easy. Annie was worn down by the loss of her children, and the dissipation of her personal fortune. She also knew that her husband had a taste for young serving girls, and a habit of making them pregnant. She was no longer prepared to play the role of the quiet, long-suffering wife, and the atmosphere in the house was tense. Palmer decided she had to go.

But first he took out an insurance policy on her for £13,000. He kept the policy going for a few months, and then poor old Annie fell desperately ill and died in September 1884. The ancient Dr Bamford signed the death certificate, saying that she had 'English cholera', and Palmer acted the part of a man in deep grief with great conviction.

The insurance company paid up, but the money was only enough to settle Palmer's most urgent debts and he was, in the words of the *News of the World*, in 'great pecuniary difficulties'. So he decided to repeat the insurance company swindle, first by insuring his brother Walter, a layabout drunkard, for another £13,000. Palmer plied his alcoholic brother with drink in the hope that he would die of alcohol poisoning, but Walter was not obliging enough to do this. In the end, he was stricken with convulsions after a drinking bout with something even stronger than brandy in his glass.

This time, though, the insurance company was suspicious and refused to pay out straightaway. Palmer was still battling to get his hands on this money at the time of his arrest. One reason for the suspicion may have been that, before Walter's death, Palmer had tried to persuade a groom working in his stables, an illiterate and simple man, to take out an insurance policy on his own life for £25,000. Palmer persuaded the man that it was to his benefit: unfortunately for the doctor, the insurance companies who were approached made inquiries about the groom, Bates, whom they had been told was a man of standing and wealth. It did not take them long to discover that he was not rich, and they refused to insure him.

Consequently, when poor Walter shuffled off this mortal coil in a haze of brandy, the insurance company which held the policy on his life started an inquiry. One of the boys working at the hotel where Walter died told them that he had seen Palmer put something into Walter's drink; on hearing about this, Palmer went to the hotel and used his great charm to persuade the youth, who ought to have known better, to have a drink with him. For several days after this the boy had severe stomach pains which eventually cleared up.

After Annie's death Palmer found consolation in the arms of serving girl, Eliza, who had a baby by him in June 1855. Eliza refused to accept a lump sum to keep Palmer's name off the birth certificate but, in the end, agreed not to name him as the father in return for an allowance to be paid during the child's life, until the baby boy was grown up. Her biggest mistake was to tell Palmer that his baby son was unwell; Palmer gave her some tablets which made the baby much worse. When she went to see her lover again to tell him that the medicine was making the baby much worse, Palmer brazenly replied that he was not surprised, that was what he expected the tablets to do. Three days later the child died.

Now Palmer embarked on what was to be his final murder. One of his best friends and gambling cronies was a twenty-eight-year-old man called John Parsons Cooke. Cooke was, like Palmer, a young man from a good family. He had been destined to train as a lawyer but, when he inherited £15,000, he gave up his studies and, as the *News of the World* put it, 'betook himself also to the turf'. He bought racehorses and gambled almost as heavily as his friend so that, by November 1855, he was also heavily in debt.

Cooke's best racehorse, Polestar, ran in the second race at Shrewsbury on 11 November 1855, and he and Palmer and two other friends were at the racetrack to see it win. Cooke had bets laid on it, and won. Palmer now had two reasons to murder Cooke: to get his hands on the winnings, and because he had forged Cooke's name as security on debts he had taken out with money lenders.

The 'friends' celebrated the victory that evening with a dinner at the Raven Hotel, Shrewsbury, with Cooke meeting the bill. The following day they were still celebrating and their two friends, Herring and Fisher, joined them for a meal. It was while drinking a glass of brandy that Cooke leapt up and shouted, 'Good God, there's something that burns my throat.'

Palmer replied 'Nonsense' and, seizing the glass, he drained the dregs of the brandy and then thrust the glass at both Herring and Fisher for them to smell it. Cooke was immediately taken ill – attacked, as the prosecution were to say in court, 'with most violent vomiting'.

The following day Cooke felt better and lent some

money to Palmer who immediately lost it at Shrewsbury races. That evening Palmer persuaded Cooke to return with him to Rugeley where Cooke took a room at the Talbot Arms. The next morning, after drinking a cup of coffee handed him by Palmer, he was taken very ill again, and remained very ill while Palmer was ministering to him. Palmer ordered broth at another hotel in the town, and his servant brought it back to his house. From there he sent it to Cooke who started vomiting after taking just a mouthful.

The next day Palmer went to London with Cooke's betting receipts and collected his friend's £500 winnings. He used it to pay off some of his own most pressing debts. While he was away Cooke was looked after by Dr Bamford and began to get better. By the time Palmer returned from London two days later, he was up and dressed. Palmer soon remedied that: he got rid of the pills Dr Bamford had prescribed and continued to dose Cooke with his own medication, probably containing strychnine or prussic acid.

But Cooke was taking too long to die, and Palmer was under enormous pressure to pay some more debts. He tried forging a cheque for £350 with Cooke's name on it, but the forgery was so clumsy the bank refused to accept it. Finally, he gave Cooke some more pills and the dose this time was so strong that the patient went into massive convulsions, doubling up in spasms of pain, and died a few minutes later. In death all his muscles were taut and his fists were tight clenched.

Palmer hastily sent for two women to lay out the body. They later told the Old Bailey that, when they arrived, they found Palmer going through his dead friend's pockets and looking under his pillow. 'Apoplexy' was the cause of death recorded on the death certificate.

Within hours of the murder, Palmer forged a document showing that his friend owed him £4000. Cooke's stepfather, who disapproved of his stepson's dissolute lifestyle but was highly suspicious of his death (Cooke was a healthy young man), refused to honour the debt and demanded an autopsy.

When the autopsy was held Palmer was present. To his consternation, he learned that Cooke's stomach was to be removed and put into a jar to be sent to London for analysis. When the doctor who removed the stomach was putting it into the jar, Palmer 'accidentally' lurched against him, causing some of the contents to be spilled. He laughed and said, 'They will not hang us yet.' Later, when the doctor asked where the jar had been put, he discovered that Palmer had spirited it to a doorway, and when it was retrieved the seal that had been placed over it had been slit in two places, although nothing had been removed.

When these ploys failed, Palmer next offered £10 to the post-boy whose job it was to take the jar to London for analysis, if he would drop and break the jar. The boy refused and later gave evidence against Palmer. No strychnine was found in Cooke's stomach, a fact that Palmer discovered to his relief when he got hold of the letter containing the results of the analysis. He sent a present of game to the coroner, pointing out that the results of the tests had been negative.

But, by this time, so much evidence had been collected that Palmer was well and truly under suspicion. As soon as word leaked out that he was being investigated, more and more people came forward with bizarre tales of their relatives dying while being treated by Palmer. The bodies of Palmer's wife, Annie, and brother Walter were exhumed.

Palmer was arrested first of all on a writ from a money-lender, and while he was in custody he became very ill – he may have been taking his own medicine. He was so ill, in fact, that he was returned to his own home and held there, under guard, until he recovered sufficiently to be taken to jail. Local feelings against him were running very high, and the police were busy day and night keeping crowds away from his home. For this reason, and for the first time in British criminal history, it was agreed that his trial should take place away from the scene of the crime – the Stafford area – because of the difficulty of choosing an impartial jury. An act of parliament was passed – known as the Palmer Act – to allow his case to be transferred to the Old Bailey.

Excitement throughout London was enormous. In the days before television, trials were a favourite entertainment, ranking alongside music halls. And if the trial was a celebrated murder case, where the accused would probably be sentenced to death, the interest was phenomenal.

To the annoyance of the court officials, it was announced that admission to the public gallery would be free – in the past they had regarded the selling of seats as one of the perks of their job. The announcement increased the demand and the crowd; people who would have stayed away, knowing that they could not afford to buy their way in, thronged the road outside the court. Despite the statement put out by the Home Secretary's office that 'It has been positively determined to discourage as much as possible the making of the court into a show,' that's exactly what did happen.

For weeks before the trial, both defence and prosecution lawyers ordered experiments with poisons; medical evidence would take up about half the twelve-day trial.

Hawkers had a field day among the crowd outside the Old Bailey; in the days before newspapers could print photographs, everyone wanted to see what the poisoner looked like. Pictures of him were sold at a penny a time, most of them bearing no real resemblance to him. One unscrupulous trader was actually selling pictures of William Cobbett, the radical politician who had died twenty years earlier; the surname was scratched off and Palmer printed over it.

When Palmer appeared in court the *News of the World* reporter wrote this description of him: 'His countenance has a fresh and florid look and the clearness of his complexion gives him a very different appearance to that exhibited generally by prisoners under a charge so serious.' His features were described as 'commonplace' and his demeanour 'remarkably tranquil, indeed cheerful'. He was, apparently, 'very stout'. He wore a black frock coat and a black silk neckerchief throughout the trial.

Despite an eight-hour address to the jury by the defence lawyer, it took the jury only an hour and fifteen minutes to find Palmer guilty. He was taken from the dock with 'a sneering expression' on his face. The judge had ordered that he be executed at Stafford, 'for the sake of example', and the night the case ended Palmer, in leg irons and handcuffs, was taken in a first-class train carriage from Euston to Stafford. He was hanged on 14 June 1856, and the rope used to hang him was made by a porter at Stafford station (who allowed his friends, for a fee, to help plait it). Extra portions of it were later sold off to the 50,000-strong crowd who turned up to witness the execution.

Palmer was self-possessed to the very end and refused to confess to his crimes. When asked straight by the prison governor at Stafford whether or not he had killed John Cooke, he claimed that Cooke did not 'die from strychnine'. He was probably playing with words; despite the wealth of medical evidence, there was no decision in court as to what poison had killed Cooke, although the judge in his summing up suggested it was strychnine. Palmer may have been correct in saying that it was not death from strychnine, but there's very little doubt that it was death at his hand.

He claimed innocence all the way to the gallows, his last words being 'I am a murdered man.' His last request in jail was to 'see to my mother and my boy'. His family stuck by him, his brother George was in court by his side every day and his mother took in the orphaned Willie. The trial was enormously expensive, costing £9000, a third of which had to be paid by Palmer's family.

It is a fitting epitaph for him – and one that he would have enjoyed – that after the trial the government condemned the fact that an estimated £200,000 had changed hands in bets on whether or not he'd be found guilty.

If Palmer was a cold and calculating murderer, Elliot Bower was the opposite. Bower killed in the heat of anger and with a fair amount of provocation. Luckily for him, although both he and the victim were English, the crime occurred in France and the French court was ready to sympathize with a man whose wife had been unfaithful to him. He was acquitted.

At the time of the murder Elliot Bower was a thirty-eight-year-old journalist working for a popular daily newspaper, the *Morning Advertiser*. He was married to Fanny Vickers, a young woman who had been widowed early in life. She had a child from her first marriage and two more by Bower. The couple had a mutual friend, Saville Morton, who had been at Cambridge with Bower and who had known Fanny since they were both children. Morton was also a journalist, working for the *Daily News* – a paper which, at the time, was being edited by Charles Dickens.

Bower and Morton were both sent out to Paris, as correspondents for their respective newspapers, and they continued to be good friends. Fanny, lonely in a foreign country, relied on Morton for companionship and English conversation.

One day in 1850 Morton arrived at the Bower apartment in Rue Seize to find Fanny in a very distressed state; she had received a letter from a woman called Isabel Laurie, giving her details about an affair Mrs Laurie had had with Fanny's husband Elliot. Mrs Laurie's motive was revenge: Elliot Bower had seduced her and then dumped her. She was not the only mistress he had taken during his ten-year marriage to Fanny, but the others had remained discreet. When Fanny accused him, he became very angry and threatened her.

Fanny was described by those who knew her as 'excitable' and she now turned to Saville Morton who seemed to be able to calm her down. Gradually, their closeness developed into an affair and Morton, who believed he should do the right thing by Fanny, consulted several lawyers in London about the possibility of her divorcing Bower. The advice was the same from all of them: she would be ruined, and so would he, if she tried to get a divorce. In those days the scandal attached to divorce was enormous, and even more so if the woman broke away from her husband.

In 1852 Fanny gave birth to another baby, her third since marrying Bower, who assumed that the child was his. Throughout the pregnancy she became more and more neurotic, a condition described in the *News of the World* report of Bower's trial as 'a state of excitement that was the precursor of the derangement which subsequently affected her intellect'.

When the baby was born she sent the concierge from the apartment block, where she and Bower lived, with a message to Morton:

'Go and announce to Mr Morton that I have been confined, that the baby resembles him, that I cannot send him a lock of its hair but that he shall have it soon.'

Morton said, 'Ah, what misfortune!' when he heard the news, but he stood by Fanny when, two weeks later, she became very ill with a high fever, a relatively common occurrence at the time in the days after childbirth. Whilst she was running a high temperature Fanny became even more deranged, and Morton rushed to her bedside, sleeping on a couch in her room. Bower agreed to this as Morton seemed to be the only person who could calm his wife down.

Fanny's family also rushed to Paris as it looked as though she was going to die. She demanded that a priest be brought to her, and she renounced the Protestant faith and became a Roman Catholic – but even the priest who received her into the Church was of the opinion that she was insane.

For most of her illness she refused to see her husband but eventually, on 1 October 1852, she called him into her bedroom while the rest of the family, including her sister and her mother-in-law, stayed in the dining-room. She was delirious and shouted at Bower that he was the cause of all her troubles; she accused him of violence and held tightly clutched in her hand the letter from Isabel Laurie. Finally, she announced:

'That baby is not yours, it is Morton's.'

'If I believed that, I would kill the infant,' cried Bower.

Then Fanny called her sister and said, 'Queen of England, drive away that man.'

Bower rushed out to the dining-room where Morton was sitting with the relatives. Bower seized a kitchen knife and rushed at him. Bower's mother tried to stop him and grabbed his coat, but he pulled away from her and it ripped. He caught up with Morton on the stairs and stabbed him with the knife in his throat below the left ear. The carotid artery was severed and Morton bled to death.

Bower went back upstairs and was described at his trial as standing there 'like one annihilated'. But after a few minutes, and with the help of the others there, he collected himself, changed his clothes, took some money and escaped down the back stairs.

He went to England where he stayed for three months. Eventually, he returned to France and surrendered himself; he was tried in Paris three days after Christmas.

Fanny had by this time recovered her sanity and was back to full health, but there were sufficient witnesses – including the priest – to testify that, at the time of Morton's death, she had been unhinged. Being France, the defence lawyer argued that, as Fanny had been unfaithful to Bower with Morton, Bower had every right to kill Morton. Being France, the argument was accepted by the court and Bower was acquitted. He would not have been dealt with so leniently under British law.

Fanny returned to England with the children and went into mourning for Morton. Because of the scandal of their private lives being so publicly exposed – the story was extensively carried in newspapers on both sides of the Channel – Bower's career was in ruins.

3. Confession to Murder

It is possible to commit the perfect murder . . . as long as you can live with your own conscience afterwards. It may seem easy at first when the relief of getting away with it is all that counts. But gradually, as the years slip by, the weight of guilt can become too great to carry – as two of the most sensational crimes of the 1860s proved. Both murders had one thing in common: they would never have been solved if the killers had not confessed. And, in both cases, the confessions came several years after the murders were committed.

One case is the story of some very mixed-up and unhappy teenagers, traumatized by the illness and death of their mother and resentful of their new stepmother. The other is the tale of a husband whose guilty conscience about the death of his first wife finally got the better of him.

The murder of three-year-old Francis Kent at his home in the village of Road, near Frome, in Somerset, took up many column inches of the *News of the World* for the whole of the second half of 1860. Francis was the son of a factory inspector, and the family lived in a large secluded house, Road Hill house, on the outskirts of the pretty village.

It was a large family by modern standards, although

not large for Victorian England. Mr Kent had been married twice, his first wife dying in 1853. She had been ill for some years and her husband had employed a governess, a well-educated young woman who was the daughter of a tradesman in Tiverton, Devon. The governess's duties were to look after and educate the two younger Kent children, Constance and William. Their two older sisters, Mary Ann and Elizabeth, were already in their twenties by the time their mother died.

Mrs Kent's ill health was mental as well as physical, and Constance, who was nine when she died, and William, a year younger, grew up with the spectre of her illness haunting the house; they had to keep quiet and they did not enjoy any normal motherly cuddles and love. The *News of the World* described their mother as 'afflicted in mind and incapable of attending to the discharge of her household duties'; this meant that she stayed in bed most of the time and took no interest in her husband or children.

The governess did her best, and the children appeared to get on well with her for the six years she was with the family before their mother died. After her death, though, there was a change. It became clear that Mr Kent had more than an employer's interest in the young woman who was caring for his children, and fifteen months after his first wife was buried he married the governess.

Constance and William resented this sudden change. The young woman who had been a paid member of the household – and therefore socially below them – was suddenly their stepmother. However much she tried to get on with them, they were determined to give her a difficult time. They resented her even more when, ten months after the wedding, the ex-governess started to produce her own children: first, Mary Amelia, then Francis, then Eveline Fanny, and by 1860 there was another one on the way.

The two older children were so unhappy that in 1856, after the birth of the first of the new family, they ran away together. William cut Constance's long hair off and she parted it at the side, like a boy, and dressed herself in some of his clothes. They set off on foot for the nearest seaport, Bristol, where they hoped they would be able to sign on as ship's boys. When they reached Bath they went to the Greyhound Hotel and asked for a room for the night. The landlord's curiosity was aroused because, he said later, of 'their respectable dress and superior manners' and the fact that one of them was wearing clothes that were obviously too small, and they were both footsore and weary. He contacted the police and shortly afterwards one of Mr Kent's servants arrived in Bath on horseback. He had been pursuing the runaways and they were taken home to face their father's anger.

Not long after this, Constance and William were sent away to boarding school and only spent their holidays at the house at Road. Constance was a good pupil, bright and well behaved, taking home the second prize for good conduct. But although she impressed the teachers, some of her schoolfriends later described her as devious, always able to make herself appear in a good light by putting blame on to others.

She told a couple of her friends that she was unhappy at home. She seemed particularly worried about her brother William, telling one friend how he was forced to push the pram with his young brother or sisters in it, which he hated, and that her father had been heard saying what a much finer man Francis would turn out to be than William. When another friend commented to Constance on how nice it was that the holidays were near, and how pleasant it would be to leave school and go home, Constance replied:

'Yes, perhaps it may be to your home, but mine is different.'

What she did enjoy about going home for the holidays was being reunited with William. In the summer of 1860 Constance was sixteen and William fifteen; they had both returned from their different boarding schools only a few days before the horrific death of their half-brother Francis who was three years and ten months old.

Francis and Eveline Fanny, who was two and a half, shared a room with their nursemaid, twenty-three-year-old Elizabeth Gough. Francis was sound asleep when the maid went to bed at 11pm and when his mother came in to kiss him about half an hour later. But when Elizabeth woke at 5am she realized he was not in his bed, on the other side of the room from her. She assumed that he had gone into his mother's room, so she lay down again for another hour.

When she got up at 6am she knocked at his parents' bedroom and asked Mr Kent if the boy was there. When his father said that he was not, the whole household started to search for him. It was then that a maid discovered that the door from the drawing-room into the garden was unlocked; this must have been done from the inside. It had been locked the previous evening. While Mr Kent rode off to inform the police, young Francis's body was found in the outside privy in the garden, over 100 yards from the house.

His body was stuffed into the toilet and his throat had been slashed so viciously that he was almost decapitated. He had also been stabbed in the chest through the blanket he was wrapped in as well as his nightclothes; there were two slight cuts on his right hand that had been made after his death. The chest blow would have required much force, according to the doctor's report. The time of death was estimated to have been before midnight – in other words, shortly after his mother had tiptoed into the room to kiss him and his sister.

It was clear, even on the most superficial examination of the evidence, that the boy had been murdered by someone from inside his own home, or someone living there had given the killer access to the house. He had been taken from his bed and the bedclothes rearranged tidily, without waking the nursemaid or the other child in the room. He had been carried downstairs, through the drawing-room, across the lawn, through the shrubbery and the stableyard, to the privy. A guard dog, a large Newfoundland hound, was loose in the grounds, and although it would not bark at anyone it knew, it would have roused the household at any suspected intruders.

Francis was apparently a large child, too heavy to be carried for long. He was described by the nursemaid, Elizabeth, as a cheerful and happy boy. Poor Elizabeth was top of the list of suspects, and before the case was over she was twice held under arrest.

On the day after Francis's body was found the local magistrates held an inquiry at the village Temperance Hall. They called Mr and Mrs Kent, the family's three maidservants, including Elizabeth, a manservant, the boy who cleaned the knives and the washerwoman and her daughter. After hearing evidence from them all, Elizabeth Gough, who had said before the inquiry that she was 'so conscious of her innocence that she would go before a hundred judges and be examined', was arrested and taken to Trowbridge Police Station. She fainted when told she was being taken into custody.

But there was no evidence against Elizabeth. The Home Secretary decided that the case had to be investigated more thoroughly, and a detective was sent from Scotland Yard to the small Somerset village – the first time in British criminal history that a Yard detective was sent outside the capital. The government also put up a reward of £100 which was matched by Mr Kent with another £100.

The detective, Inspector Jonathan Whicher, soon freed Elizabeth Gough and told her that she could go wherever she pleased; she returned to her work at the house at Road Hill. Whicher quickly tracked down two ex-servants who had been dismissed by Mr Kent, and might have a grievance against him, and found they both had watertight alibis. He also carried out an experiment by removing a sleeping child from a room where adults were asleep and found that it was easily possible.

His suspicion fell on Constance, and four weeks after the date of the crime she was arrested. The main reason for suspecting her was a missing nightdress. Constance's clothes, with those of the rest of the family, were regularly collected by a washerwoman who laundered them at her own cottage in the village. A maid at Road Hill house counted them all into the bundle, checking them against a list given her by each of the older members of the family, including Constance. But by the time the bundle reached the home of the washerwoman a nightdress of Constance's was missing. The maid said that, after making up the bundle in the lumber room, Constance came in and, after a few moments, asked the maid to fetch her a glass of water. Whicher believed that during the minute that the maid was away she removed her own nightdress and returned it to her room.

The reason for this action, he argued, was that she had destroyed the nightdress she wore to commit the crime, and wanted to cover for its loss by arranging to 'lose' another in the wash.

The *News of the World* claimed that Constance shouted out, 'I am innocent,' when she was arrested. 'She walked with a firm step from her father's house but she was in tears.'

She was remanded in custody for a week and taken to the county jail at Devizes but, at the end of the week, she was released. While she was held, the magistrates heard evidence about her relationship with her little half-brother – and heard two completely different stories. One of her schoolfriends said:

'She said she disliked the child, and that she liked to tease it more for fun than anything else; she did not express any ill feeling towards this child more than to the other two young ones.'

She claimed that Constance had told her that the second family was better treated than the first, and that her stepmother would never let her choose dresses that she wanted, but would insist on her having colours and styles that the stepmother preferred.

Constance, however, described her stepbrother in the following terms:

'Francis was a merry, good-tempered child, fond of romping. I had played with him that day,' Constance said. 'He appeared to be fond of me and I was fond of him.'

A defence solicitor, engaged for Constance by her father, told the magistrates that there was 'not a tittle of evidence against her'. He said that although an atrocious murder had been committed, arresting Constance was 'a judicial murder no less atrocious'. His words swayed the magistrates who released Constance against Inspector Whicher's better judgment. Her father was ordered to put up £200 bail, guaranteeing that Constance would appear before the court should they want to call her again. The day she was released her stepmother gave birth to another baby, a boy called Samuel.

The press now turned on Whicher, taunting him with falsely accusing Constance and nearly causing a gross miscarriage of justice. Whicher was recalled to London, deeply hurt by the criticism. He retired from the police three years later.

Rumours were now rife and Child Killing at Road was a headline that appeared every week in the *News of the World*. In the middle of August there was a sensational development when a man, claiming to be the murderer, gave himself up to the police, but it was quickly obvious that he knew nothing about the crime. He was an epileptic, suffering from depression because his wife had left him. He was held in custody for a week and then given his fare back to London.

Suspicion now switched back to Elizabeth Gough but

this time she was linked with Mr Kent; it was broadly hinted that Mr Kent was her lover, and that Francis had woken up and witnessed them making love in the nursery and he had been killed to stop him talking. One of the magistrates said: 'The deceased had witnessed something improper and that is what led to the commission of the foul deed.'

Elizabeth could take the gossip no longer, and gave in her notice. She said she was 'constantly watched and distrusted', and complained that nobody was allowed to sleep with her – the other young children were sleeping in their parents' room, and none of the other domestic staff was willing to share a room with her.

Life must also have been hell for the rest of the family at Road Hill house; the police constantly had to clear away crowds of sightseers who made daytrips in their ponies and carts to view the place. Three young men had to be evicted from the garden by Mr Kent. When he challenged them they retorted that, as there was a £50 reward for the recovery of the missing nightdress, they had to be given the opportunity to look for it.

Every member of the family was subject to rumour and speculation. The second Mrs Kent was reported to be 'a common mill girl', and to have been cohabiting with Mr Kent before his wife's death, and even to have given birth to her first child within a few weeks of her marriage to him – there was no evidence to support any of these rumours.

Yet another inquiry into the whole affair was set up, this one run, at the government's instigation, by a solicitor from Bath. By this time, fifteen-year-old William was being touted as the prime suspect, but he dropped down the list of favourites when Elizabeth Gough was once again arrested. Again, the only evidence was very flimsy. A piece of flannel found in the privy when the body was discovered was believed to be a 'chest flannel' worn by Elizabeth – in those days women frequently placed a piece of warm material under their clothes to keep them from chest infections. It was not enough to justify holding Elizabeth, and once again she was released.

Gradually the story slipped out of the headlines. It became one of many unsolved crimes, although it was a particularly intriguing one because the number of suspects was so small and they were all intimately connected with the victim.

Mr Kent and his family moved away from the area, first to a house they owned at Corsham, near Chippenham, and then to Wales. Constance left the family home and joined a religious community at Dinan, in France, where she stayed for two and a half years. She returned to England in 1863 and went to live at St Mary's Home, a home for religious ladies, in Brighton. While she was there she fell very much under the influence of the Mother Superior, Miss Greame, and the curate from St Paul's Church, Brighton, the Reverend Arthur Wagner.

To the astonishment of the whole nation, at Easter 1865 Constance Kent walked into Bow Street magistrates court in London and handed the magistrates a written confession to the murder of her half-brother. It said:

I, Constance Kent, alone and unaided, on the night of the 29th June 1860 murdered at Road Hill house, Wiltshire, one Francis Saville Kent. Before the deed no-one knew of my intention nor after it of my guilt. No-one assisted me in the crime nor in the evasion of discovery.

Constance had told Arthur Wagner a fortnight earlier that she intended to confess. She had written to her father to prepare him and then, in the company of Miss Greame and Mr Wagner, travelled to London. The Bow Street magistrates decided that her confession had to be heard in Trowbridge, near the scene of the crime, and she was taken there.

The story in the *News of the World*, The Road Murder. Confession and Surrender of Constance Kent, was carried on the same page as – and merited as many column inches as – the announcement of the assassination of Abraham Lincoln, the American President.

When she appeared in court before the Trowbridge magistrates the *News of the World* reporter described her as short and stout and 'possessing none of the delicacy of figure or appearance that has been attributed to her'. He said she seemed to be much healthier than she was in 1860; in Victorian times, being 'stout' was regarded as being in good health. The confession, he reported, was written in beautiful handwriting but on very ordinary notepaper. When it was read out in court Constance broke down in floods of tears.

She was taken to Devizes jail again, this time to await trial at Salisbury Assizes. Her small bare cell would have been very similar to the ones she was used to in her religious life, and friends were allowed to supply her with a bed and books. Her father visited her in jail and, although the meeting was described in some daily papers as very emotional, the *News of the World* was at pains to correct that impression. Constance, the report said, had been very calm and composed with her father.

The case came to trial five years and three weeks after the death of the three-year-old boy. The court was very crowded but the spectators were disappointed; because Constance confessed to her crime, no witnesses were called, the details of the crime were not elaborate, and the whole thing was over within a couple of hours. The most dramatic moment came when the judge put on his black cap to pronounce the death sentence. He was, apparently, trembling and crying as he said the words. This reduced Constance to tears, too, and they both sobbed loudly.

One of the spectators at the trial was the hapless Elizabeth Gough who had twice been held in custody for the murder. Despite rumours that she had emigrated and married a rich Australian sheep farmer, she had been living in London and working as a barmaid. The magistrates at Trowbridge organized a public collection for her as compensation for the suspicion she had remained under until the day of the confession.

The death sentence on Constance was commuted to life imprisonment because Constance was so young at the time the crime was committed. She did not, herself, reveal details of the murder, but a letter was published in *The Times* from a doctor who was called to examine her mental state. He was asked to determine whether or not she was sane, and his conclusion was that she was. It is possible, though, that had she wished she could have pleaded hereditary insanity; not only was her mother of unsound mind but so, too, was her grandmother and her uncle. She chose not to: Constance had decided that she wanted to face the music.

The doctor's letter explains her version of how she killed Francis. She took and hid one of her father's razors some days before the murder, and also hid a candle and matches. She carried the child out of his bedroom and through the house and garden and killed him in the privy, afterwards realizing that her nightdress was stained with blood. She tried to wash it out in the water bowl in her room, but when she held it up to the light could still see the stains. Eventually she burned it in her grate and tried to shift the blame for its loss on to the washer-woman. Her motive was revenge against her stepmother for making disparaging remarks about the older children.

Constance served twenty years in prison; she was released in July 1885. She was still only forty-one years old. She changed her name to Ruth Emilie Kaye (Emilie was her middle name, and the surname was K for Kent) and went to live in Tasmania with her brother William and his wife, later moving with them to Australia. She worked as a nurse and lived until April 1944, dying shortly after her 100th birthday.

The real truth about the murder of little Francis died with her, because she never confided in anybody about it, even after William's death. Did she do it alone? Or did she do it with her brother? Inspector Whicher believed they were in it together. Certainly, if Constance did it on her own, she exhibited much strength and determination.

If she did it with her beloved William, she remained true to him to the very end.

Constance Kent served twenty years behind bars for a crime she could have got away with: William Sheward is another murderer who could have lived out his life in freedom if his conscience had not got the better of him. He was hanged for his confession to a murder he committed almost eighteen years earlier.

Sheward, who was described by those who knew him as 'quiet and inoffensive', was first married to a woman called Martha Francis who was fifteen years older than him. He met her when she worked for him as a housekeeper in Greenwich. After their marriage the couple moved to Norwich, not far from Martha's family home. Sheward worked as a tailor and scraped a living for the two of them, but they were not happy. Martha, who was a neat, well-dressed woman with long, curly hair, was a bit of a shrew who believed her husband was careless with money. They were also sexually incompatible: he was highly sexed and she was not, and the age difference meant that they would never have the children which Sheward wanted.

On 15 June 1851 the couple had a vicious row about money. Sheward had given a mutual friend £400 to look after for them and, unknown to his wife, he had also given the friend permission to borrow some of the money. Martha Sheward wanted the money back and was threatening to go round to the friend's house to retrieve it. They rowed violently and Sheward snapped; he grabbed a razor with which he cut her throat.

He was remarkably composed, covering the body with an apron, and settling himself on the sofa for a night's sleep. The following day, a Sunday, he had promised to go to Yarmouth on an errand for a friend, and he did, spending another night in the same room as his wife's corpse. On Monday, he got up and went to work at his tailor's business. By the time he returned home the house had begun to smell, and he realized he had to get rid of the body.

This is where the crime becomes gruesome. Sheward took a sharp knife and began mutilating the body, chopping it up into smallish pieces. Between 9.30pm and 10.30pm he walked around the Thorpe area of Norwich disposing of the bits. He returned home, had another night's sleep, went to work the next day and repeated the procedure the following evening. He did this all week. He cut off his dead wife's hair and let the wind blow it away. He tried to boil certain portions of the body, including the hands and feet, in a bid to make them unrecognizable, and on one evening he emptied a pan full of entrails down a drain in one of the city's main streets. On the sixth night he burned all the bloodstained sheets and blankets, and his wife's clothing.

The first the public knew about Sheward's grisly missions was when a dwarf, taking his dog for a walk in the countryside near the city, noticed the dog emerging from a hedgerow carrying something in its mouth. When they got home the lump of rotting flesh was clearly identified as a human hand. Over the next two months forty pieces of the unfortunate Mrs Sheward were retrieved, including both hands (one with the ring finger cut off) and both feet, but no head. Some bits of the body were pickled in spirits of wine and preserved at the Guildhall in Norwich.

The citizens of Norwich were convinced there was a sex killer loose in their midst, an impression that was increased when the police put up notices asking for information. On the posters the dead woman was described as between sixteen and twenty-six. This deflected attention from William Sheward's missing wife who was fifty-four at the time of her death. Gradually, when the discovery of pieces of corpse ceased, and there was no information about any young girls in the right age group being missing, the public lost interest in the case. (One serving girl who had eloped with her sweetheart was popularly supposed to have been the victim, but she turned up safe and well.)

Sheward was able to convince friends and his wife's family that she had left him, taking all their money, and had gone to live in Australia or New Zealand. Her brother was suspicious, but unable to prove anything. After Martha's death Sheward set up in business as a pawnbroker, but he was no more successful at this than he was at tailoring.

A year after Martha died he met a much younger woman and they lived together for a few years. Eventually, in 1862, they married. By this time they had three children and another three were born in the next eight years. Sheward's business failed and, in 1868, he and his wife and family moved to the Key and Castle Tavern in St Martin-at-Oak, Norwich, where he was the publican. Again, his lack of business sense meant he failed to make a good living, and the family lived in acute poverty.

Just after Christmas 1868 he was depressed and he told his wife that he was going to London to see his sister. Instead, he spent two days wandering around the capital trying to pluck up the courage to commit suicide. But in those days suicide was regarded as a very serious sin – and a crime – and it seems that Sheward preferred to clear his conscience before going to his Maker. On New Year's Day 1869 he walked into Wandsworth police station, unshaven and dirty and probably also hungover, and told the startled station officer that he wished to confess to murder.

He was taken before Lambeth police court to make a full confession. Afterwards, he wrote a letter to his wife saying that he was in trouble and that she would soon find out just how much trouble he was in.

Sheward, who was by then fifty-seven and severely crippled with rheumatism, was taken back to Norwich to stand trial. He pleaded not guilty, having tried to retract his confession when he fully sobered up. In the dock he was asked about the disposal of the body and he broke down and sobbed, 'It is too horrible to talk about.' The prosecution tried to argue that he had already met his second wife at the time of the murder, but they failed to prove it.

He was sentenced to hang. From prison he wrote to his wife, who was left to cope with children aged from eight months to fourteen years:

I want you, by God's help, to forget me, save knowing that I have gone to eternal rest ... I am very sorry and heartily grieved that I should have been the instrument of drawing you into all this trouble and affliction, and I sincerely thank you from the bottom of my heart that you have been able to forgive me, so that now I shall be able to rest in peace with God and man ... I think if you look back for this past two years you will see the handywork of the Almighty in reducing our stock and trade and taking nearly everything from us as a judgement on me for my hidden crime.

He was executed inside Norwich Castle on 20 April 1869. For a few years after the case the name 'Sheward' was used as a slang expression to describe anything gruesome, and just the mention of the word was enough to have delicate ladies reaching for their smelling salts.

4. 'A Bad, Bad Man'

'Quick, Dad, the police are coming!'

The small, wizened little man with the dyed hair did not need to be told twice. He pushed his plate of mutton stew away, darted out of the back room of the café, upstairs and out of the bedroom window. With astonishing agility he shinned up a drainpipe and on to a roof where he hid behind some high chimney stacks. He stayed up there until he saw the two cops leave the café. They were questioning his wife about where he was – she swore she hadn't seen him for days.

As soon as they'd gone he came down off the roof by the same route. His stew was still warm, so he finished his meal and was just settling down to smoke his pipe when the warning came again: somebody had tipped them off and the police were coming back. This time the little man did not lurk behind the chimneys but was off over the rooftops and away.

Charlie Peace was a double murderer, a thief, a liar, a hypocrite and a philanderer. He was ugly, yet he was attractive to women. He was a good musician, a good storyteller, a good companion. He was daring and clever, a master of disguises who avoided capture for many years with insolent ease.

He claimed to be religious – but he was prepared to let another man go to the gallows for one of his murders.

For many years after he was hanged at Armley Jail, Leeds, in 1879, the story of Charlie Peace was part of criminal folklore. If Jack the Ripper had not knocked him off his perch, he would have been the most celebrated criminal of the nineteenth century.

Peace was born in Sheffield in May 1832. His father was a respected tradesman in the city, running a shoe-making business. He sent his son to school, but the boy was not interested in learning and acquired only a basic ability to read and write. He showed early on, though, that he was good with his hands. At thirteen he was apprenticed at a steel mill in Sheffield, but was badly injured when a red-hot steel rod rammed into his leg. He was helpless for eighteen months, unable to walk and initially not expected to live. But eventually he recovered. He was bandy-legged which, coupled with the limp left by this injury, gave him a very peculiar lopsided gait.

Work did not suit Peace. He wanted money, but he wanted it the easy way and, by the time he was twenty, he had embarked on a life of crime. He could play the violin well – well enough to be billed the Modern Paganini at the local music halls – but he found that this did not bring in a steady income, and he took to housebreaking. At the beginning he wasn't very good at it and he was caught four times and sent to jail, the sentences increasing in severity. Eventually, after serving six years, he was caught again and sentenced to ten. He became involved in a prison mutiny, for which he was flogged, and was sent to finish his sentence in the penal colony on Gibraltar. He behaved himself there and, after six years, he was released and returned to Sheffield. He was always fascinated by firearms and had blown off one of his own fingers while messing about with a pistol.

He married a woman called Hannah Ward, a widow with a son, and they had two more children. Outwardly, Peace was a respectable man with a picture-framing and gilding business in the village of Darnall, close to Sheffield. He sent his children to Sunday school and attended church regularly with his wife. As well as picture frames he also dealt in musical instruments and curios. He was popular with his neighbours because, despite being a small, ugly, monkey-like man, he had a lot of charm and was very hospitable with plenty of drink in the house.

His neighbours did not realize, however, that Peace bumped up his income by regular burgling forays into the city and neighbouring towns. He was extremely agile, small enough to fit through tiny windows, as happy walking along narrow rooftop ledges as he was along the ground, and well versed in the ways in which the police worked.

On one occasion, when he found a policeman drunk on his beat, he realized it was his lucky night and burgled six houses in a row. On another occasion, when he found a safe in a downstairs room, he cheekily went upstairs, removed the keys from the trouser pocket of the house-owner as the trousers lay on the bed in which the man was sleeping, went back downstairs and made off with the family silver.

One vicar who came to the church at Darnall knew Peace – he had been a prison chaplain while Charlie was inside. He thought that Peace had mended his ways and promised to say nothing about his past as long as Peace continued to lead an honest life. Peace swore he would. Three weeks later he burgled the vicarage.

While the family was living in Darnall Peace fell desperately in love with a woman called Catherine Dyson who lived with her husband and five-year-old son two doors away from him. Kate Dyson was young, very pretty, plump and liked a good time. She was Irish, but had met and married her husband Arthur in America. Arthur, who was 6′5″ tall – a phenomenal height in those days, which caused him to be stared at in the street – was a civil engineer who worked for railway companies. Kate had been nineteen when she married him in Cleveland, Ohio. They returned to his native Sheffield seven years later and had been living in Darnall for two years when they came to know Charlie Peace.

Arthur Dyson was a clever, gentle man, who disapproved of drink and was devoted to his family. Kate felt that marriage to him had deprived her of a lot of fun: she was very fond of drinking, loved the music halls and generally wanted a more exciting life than Arthur gave her. So when the odd-looking Peace began to pay attention to her, she was flattered – and game. They started to meet secretly in an attic above the empty house between the two they lived in, in Britannia Street. As far was Kate was concerned, she would bestow her favours on Charlie in return for the one thing he could provide: drink. Sometimes she left notes for him begging him to bring her a drink; at other times her notes warned him when her husband was around.

When Arthur was at work, the two of them would go openly to local pubs together, and even had their photograph taken together at a fun fair. But Peace got too cocky and began to turn up at the Dyson home. Arthur Dyson at first welcomed him, enjoying the company of the strange little man who told good stories. He even gave Peace work, framing some pictures for him. But Arthur began to get suspicious of Peace and his wife, and also just plain irritated, especially when Peace continually interrupted the Dyson family evening meal. Hints did not work, so eventually Arthur wrote a note on his visiting card. 'Charles Peace is requested not to interfere with my family,' it said. He threw it into the yard of the Peace home.

Charlie was unabashed, especially as, for a little while, it looked as though Kate was still willing to see him secretly. But she was bored with him and also genuinely afraid that her husband would find out. Worse, Peace was pestering her to leave Dyson and go away with him, and Kate had no intention of doing that, so she told him to leave her alone. Peace was furious.

'If I make up my mind to a thing I am bound to have it,' was one of his familiar sayings, and he was not going to let Kate Dyson get through his fingers so easily. He mounted a terror campaign against the Dysons, peering through their windows at all hours of the day and night, following Kate down the street. One day in July 1876 he deliberately tripped up Arthur Dyson in the street, and that evening he pulled out a pistol and threatened to shoot Kate Dyson and her husband. 'I will blow your bloody brains out and your husband's, too!' he said, in front of witnesses. The Dysons, who were genuinely frightened of him, reported the matter and a warrant was taken out for Peace's arrest.

Peace, his long-suffering wife Hannah, and their children fled to Hull where Hannah found a job running a café. But the Dysons were not rid of him: he would turn up in Britannia Street when they least expected him, but would vanish again before anyone could call the police. Eventually, Arthur moved his family to the other side of Sheffield, to a house in Banner Cross Terrace. If they breathed a sigh of relief it was premature; when they arrived at the new house where their furniture was being unloaded, Charlie Peace walked out of the front door to greet them, like something out of their worst nightmare.

'You see, I am here to annoy you wherever you go,' he said. When Arthur Dyson reminded him that he was wanted by the police, he coolly replied that he 'did not give a fig for the police', a prophetic statement.

On 29 November 1876 Charlie Peace was again seen near the Dyson home. He asked a woman to take a note to Kate Dyson for him, but she told him to take it himself, and he poured out his troubles over Kate to a labourer he met at the nearest pub, showing the man the letters she had sent to him in the past (as the labourer could not read it was a pointless gesture).

That evening, at about eight o'clock, after settling her son to sleep, Kate put on her clogs and went to the toilet, an outside privy shared by all the houses in the terrace. She had to go down a passage to the end of the row of houses. As she came out of the privy, to her terror she encountered Peace, brandishing a gun. He said, 'Speak, or I'll fire.' Kate screamed and slammed herself back into the privy. Arthur Dyson, hearing his wife's scream, came rushing out and ran down the passage after Peace who turned and fired at him. His first shot missed Dyson, the second shot hit him in the forehead and, although he was still alive when he was carried back into his home by neighbours, he died two hours later.

Peace ran away but dropped the bundle of love letters from Kate that he had earlier been showing to the labourer. Among them was the warning from Arthur Dyson to keep away from the family, as well as billet doux from Kate promising him a keepsake and arranging assignations. More desperate notes from her pleaded with him to 'Send me a drink, I am nearly dead.'

Knowing he was now in deep trouble – if caught he would be hanged – Charlie Peace took care with his escape, doubling around the countryside for a couple of days.

He ran across fields, hailed a cab to another area of Sheffield, then walked to a suburban railway station (he guessed that there would be police looking for him at the main station) where he took a train to Rotherham. He boarded another train for York that evening where he lay low for two days. During that time he disguised himself.

One of Peace's cleverest tricks was to change his appearance, chameleon-like, whenever he needed to: no mean feat for someone so odd-looking. Because he knew the description of him on the wanted posters would include his missing finger, he made a tube for his arm, with an iron hook on the end, so that it looked as though he had lost an arm and hand. He shaved off his beard, bought some spectacles, dyed his hair black and used walnut juice to stain his skin dark. He had broken his jaw badly in his early life and he was able to make his lower jaw protrude oddly, completely changing the shape of his face.

He went from York to Hull, to the café which his wife, Hannah, was running. The disguise was so good that his daughter Jenny did not recognize him at first. It was here that he settled down for his mutton stew, but was disturbed by Jenny's warning that the police were coming. After fleeing to the rooftops for the second time Peace decided to leave the area until things cooled down.

He took a train to Manchester, travelling in the same compartment as a police sergeant, with whom he chatted during the journey (on another occasion he cheekily read out the poster offering £100 for his capture to a policeman who was standing nearby). He moved on to Nottingham, and there met a woman called Susan Grey. Sue was about thirty and her own life had been far from blameless. She was known by at least two other names – Bailey and Thomson – from other men she had lived with, and she was a heavy drinker. Peace himself described her as 'a terrible woman for the drink and snuff'.

They set up home together, Peace calling himself Mr Jack Thomson. But Charlie Peace still wanted to be near Hannah and his children, so he moved with Sue to Hull, taking lodgings astonishingly with a policeman. He supported them by burglary and, in February 1877, he was nearly caught when a family woke to find him rifling through their belongings. They chased him and Peace drew a gun, shooting at the man of the house twice.

On another occasion a policeman stopped Peace as he left a house he had burgled. He fired at the policeman and escaped. Hull was getting too hot for him, so he and Sue returned to Nottingham where he continued breaking and entering. Eventually the police were tipped off and came to the house he was sharing with Sue: the couple were in bed together at the time. Peace persuaded the police that he was Sue's illicit lover, not the man they were looking for. He said he was a hawker and that he would show them his hawker's permit which was downstairs. They went downstairs to wait for him until he was dressed but, inevitably, he never came: he had climbed out through the window and disappeared over the rooftops.

After a flying visit to Hull to see his family he decided the north of England was no longer safe. There were now several rewards out for his arrest for different crimes, although the police did not realize it was the same man they were looking for.

Peace now based himself in London and Sue Thomson joined him there, in lodgings in Lambeth. From there he made nightly burglary jaunts and he was so successful that he was beginning to be wealthy. In one raid on a house in Southampton he got away with a large haul of silver.

He rented a house in Greenwich, and it was there that Hannah and their youngest child, a boy, joined him and Sue. The two women understandably did not get on, and there was plenty of squabbling. Hannah on one occasion triumphed over Sue with her ultimate hold on Charlie; she knew he was 'the Banner Cross murderer', as Arthur Dyson's killer had been dubbed. Peace made both women swear on a Bible that they would protect him from discovery, and used his consummate charm to keep both of them happy.

The strange family moved to a bigger house in Nunhead, near Peckham, where Hannah and her son lived in the basement and Peace and Sue lived upstairs.

The house was elaborately furnished and they lived well, better than most of their neighbours. Peace had a pony and trap, which set him a cut above most local residents, and he was referred to as 'our carriage neighbour'. He used the pony, Tommy, to take him around the town during the day, sizing up properties that he would later break into. At night the pony and trap were stationed not too far from the scene of the crime to drive him and his booty home. He always dressed well when he went out thieving, and carried his housebreaking tools in a violin case. 'The police never think of suspecting someone who wears good clothes. In this way I have thrown them off their guard many a time,' he said later.

Peace went to church every Sunday and was popular with local residents, mainly because he was generous with his hospitality. He also loved singing and music making, and telling stories. Despite his odd appearance – he looked at least ten years older than he was – he was well respected, and he explained away his odd menage by pretending that Hannah was his sister.

Sue Thomson gave birth to a baby boy and Peace, who was devoted to animals, filled the house with cockatoos and parrots as well as dogs and cats and rabbits. Local children enjoyed visiting, and Peace relished an audience. His love of musical instruments surfaced again, and he acquired a collection. He explained away his absences from home during the night to his neighbours with an inspired lie: he claimed he was patenting the design of an unsinkable boat and that he was going down to the Thames to experiment with it when there was nobody around to steal his ideas. It was so bizarre that it was accepted.

The police, too, were miles away from catching him. They believed there was a highly skilled gang at work in London: Peace, in fact, never worked with any other criminals. He even disliked having to use third parties to get rid of his stolen property, and at one stage he experimented with melting silver down in his own home. He gave up that idea because he believed it would make the neighbours suspicious.

He was finally caught and arrested in Blackheath. A policeman noticed a light flickering in the downstairs room of a house at 2am. He called for assistance and, while one policeman knocked at the front door of the house, two others stationed themselves behind the garden wall. Peace made a rapid exit when the bell rang, right into the arms of the waiting police.

He pulled his gun out and shouted to them to stand clear or he would shoot them. One, PC Edward Robinson, chased Peace, who turned and fired five shots, the fifth hitting the young policeman in the elbow. But Robinson did not give up and managed to get the revolver off Peace. By this time the other two policemen had arrived and overpowered Peace. He struggled to escape, and had to be knocked out with a police truncheon.

At the police station he gave his name as 'John Ward' and, when asked for his address, replied, 'Find out! That's your business.' Nothing the police could do, even threatening him with violence, could persuade him to give any details about himself. Scotland Yard had only recently formed its CID branch, and two of its top detective inspectors were assigned to try to find out the identity of 'Ward'. They even tried dressing a policeman up as a criminal and roughly shoving him into a cell with Peace, but all the young officer got was a lecture from Peace about how to handle the police, and a few entertaining stories. He gave nothing away about his true identity.

While awaiting trial, though, Peace sent a letter to one of his neighbours, asking the man to visit him in Newgate jail. The neighbour, a respectable map-maker, was astonished to find his friend in prison. He was even more astonished to find that he was followed home by two detectives who asked for his help in establishing 'John Ward's' true identity. The neighbour knew him as John Thomson, and was able to tell the police that the two women who had lived with Peace had split up, Hannah returning to Sheffield and Sue visiting relatives in Nottingham. Sue was thought to be returning to stay with the neighbour and his wife, and the police arranged that, when she did so, the neighbour would alert them with a telegram.

When they interviewed her, though, Sue Thomson gave them little help. She refused to cooperate until she was told that she would be charged with receiving stolen property: a silver watch had been found among her things and was identified as part of one of Peace's hauls. Scared that she would find herself facing a court, Sue Thomson told the police that she had taken an oath not to tell 'Ward's' true identity; they helped her through this crisis of confidence by persuading her that writing it down was not 'telling'. She wrote:

'I know that 'is name is not Ward. It is Charles Peace of Sheffield.' Sue Thomson was eventually given the £100 reward that was on offer for the capture of the Banner Cross murderer.

But, at first, the London police did not realize the

importance of their catch. They sent a Detective Inspector Phillips up to Sheffield; this was a memorable trip for the policeman who had never been out of the capital before and who was bowled over by northern openness and hospitality. He discovered that the local police believed Charlie Peace had been killed in a mining accident in Derbyshire – a rumour that Peace himself had put about, to take the heat out of his pursuit. But as soon as Phillips described the missing finger and chose a photograph of Peace from among a selection, they were convinced. They sent one of their own men to London to make doubly sure but, in the meantime, they helped Phillips trace Hannah who, by this time, was a woman of fifty. She was living in a cottage near Darnall with her daughter and son-in-law, and the tiny house was stuffed full of stolen goods that her husband had taken. She was arrested and charged with receiving stolen property.

When he heard that she was in custody, Charlie Peace wrote a letter to a lawyer in Sheffield, begging him to do everything he could for Hannah because 'she is inesent'.

Ten days later, on 19 November 1878, Peace was tried at the Old Bailey (under the name of John Ward) for attempting to murder PC Robinson. Although by this time the police knew his true identity, they did not reveal it in court as they were still making inquiries. It took the jury four minutes to find him guilty and, despite an impassioned speech by Peace in which he claimed he had only been using the gun to frighten the police and had not intended to harm anyone, he was given a life prison sentence.

Hannah was taken to London and held in custody until January 1879 when the case against her was dismissed, on the grounds that she was Peace's wife and acted under pressure from him (in Victorian England a husband was deemed to have complete control of his wife).

By this time the police were ready to transport Charlie Peace to Sheffield, to face trial for the murder of Arthur Dyson.

With the dice so heavily loaded against him, most criminals would have gone quietly. But Charlie Peace was the stuff of legend and he had, by no means, lost his will for a fight. He was, according to the two warders who escorted him from Pentonville, troublesome all the way, but it was when the train was near to Sheffield that he pulled the biggest stunt of his colourful career.

He told his guards that he needed to urinate and they lowered the window to allow him to lean out. His hands were in chains which meant that he could not move them more than 6″ apart, but it was sufficient movement for him to suddenly dive out through the window. The train was running alongside a canal which Peace, who knew the Sheffield area well, was perhaps hoping to dive into, breaking his fall from the speeding train. He was foiled, though, by one of the warders who grabbed his foot. Peace kicked off his shoe and plunged out, hitting his head on the footboard and falling on to the line.

The communication cord on the train did not work, but eventually the train did stop and the two warders ran back along the track for a mile until they found Peace, unconscious on the snowy ground. He may, in fact, have been attempting suicide, because in his pocket was a piece of paper that read, 'Bury me in Darnall.' But it is more likely that he was desperately trying to escape.

The warders were able to stop a slow train that was also heading for Sheffield, and they bundled Peace on board. He was seriously injured. In the meantime, the first train arrived in Sheffield where a huge crowd had gathered to see the murderer. News that he had escaped was greeted with disbelief; the spectators thought it was a trick by the police to get them to disperse. But when they saw the empty carriage they were convinced, and rumours flew around about how he had spirited himself away.

The magistrates court was waiting for him to appear, to be remanded for trial, but when he did arrive in Sheffield he was in no condition to stand in the dock. He had severe concussion and a head wound. He also seemed to have caught a chill, and shivered constantly and asked for more blankets.

His spirit was not subdued, though. He was as difficult as he could be for the prison guards who were detailed to look after him. When ordered to drink brandy to revive him he complained that he would prefer whisky. Two days later he was still in no condition to attend a court hearing, so the court was brought to him: the magistrates came to the cell in the police station where he was held and, by candlelight, heard the case against him.

Kate Dyson, whose husband he had murdered, had been brought back from America where she was now living to give evidence against him, which she did with confidence, despite being so close to him. It was hard for any of those present to believe that the shrivelled little old man wrapped in blankets, who moaned and cursed throughout the hearing, could be a desperate and dangerous criminal.

But the police were taking no chances. When Peace

appeared at Leeds Assizes on 4 February 1879 he was flanked by two policemen, and another six sat behind him. They were obviously expecting another dramatic escape bid. As the *News of the World* described it: 'If the little criminal fidgets, they all look anxious.'

The trial was a celebrated affair with the public galleries crowded. Well-connected ladies, armed with opera glasses in order to see Peace better, jostled for front seats in the side galleries which were reserved for 'people of privileged rank'.

Peace was described by the *News of the World* as 'a wizen-faced little old-looking man' who 'looks quite sixty', although he was actually only forty-seven. A vivid red scar could be seen through his short grey hair, the result of his plunge from the train. Although he was small, only 5'4", he was described as having a closely-knit, muscular frame.

His forbidding face, rendered even more repulsive by an unshaven beard and moustache, the grey bristles of which stand out nearly straight, evinces little sign of emotion. The eyes are sunken, the lower lip protrudes, the cheeks have fallen in, but there is an actual smile on his countenance. The owner of it is apparently most at his ease.

The case revolved around whether Peace shot Arthur Dyson by accident, as part of a struggle, or whether he cold-bloodedly aimed at his love rival and pulled the trigger. He made no attempt to deny that he was at the scene of the crime; the evidence of the woman and the labourer with whom he had talked earlier in the evening placed him firmly there. But it was Kate Dyson's evidence that was crucial, and she maintained that Peace had not been close enough to her husband to struggle with him.

His defence made a great deal of capital from their relationship, trying to prove that, at the time of the murder, Kate was still seeing Peace and had been in a pub with him the night before the murder. Although she could not deny having associated with Peace, Kate stood up during rigorous cross-examination, insisting that she had done nothing more than have the occasional drink with him. She denied having a habit of drinking too much. She was unflustered, despite the fact that Peace stared at her intently throughout her evidence; she obviously enjoyed the attention she was getting.

It took the jury just twelve minutes to find him guilty and he was sentenced to be hanged at Armley Jail, Leeds. But the Charlie Peace story was by no means over; there was another even more dramatic turn of events to come.

From the condemned cell Peace, who had always claimed to be a God-fearing man, sent for the vicar of the village of Darnall, the Rev. J. H. Littlewood, and confessed that he had committed another murder, one for which a young Irishman had been sentenced to life imprisonment. Peace had been sitting in the public gallery of the court in Manchester when the young man was sentenced to death, and admitted that he would have been prepared to watch him go to the gallows if the sentence had not been commuted to life.

The murder was the shooting of a policeman who had tried to arrest Peace as he went about his profession of breaking and entering. The killing had been carried out in Manchester in August 1876 – before the murder of

Arthur Dyson. It was the day after he heard the innocent Irishman, William Habron, being sentenced to death that Peace pulled out his pistol again and shot his lover's husband.

William Habron and his three brothers had come over from Ireland in 1870 and they worked on farms in the Whalley Range area of Manchester, now a suburb but then an area of large houses interspersed with fields. Three of the brothers worked for one farmer, Frank Deakin, who found them to be very good employees. They were simple, hard-working lads, they caused no trouble and regularly sent their wages home to their parents in Ireland. Occasionally they got drunk and, on the day of the murder, two of them, John and William, had appeared in court, but the charge had been dismissed. That evening in their local pub William was heard to say, 'Damn the bobbies.' That remark on its own was almost enough to have him condemned to hang.

Later that night Police Constable Nicholas Cock, the policeman who had arrested the Habrons for drunkenness, was shot dead. An hour later three of the brothers were arrested, but one was immediately released. The other two went on trial: John was found not guilty but William, the youngest and only nineteen, was found guilty, despite the judge in his summing up attempting to persuade the jury that William, too, was not guilty. The witnesses, including another policeman, said there had been two men at the scene of the murder, and that the man they had seen most clearly was tall and straight, like William Habron. Only one man, a passerby who had been talking to the policeman when the murderer was seen, described him as small, elderly and stooped – a better description of Charlie Peace than of Habron.

In his cell Peace gave a detailed confession to the crime:

I was in Manchester in 1876. I was there to work some houses.
I went to a place called Whalley Range. I had spotted a house
there that I thought I could do. On my way to the house that
night I passed two policemen in the road. There were some
grounds around the house and my object was to get into these
in the dusk and wait a chance of getting into the house. I
walked into the grounds through the gate and before I was able
to begin work I heard a step behind me. Looking back I saw it
was one of the policemen I had passed on the road. I doubled
back to elude him. For the moment I succeeded and taking a
favourable chance I jumped on the wall and, as I was dropping
down, I all but fell into the arms of the second policeman who
must have been planted for me.

This policeman – I do not know his name – made a grab at
me. My blood was up, being nettled that I had been disturbed,
so I told him, 'You stand back or I'll shoot you.' He did not
step back and I stepped back a few yards and fired wide at him,
purposefully to frighten him that I might get away. Now, Sir, I
want to tell you and to make you believe me when I say I
always make it a rule during the whole course of my career never to take life if I can avoid it. Whether you believe me or not I
never wanted to murder anybody and only wanted to do what
I came to do and get away; and it does seem odd, after all, that
in the end I should have been hanged for taking life, the very
thing I was always so anxious to avoid.

I have never willingly or knowingly hurt a living creature.
That is why I tell you I fired wide at him, but the policeman
was as determined a man as myself and after I fired wide at him
– it was all the work of a few moments, Sir – I observed him

seize his staff which was in his pocket and he was rushing at me and about to strike me. I saw I had no time to lose if I wanted to get away at all. I then fired the second time, but all I wanted to do then was disable him in order that I might get away. I had no intention of killing him. We had a scuffle together, I could not take as careful aim as I would have done and the ball, missing the arm, struck him in the breast and he fell. I know no more. I got away, which was all I wanted.

Some time after I saw in the papers that certain men had been taken into custody for the murder of this policeman. That interested me. I liked to attend a trial, and I determined to be present. I left home for Manchester, not telling my family where I had gone. I attended Manchester Assizes for two days and heard the youngest of the brothers sentenced to death. The sentence was afterwards reduced to penal servitude for life.

Now, Sir, some people will say that I was a hardened wretch for allowing an innocent man to suffer for my crime. But what man would have done otherwise in my position? Could I have done otherwise knowing as I did that I should certainly be hanged for the crime? But now that I am going to forfeit my own life and feel that I have nothing to gain by further secrecy I think it is right, in the sight of God and man, to clear the young man who is innocent of the crime.

That man was sentenced to death the day before I shot Mr Dyson.

Peace went on to say that, if the police wanted proof, they should match the bullet that killed PC Cock with his gun which was in their possession. He also pointed out that all the witnesses, with the exception of the passerby, had perjured themselves in the case against Habron.

He continued to claim, as he had done in court, that the shooting of Dyson was an accident, the gun going off as he struggled with him, just as he claimed it had with PC Cock. He pointed out that if he had set out to murder Dyson he would have been careful to prevent anyone seeing him in the neighbourhood that day, and would have shot his rival in his own home, not outside in a public place.

From prison Peace wrote to his wife, Hannah, saying that he had been 'a bad, bad man to thee for many years'. He claimed he was glad to be going to the gallows, as he would have died within a couple of years in prison anyway. He enclosed a verse he had written when he heard that his son – by Sue – had died while he was in prison:

> *Farewell my dear son, by us all beloved*
> *Thou art gone to dwell in the mansions above.*
> *In the bosom of Jesus who sits on the throne*
> *Thou art anxiously waiting for us to come home.*

He did not communicate directly with Sue after the Dyson trial. When he had discovered that she had given the police his true identity he had tried to implicate her in his crimes, and then before his trial he had written to her asking her to sell his property to raise money for a lawyer for him. She had replied that there was no property left to sell, and she had used any money she had to live on. Peace had asked her to come and see him 'as you have been my bosom friend and oft times said you loved me and would die for me', but she did not visit.

Peace was hanged on 25 February 1879, at Armley Jail.

He was a troublesome and insolent prisoner to the end. When a warder told him to hurry up in the lavatory on the morning of the execution he shouted, 'You're in a hell of a hurry. Are you going to hanged or am I?' Unlike many prisoners waiting to go to the gallows, Peace had a large breakfast, commenting, 'This is bloody rotten bacon.'

There were four reporters present to take down his last words:

I know that my life has been base and bad. I wish you to ask the world, after you have seen my death, what man could die as I did if he did not die in fear of the Lord . . . My last wishes and respects are to my dear children and their dear mother. I hope no person will disgrace them by taunting them or jeering at them on my account.

During the final religious service he constantly inter-rupted, asking for a drink. He was not given one. The *News of the World* reported that death was 'as near as pos-sible instantaneous'.

William Habron was released from prison a month later and given £1000 compensation. His employer, Deakin, who had stood by the boy and never lost faith in his innocence, met him in London when he was released. He had to break the bad news to him that his father in Ireland had died broken-hearted.

PC Robinson, the one who finally caught Peace and was shot in the arm by him, suffered more than just a bullet wound. The instant celebrity he attracted meant that everywhere he went people insisted on buying him drinks, and he was eventually sacked from the police after being found drunk on duty several times. He worked for a time in Canada, but eventually came back to England where he spent his last years, in poor physical and mental health, in the workhouse. By the time of his death in 1926 he was so confused that he thought his own name was Charlie Peace.

5. Deadly Wives

When the pretty French schoolgirl was told that she was to marry a man who was eleven years older than her, all her dreams were shattered. There was nothing glamorous about Edwin Bartlett. He was not good-looking and he had rotten teeth which made his breath smell. He was a shopkeeper which, although it was a secure job in the 1870s, was hardly romantic. And as far as whispering sweet words in her ear, Edwin was not as well educated as his young bride, and his inferiority complex made him keep his mouth firmly shut (probably to hide his teeth, too), unless he got carried away on one of his favourite subjects. One of those subjects was sex – but Edwin was not a dynamic lover. What turned him on was the thought of his beautiful wife in the arms of another man . . .

The story of Adelaide Bartlett – dubbed The Pimlico Mystery by the *News of the World* – was a tale with kinky sexual overtones that riveted the nation, even though very few of the details could be published. Adelaide's husband, Edwin, was a voyeur who was excited by the idea of his wife with another man, and even selected the man for her. He bought the sort of books and pamphlets which nowadays would be sold from the top shelf of the newsagent, but which in those days – the couple were married in 1875 – were under plain covers. In today's terms, they were sex manuals, and probably would be thought very tame. By the standards of the nineteenth century they were shocking.

Adelaide was born in Orleans and her maiden name was Adelaide Blanche de la Tremoile. Her mother came from a reasonably high-ranking family, but had given birth to Adelaide illegitimately. Adelaide's father was rumoured to be a titled English gentleman who paid for her upbringing, including her schooling in England. It was while she was living with a guardian in Richmond that Adelaide met Edwin Bartlett, her future husband. She was eighteen at the time and he was twenty-nine.

Edwin was a self-made man. His mother and father had been able to provide him with a rudimentary education, but they did not have the money to give him a leg up in a career. He worked very hard, however, and with a partner, Edward Baxter, he owned a chain of six grocer's shops, in the Brixton and Dulwich areas of London, by the end of his twenties.

He met Adelaide at his brother's house in Kingston: Adelaide was a schoolfriend of his niece. She was dazzlingly beautiful, with dark curly hair and large dark, expressive eyes. Edwin was not a good-looking young man and the attraction was all one-sided: he quickly fell in love with her. He was attracted not just by her looks but by her education and upbringing which were on a plane above his. In Victorian England this would have meant that a match between them was out of the question. But when he discovered that she was illegitimate he realized that he might have a chance of marrying her; at that time legitimacy mattered a great deal and she would be unlikely to marry into the aristocracy.

Edwin pursued her and was able to persuade her guardian that he would make a good husband. He was relatively prosperous and seemed a steady young man; no doubt Adelaide's mysterious father would be relieved to see her married and off his hands. Adelaide later claimed that she brought money with her into the marriage, and that is probably true. But Edwin was so determined to have her that it is unlikely he haggled for much of a dowry, and when she later said that it was her finances that paid for his business she was not telling the truth. He had been in the grocery business for thirteen years before he married Adelaide, and he worked very hard in his shops.

Persuading her guardian to give them permission to marry was easy compared with persuading Adelaide. She did not fancy Edwin at all, and only agreed on the basis that their relationship should be, and remain, platonic. Part of the deal was that Edwin should pay for her to continue her education; she spent the two years after their wedding at a finishing school in Stoke Newington and a convent in Belgium, only spending holidays with her husband.

It was an odd arrangement, but Edwin was content to go along with it. He had a tremendous inferiority complex about his own lack of education, and was constantly trying to remedy it by reading everything he could get his hands on. One way of compensating for it, he thought, was to have an educated and accomplished wife. He set her on a pedestal: she was beautiful and untouchable. Although she was fond and affectionate, theirs was not a passionate sexual relationship.

Soon after Adelaide finished her schooling, she moved into a flat above one of Edwin's shops, in Herne Hill. Within a few weeks Edwin's mother died and he invited his father to live with them – a major mistake. Living with in-laws was no easier then than it is now, and the old man, who was quarrelsome and difficult, and Adelaide, who was young and used to having her own way, disliked each other. Old Bartlett had disapproved of his son's choice of a bride and had refused to attend their wedding.

Three years after they were married, Adelaide could stand it no longer and ran away. The only place she knew where she would be welcome was at the home of her old schoolfriend, the daughter of Edwin's brother Charles. She stayed there for a week. Living in the same house was another of Edwin's brothers, Frederick, and he, too, fell under Adelaide's spell. Whether they had a romance nobody now knows: Edwin's father was sure that they did and publicly accused them. Edwin believed his wife when she said they did not. Frederick's views are not known, but he emigrated to America a month or so afterwards, perhaps out of guilt. Edwin was so frightened of losing Adelaide that he made his meddlesome father write a letter of apology to her, and he had it witnessed by a solicitor.

The household got back on to some sort of even keel, and Edwin obviously persuaded his wife that married life should be more than platonic. She later claimed that they only made love once, and the result was a pregnancy. Unfortunately, at Christmas 1881, the baby was still-born. Adelaide was in terrible pain; it was a long and difficult birth, and the midwife begged Edwin to call a doctor. Edwin refused; he said he did not want another man 'interfering with her'. By the time he capitulated the baby was dead and Adelaide was very ill. She would have been justified in never forgiving him, but afterwards they seemed to become very loving and tender with each other.

Adelaide wrung from Edwin an agreement that they would not have any more children; she did not want to go through that ordeal again. She claimed her decision not to have any more babies meant that they went back to a platonic relationship but, when Edwin died, contraceptives (scandalous objects that were difficult to obtain) were found in his pocket. They were, according to the judge, the other 'very unpleasant aspect' to the case and proved, he said, that the Bartletts had not been living together 'as man and wife'. He implied that Edwin was using the contraceptives for extramarital sex: in fact, he was probably hoping to use them (as millions do today) with his wife and so prevent her having to go through the torture of another childbirth.

In the next couple of years Edwin and Adelaide moved house twice, and they were careful to choose homes without room enough for Edwin's father. When they moved to a cottage at Merton Abbey, near Wimbledon, they started to attend a Wesleyan chapel where they met a young preacher called George Dyson. Edwin was very impressed by Dyson, as he was impressed by anyone with more education than he had himself, and before long Dyson was a regular at the Bartletts' supper table.

By this time Edwin Bartlett, who had been married to Adelaide for ten years, and (if you accept her version) had only made love to her once, was developing some strange views about sex and marriage. One of his favourite theories was that a man needed two wives, one for intellectual stimulation and companionship and the other for 'service', by which the frustrated Edwin probably meant sex. He had also bought the book that would so horrify the judge at Adelaide's trial. It was called *Esoteric Anthropology* and dealt with sexual techniques and perversions. Both he and his wife read it from cover to cover; this suggests that the relationship between them, while perhaps not sexually normal, was not a frigid, silent one. They shared a great interest in sex, even if they did not share a bed.

They were also both interested in hypnotism, in those days called 'mesmerism' (after the French student, Franz Mesmer, who experimented with it and made it popular). Hypnotism was a Victorian parlour craze, with much amateur dabbling.

George Dyson became a fixture in their lives. Edwin paid him to teach Latin and geography to Adelaide, which he did during the day while Edwin was at work. For a man who was so possessive that he did not even want a doctor to go near his wife professionally, Edwin was now encouraging her to spend hours alone with another young, attractive man.

Perhaps he hoped that the excitement of being with Dyson, who soon fell in love with her and wrote poems for her, would turn Adelaide towards him. Or perhaps he hoped that she would have an affair with Dyson and free him to have an affair with someone else – although there is no evidence of Edwin ever being unfaithful. Or perhaps – and this seems in some ways the most likely explanation – he enjoyed a sexual frisson at the thought of his wife in the arms of another man.

He laid everything on for Dyson. When the couple went to Dover on holiday, he wanted Dyson to go with them. When the preacher could not, because of his duties, Edwin wanted to buy him a first-class season ticket so that he could pop down whenever he was free. When Dyson refused even that, Edwin used to go up to London by train and persuade his friend to return to Dover with him.

When the Bartletts moved to lodgings in Victoria, not so close to Dyson's chapel in Putney, Edwin presented him with a season ticket and told the new landlady that there would be a frequent guest calling to have supper with them. The Bartletts kept a pair of slippers and a lounge coat for Dyson to change into for comfort when he was with them. All three were on Christian-name terms, and the maids working in the house saw Adelaide sitting at George Dyson's feet with her head on his knee. On one occasion they noticed that, when Adelaide and George were alone, the curtains were not just drawn but were pinned together.

George admitted he had kissed her, both in front of her husband and when they were alone. Edwin, it seemed, like to see them kiss. George, who was understandably rather confused by all this, even talked to Edwin about how his affections for Adelaide were growing. Edwin, instead of being possessive or shocked, seemed to encourage him.

Edwin showed George a love letter that Adelaide had sent to him, her future husband, before their marriage. Then he told George that 'I should like you to get her into that frame of mind and disposition of heart' and talked to George about him marrying Adelaide after his own death. He got George to be one of the executors of his will, leaving everything to his wife.

So Edwin, it seems, colluded with Adelaide and George Dyson in their affair – if it ever was a real affair – all the way along the line. The mystery is why he thought he was going to die. He was a healthy forty-one-year-old and had only been ill once before in his life: the year Adelaide lost the baby Edwin had a minor nervous breakdown which he put down to overwork.

But in December 1885 he became ill. At first it seemed as though his new illness was a recurrence of nervous problems: Edwin was a hypochondriac who imagined symptoms where doctors could find none. But he had a very real reason to feel ill; a few years earlier a dentist had filed away his rotting teeth and had fitted him with false ones. But the stumps of the bad teeth had been left in the gums and were giving him hell.

When the doctor, Dr Alfred Leach, called to see him, he also had sickness and diarrhoea, but these did not last long. Dr Leach found blue marks in Edwin's mouth, which could have come from mercury poisoning, or could have been connected with the rotting teeth. His breath, according to the doctor, smelt foul, and was probably one reason that Adelaide insisted on keeping their marriage platonic.

The removal of so many teeth, and the stomach upset, laid him low, but Dr Leach was sure he would make a full recovery. Edwin, though, appears to have convinced himself there was something more seriously wrong. When he discovered he had a roundworm he became obsessed with the idea that there were worms inside him that would crawl up his throat.

As December wore on, he stayed in bed. But Dr Leach, who visited regularly, thought he was improving well. He and Adelaide were sleeping in separate rooms because of his illness, but Adelaide was, according to everyone who saw them, a devoted wife. She would often fall asleep cradling Edwin, and she would feed him with a spoon as if he was a baby. She once told Dr Leach, in Edwin's presence, that she wished they were not married so that they could have the pleasure of getting married again.

It was on the 27th of the month that Adelaide made a strange request to George Dyson: she asked him to buy a large quantity of chloroform for her. George knew he would not be allowed to buy so much at one shop, and actually went to three different chemists to get it for her (small amounts could be bought as stain remover or to ease toothache, but large amounts were only sold to doctors). She explained later that she was using it to help her sick husband sleep, especially as he, for the first time, was demanding sex with her on a regular basis and she could not stand it. But according to George, she told him at the time that Edwin rubbed it on externally to soothe his limbs.

Three days after George gave the chloroform to Adelaide, Edwin died of chloroform poisoning. The post-mortem found chloroform, which had been used by the medical profession in Britain for over forty years at that time, in his stomach, but not in his lungs. There were no signs of it in his mouth or throat where medical experts agreed there should have been burn marks. The doctors agreed that anyone swallowing it would almost certainly vomit, and that if it had been poured down the throat while the victim was asleep the fumes would have got into his lungs.

There had also been no sound from Edwin when he either took it himself, or had it administered to him by his wife. It would have hurt like hell, yet the first the landlord and landlady and their maid knew about it was when Adelaide roused them at four o'clock in the morning.

She claimed then, and at her trial, that she had been asleep holding her husband's foot and had woken when she had cramp. She had discovered Edwin was dead but had tried to revive him with brandy, pouring half a pint down his throat. Foot holding seems to have been one of the odder practices that the Bartletts indulged in; at one point Edwin had told his doctor about it and the doctor described it to the court as 'their habit of toe holding and all that sort of nonsense'.

Edwin's father was quickly on the scene the next morning, 1 January 1886, and he was as troublesome to Adelaide as ever, demanding a post-mortem. There would have been one anyway: Dr Leach found the smell of chloroform in the room overpowering, and was suspicious.

Adelaide left to stay with some friends, Mr and Mrs Matthews, and it was George Dyson who took her there. By this stage George was a very worried man; he had bought the chloroform and he was having a relationship of some sort with the dead man's wife. His career would be ruined and, what's more, he could find himself facing murder charges. He threw the remaining chloroform bottles in his possession away, later saying at the court case that they were 'hateful to me'. He also asked Adelaide to return the poetry he had written about her.

They were both arrested but, when the case opened at

the Old Bailey in April 1886, the charges against George Dyson were withdrawn. He and Adelaide were by this stage no longer even on speaking terms – they sat as far away as possible from each other in the dock. When the minister was released, he became the main prosecution witness against Adelaide. Not only did he admit supplying her with the chloroform, but he claimed that she asked him, after Edwin's death, to say nothing about it.

Adelaide's defence was led by a famous – and very expensive – barrister, Edward Clarke. Rumours rushed around London that her mysterious father was paying her legal fees, as Clarke was outside the pocket of a grocer's wife. Whoever paid, it was worth the money. Clarke's speech in defence of Adelaide had her and all the other women in the courtroom in tears; he movingly told how she nursed the sick Edwin, how she spared no expense on a post-mortem, how she had done everything possible to help the inquiries into her husband's death.

According to Clarke, Edwin was eccentric almost to the point of insanity. He had thrown his wife into George Dyson's arms, but then, whilst ill, had started to demand sex with her himself. Adelaide had been using chloroform to get him to sleep, as by this time she felt – with her husband's blessing – that she belonged to Dyson.

Adelaide won everyone in court over to her side. She sat in the dock quietly and composedly, her beautiful face turning to each of the witnesses as they gave their evidence. Unlike most women prisoners of the day, she did not hide behind a hat or a veil, but sat bare-headed, wearing a simple black silk dress and black gloves. By the end of the trial she had jurors, lawyers, spectators and the judge eating out of her hand, even though she did not speak after uttering her plea of Not Guilty. Adelaide had never found it hard to attract admirers; her skill at it may have saved her from the gallows.

The judge summed up in favour of her and took a swipe at George Dyson by saying that he should not have allowed himself to get romantically involved with a married woman. The fact that Adelaide and Edwin read Edwin's sex books 'with avidity' was, according to the judge, one of the 'unpleasant aspects of this case'. He said that he 'pitied a woman who had a husband who taught her with such disgusting works as this'.

It took the jury two hours to decide that Adelaide was not guilty of killing her husband, although they added that this was 'a case of great suspicion'. If it had been tried in Scotland the verdict would have been Not Proven. What the jury was saying was that there was not enough evidence to convict Adelaide, but they did not necessarily think she was innocent. The crowd outside the court did, though. When the news of her acquittal spread a great cheer went up and, to the annoyance of the judge, even the spectators in the public gallery of the Old Bailey clapped and shouted.

Adelaide walked free and left behind one of the greatest mysteries in forensic history. How did the chloroform get into Edwin's stomach? It is probable that he swallowed it himself, either in a suicide bid because he believed he was dying (and Adelaide may have encouraged him to believe he was much more ill than he was) or because she hypnotized him into swallowing it. That would explain the absence of fumes in his lungs and possibly, if Adelaide was able to put him into a deep trance, the fact that he did not cry out in pain. But nothing explains how he managed to get it down without it touching his mouth or his throat. One of the medical experts who gave evidence at her trial said that she should, 'in the interests of science, tell us how she did it'. But Adelaide never did tell them.

Florrie Maybrick was not as lucky as Adelaide. Her trial took place three years later, in July 1889, and she drew the short straw as far as judges go. Mr Justice James Fitzjames Stephen was famous as a hang 'em and flog 'em old reactionary: not long after Florrie's case he was carted off to a lunatic asylum where he died a couple of years later.

He sentenced Florrie to be hanged, despite the fact that there was no clear evidence that her husband James had been murdered. In a two-day rambling summing up it became clear that what the judge really objected to was Florrie having had an affair with another man. He referred to this as a 'degrading vice'.

There was uproar across Britain at the sentence – the judge and jury were booed and the wagon that took Florrie to prison was cheered the length of its route. There were public meetings to protest about the sentence, and several people came forward and offered to be hanged in Florrie's place. Eventually, just three days before she was due to go to the gallows, which she had heard being built from her cell at Walton Jail, her sentence was changed to life imprisonment.

Florence Maybrick was born in America. Her mother was French and her father was American. Her mother, the Baroness von Roques, was considered not quite respectable by British society because she had been married three times. So when James Maybrick, a prosperous forty-two-year-old cotton merchant, announced to his family that he was going to marry the beautiful eighteen-year-old Florrie, they were not pleased. The wedding went ahead and, after a couple of years based in Alabama (the heart of the cotton-growing territory of America, and Florrie's home state), the couple moved in 1884 to live in Liverpool, the English base for most of the sea trade in cotton.

The Maybricks bought a large house, Battlecrease House, in the Aigburth suburb of the city. It was an impressive home with spacious rooms and all mod cons, including a new-fangled invention, flush lavatories. They had five servants, including a nanny to look after their two young children, and they wined and dined friends lavishly.

But James Maybrick was mean and difficult. He kept Florrie very short of money, yet expected her to provide a luxury lifestyle. He was a hypochondriac and for years had been dosing himself with ever-increasing amounts of patent medicines, including some containing arsenic and strychnine. Whenever he could get hold of it, he took arsenic in his tea, believing it made him stronger.

He kept a mistress, giving her as much to support herself as he gave Florrie to run the large house, the servants and two children. Not surprisingly Florrie, a very pretty girl who had no experience of making do on a tight budget, ran up debts. She also took a lover, one of her husband's friends, a young man called Alfred Brierley.

She may have launched into the affair to get even with James but, before long, she was head over heels in love with Brierley. She was even prepared to book a hotel room in London and spend a weekend with him. They had planned to be away for a week, Florrie saying she was visiting friends, but after three days she and Brierley quarrelled. He had found a girl he wanted to marry and he was worried about his affair with Florrie becoming a scandal. Rather than that, he told her, he would blow his brains out. Florrie agreed they should end their affair.

But when, a few days later, she and her husband bumped into Brierley at the Grand National at Aintree, Florrie couldn't contain herself and got out of her husband's carriage to walk along the course with Brierley. James – and much of Liverpool society – was scandalized. When they got home that night he physically laid into her, giving her a black eye and a lot of bruises. The servants heard the fight. Florrie called a cab and threatened to walk out; James told her that, if she did so, she would never be allowed to return or see her children again. She stayed.

The following day Florrie called the family doctor. He saw to her physical injuries and also discussed her other problems. In the end, he brought her and James together, and they both promised to forgive and forget. James even agreed to pay off Florrie's debts.

From then on, James Maybrick's health went into decline and eventually, a month later, he died. It was a slow and painful death, and the servants and friends of the family were worried enough to send for his brothers. They suspected Florrie was trying to poison him with arsenic. She had bought some fly papers, which contained arsenic, and had left them in water to soak out the poison.

When James finally died – and, by that time, Florrie

was so much under suspicion that she was not allowed to nurse him – he was found to have strychnine, hyoscine, prussic acid and morphia in his body, as well as traces of arsenic. All of these chemicals are poisonous, and all of them had been contained in the different potions and medicines with which James was constantly dosing himself. He would have needed four times as much arsenic to have killed him as was found in his body, and there was enough arsenic in the house (concealed about the place in bottles and jars) to kill fifty people. If Florrie was trying to kill him with arsenic she had the means, but she certainly did not go about it very enthusiastically.

After his death, his brothers pushed hard for Florrie's arrest. She was charged with murdering James. At her trial the medical experts could not agree what had caused the gastroenteritis that had killed James: was it because he had a chill, or because he was full of his own noxious medicines, or did he eat something that was off, or did his wife kill him? The defence argued that Florrie would not have needed to soak fly papers to get arsenic. She claimed she was using the water from this as a cosmetic (it was believed in fashionable circles to be a depilatory, for removing facial hair, as well as whitening and clearing the skin).

The judge at Liverpool Assizes came down heavily against her, and it took the all-male jury just three quarters of an hour to pronouce her guilty. When she heard the death sentence, according to the *News of the World*, 'the poor creature sat sobbing like a child' and 'strong men could be seen stealthily wiping their eyes'. She was only twenty-six years old.

In the spectators gallery, a group of women held an

enormous bouquet which they had been planning to give her when she was acquitted. The judge refused to allow them to hand it into the dock.

After she was granted a reprieve from the death sentence, Florrie served fifteen years in prison, despite efforts by her supporters to get her out sooner. Her French mother visited her when she was being held in solitary confinement, and afterwards told the *News of the World*:

She is all broken down. She is dressed in a prison dress of very washed-out coarse blue homespun, made without any shape. Around her shoulders was a cape of brown felt as stiff as a board. I could not kiss her or touch her. She was particularly anxious about her children, and when I left she was weeping bitterly.

After her release Florrie visited her mother in France, and then spent the remaining thirty-seven years of her life in America. She wrote a book, *My Fifteen Lost Years*. She died at the age of seventy-eight, a recluse living in a small house overrun with cats.

6. Murder by Gaslight

Polly Nichols, a prostitute with a huge appetite for drink, had been working hard all day. She was 'on the game', but it was no game for the streetwalkers of the East End of London in the 1880s. Every day they had to earn the money for their bed that night, and the way they earned it was by going into back alleyways and deserted yards with strange men. Polly, whose real name was Mary Ann, was forty-two and looked older, ravaged by the terrible life she led. Yet she still clung to the memory of herself as a pretty, young girl. She had spent some of her earnings on a new bonnet which she showed off proudly to the other women who worked her patch. She had earned more than a shilling altogether that day, but most of it had gone on booze. By the end of the evening she was broke again and needed to find another punter to give her the 4p to pay for somewhere to sleep.

Polly found her punter – and she never again needed to pay for a room in a lodging house. The client who took Polly into a dark gateway in narrow, ill-lit Bucks Row in Whitechapel in the early hours of the morning of 31 August 1888 was Jack the Ripper, the most notorious criminal in British history. The killing of Polly Nichols was the start of his three-month reign of terror.

She was last seen alive staggering drunkenly down the

Whitechapel Road at 3.45am. An hour and a half later her mutilated body was discovered by a market porter on his way to work. He thought she was drunk but, after calling a friend across, the two workmen realized they were looking at a corpse. They must have been on the scene very soon after her killer; a doctor called in by the police found that Polly's legs were still warm and estimated she had been killed no more than half an hour earlier.

Polly's throat had been savagely but expertly cut from ear to ear, her stomach had been slashed from top to bottom and loops of her intestines had been dragged from inside her. There were two stab wounds in her genitals and bruise marks on her throat where she may have been strangled before being attacked with the knife.

It appeared to be a motiveless killing: Polly was a quarrelsome, noisy drunkard, but nobody hated her enough to perform such a brutal mutilation. It was also a murder with very few clues. One woman living a couple of doors from the murder scene had woken her husband when she heard gasps and moans in the street, but these had not been loud or lasted for long. A nightwatchman at a nearby warehouse saw nothing.

Polly's murder came within months of two other savage prostitute killings in the East End and, for a while, the deaths were linked together. But even in those days, when forensic science was in its infancy, the police and doctors were soon able to rule out a connection. Polly, by every expert's agreement, was the first of the Ripper victims, and the other two who died, Emma Smith and Martha Turner, were casualties of the everyday violence of the area.

The East End of London was a rough and dangerous

place in the 1880s: respectable citizens tended to stay at home behind locked doors in the evenings. Old people were regularly mugged, the maze of alleyways provided easy escapes for gangs of thieves who roamed the streets. Violence was accepted as one of the occupational hazards of being a prostitute. Most of the women who earned their livings on the game had no homes of their own, but lived in common lodging houses – tenements with rabbit warrens of rooms, one of which they rented for a few pence a night. Many stayed regularly in the same room and were able to leave their few belongings there on a permanent basis. But there was no security because it was strictly 'no pay – no bed', and most of them went out each evening to earn the money to buy them that night's sleep. They trawled around the local pubs looking for customers, and many of them dealt with the misery of their lives in the only way available to them: they got drunk. The lodging keepers were tough men used to dealing with the disorderly behaviour of their customers. The Metropolitan Police estimated that there were about 1200 women earning a living from prostitution in Whitechapel alone in the 1880s.

Conditions for the residents who were not prostitutes were just as bad. There was an average of five people to each room in the East End, and more than half of all children unlucky enough to be born there died before they were five years old. Violence was so commonplace that the death of a prostitute did not make big news.

Emma Smith, who was murdered in April, died after some implement, not a knife, had been thrust into her vagina, causing such severe internal damage that she died the following day from peritonitis and loss of blood. The forty-five-year-old prostitute claimed before she died that she had been attacked and robbed by a gang of four men, and it is hard to see why she would lie. Although her killing was particularly nasty and sexual, it bore none of the Ripper's trademarks.

The death of Martha Turner was also different from the typical Ripper murder. Martha, a thirty-five-year-old prostitute who had very few friends, was found with thirty-nine stab wounds, probably inflicted by two implements. The doctor who examined her body thought one of them was possibly a surgical instrument, but there was none of the sexual mutilation that was the Ripper's trademark. It was probable that Martha was killed by more than one person.

It was three and a half weeks after Martha's death that Polly was killed. In the following three months, the Ripper killed randomly and viciously another four times, making five deaths in all. Every time he managed to evade capture, sometimes by the narrowest of margins.

Eight days after Polly's death, another prostitute, 'Dark Annie' Chapman, was knifed to death in a yard at the back of a lodging house in Hanbury Street. Dark Annie was popular, and although she drank too much she was driven to it by the terrible circumstances of her life. Her husband, from whom she was separated, died, and with him died the small allowance he paid to forty-five-year-old Annie for their two children. She struggled to earn a living by reputable means – selling flowers and doing crochet work – but failed; the children were put in homes and Annie took to the streets. She never recovered from the loss of her children and drank to cope with her unhappiness. For a time she lived with another man, who worked as a sieve maker, so she had the nickname 'Sivvy' among the other prostitutes. She did not swear – which was unusual among women on the game – and she was known to the others as a kind and gentle person.

On the day of her death Annie was in a bad way: she had been in a drunken brawl with another prostitute over a piece of soap, and she'd come off worse, losing her bonnet and her shawl to the other woman. She was a regular at one of the 230 lodging houses in the East End, and so the lodging-house keeper, who liked her, allowed her in to clean herself up. She told him she did not have enough money for her bed, but was going out to earn it. She told a friend:

'It's no use my giving way. I must pull myself together and go out and get some money, or I shall have no lodgings.'

Many of the houses in the Whitechapel area had passages through the ground floor which were left open, front and back, for the floating population of tenants: prostitutes made use of these to take customers through to the yards or up to the landings to do business. Dark Annie and her client had gone through to the yard at the back of a three-storey house in Hanbury Street, and that is where her body was found at six o'clock the next morning by one of the men who lived in the house. Again, she was probably discovered within half an hour of her murder; a passerby had seen a woman and a man outside the house at 5.30am, and her body was definitely not there at a 4.45 when one of the men who lived in the house had been out into the yard.

Dark Annie's injuries were similar to Polly's, and greater. Her throat had been cut right back to her backbone, her stomach opened and her intestines dragged out and looped up to her left shoulder. Her womb, ovaries, part of her vagina and part of her bladder had been removed entirely. Her two cheap brass rings had been taken from her fingers and, together with some coins, left near her feet – details which over the years would give rise to endless speculation about a ritual element to the killing. There were several other 'clues' near the body, including part of a letter (which proved to have nothing to do with the crime), a comb and a bloodstained leather apron.

News of the murder spread rapidly through the densely populated streets of the East End. Crowds gathered, and any suspects taken into custody by the police were screamed and jeered at. The leather apron found near the body led to a man who worked in a boot-making shop; he was arrested. It turned out that the apron belonged to one of the tenants at the lodging house where the body was found.

The missing organs – and the expertise with which they were removed – led the coroner to suggest that the woman had been killed for the sale of her uterus which he claimed would fetch £20 at the disreputable end of the medical profession. There was no other evidence, apart from his statement, of a market in female organs. But he confirmed what was already apparent: the Ripper had a good knowledge of female anatomy. The rumour that the killer was a doctor spread around the East End like wildfire, and anybody seen with anything resembling a doctor's black bag was followed and taunted in the streets.

The Home Office refused to put up a reward for The

Whitechapel Murderer as the *News of the World* dubbed him, but local people clubbed together into vigilante groups and raised their own funds for rewards.

Feeling in the area reached hysteria level when, three weeks after Dark Annie's murder, the killer struck again, this time murdering twice on the same night.

In the early hours of Sunday, 30 September, two women were killed and their bodies abandoned within three quarters of a mile of each other. The Ripper was obviously interrupted at his first murder of the night and, hungry for the rite of mutilation that went with his killings, chose another victim just a few streets away. He was either in the grip of a madness that made him reckless about capture, or supremely clever and self-confident.

The body of forty-five-year-old Elizabeth Stride, known around the East End as Long Liz, was found by a club steward who was returning to the Working Men's Educational Club, in Berner Street, where he lived, with his pony and cart. As he turned into the dark courtyard next to the club at 1am the pony shied and refused to go on. Getting down to investigate, the steward poked about in the darkness with his whip and found something which, with the help of a light from a match, he could see was the body of a woman, blocking the way. Thinking she was an old drunk, he went into the club to get help but when he and several others lifted her they realized with horror that her throat had been cut. It is possible that the killer was still there when the pony shied, and it was his presence in the darkness, rather than the body on the ground, that frightened the animal. But by the time the steward returned with help, he had escaped. The doctors who were called to the scene by the police found no other injuries on Liz.

Liz was only a part-time prostitute. She was Swedish by birth, had been married to a carpenter and had nine children. She claimed to other East End residents that her husband and two of her children had drowned when a ship sank in the Thames, but there was no record of her family among the dead; she probably claimed his death to cover the fact that they had separated. Liz had a regular relationship with another man but, when she was drunk, they would fight and she would walk out for a few days, supporting herself by prostitution.

Liz's last movements were uncertain, although she was seen with a man at 11.45, and possibly seen again twice after that. Descriptions of the man varied, and it's possible that she had more than one customer in the hour before her death.

Catherine Eddowes did not escape mutilation. Her body was found three quarters of an hour after Liz's, her throat slashed and her stomach hacked open, and her entrails pulled out. Her face had been gashed across the nose and down the cheek, her eyelids nicked, the tip of her nose sliced off and there were several other cuts on her face. Her left kidney and her womb had been completely removed. The lack of bleeding from her massive stomach wounds meant that these cuts had been made after her death.

The murder must have occurred between 1.30am and 1.45am because the square where Catherine died was patrolled every quarter of an hour by a policeman who discovered the body. Catherine, who was also known as Kate Kelly, had been in police cells only an hour and a half before her death, being held for being drunk. She had asked to be released and had walked out into the night to her death.

Forty-three-year-old Kate was described by those who knew her as a jolly woman who earned her living by hawking and cleaning, working as a prostitute only when she could find no other way of raising the meagre amount of money she needed to live on. She had two children, although she had never married, and on the day of her death had left the man she lived with, saying that she was going to see her grown-up daughter. Instead, she obviously got drunk and ended up in police custody, being released to her death (a fact that led to a great deal of criticism of the police).

Part of her apron had been cut off and this was found a few streets away. It was bloodstained and had probably been used to wipe clean the murder weapon. More significantly, near to where it was dropped, was a message written in chalk on the hallway wall of a tenement block. It said, 'The Juwes are The men That Will not be Blamed for nothing.' Was it written by the Ripper? Unfortunately, it was wiped clean on the orders of an over-zealous police chief who felt it might whip up racial hatred against the Jewish population.

The police also found traces of blood in a public sink nearby where the killer had washed his hands. The doctor who gave evidence at the inquest stated firmly that he believed the killer had a good knowledge of anatomy; there was a suggestion that the way Kate's innards had been placed about her body could be ritualistic (it was later suggested that the killer was a Freemason).

Up to this point the murderer was a nameless terror

who stalked the East End. But shortly before the night that Liz and Kate died, a letter was delivered to the Central News Agency, claiming to be from the murderer. This was followed by a postcard a couple of days later. Neither were published until after the double murder, which the killer referred to as 'a double event'. Both the letter and card were signed Jack the Ripper. The letter said:

Dear Boss,

I keep on hearing the police have caught me but they won't fix me just yet. I have laughed when they look so clever and talk about being on the right track. That joke about Leather Apron gave me real fits. I am down on whores and I shan't quit ripping them till I do get bucked. Grand work the last job was. I gave the lady no time to squeal. How can they catch me now. I love my work and want to start again. You will soon hear of me with my funny little games. I saved some of the proper red stuff in a ginger beer bottle over the last job to write with but it went thick like glue and I can't use it. Red ink is fit enough I hope, ha,ha. The next job I do I shall clip the lady's ears off and send to the police officers just for jolly wouldn't you. Keep this letter back till I do a bit more work, then give it out straight. My knife is nice and sharp. I want to get to work right away if I get the chance. Good luck. Yours truly,

JACK THE RIPPER

Don't mind me giving the trade name. Wasn't good enough to post this before I got all the red ink off my hands curse it. No luck yet they say I am a doctor now ha, ha.

The postcard was received the day after the double murder. It said:

I was not codding dear old Boss when I gave you the tip. You'll hear about Saucy Jack's work tomorrow. Double even this time. Number one squealed a bit. Couldn't finish straight off. Had no time to get ears for police. Thanks for keeping last letter back till I got to work again.

JACK THE RIPPER

Although the card arrived at the news agency the day after the double murder, there had already been some details published in the newspapers and there was nothing to prove that either letter or postcard had been written by the murderer. Catherine Eddowes's facial mutilations included cuts near her ears, but they had not been severed. In retrospect, the police believed the letter and card were the work of a journalist, trying to increase the tension in the story. Nevertheless, whoever wrote them coined the name that would go down in history.

More horrifically, the local East End man who had set up a 'vigilance committee', a sort of early Neighbourhood Watch scheme, was sent a parcel containing half a human kidney which doctors said matched the other kidney left in Kate Kelly's body. The writer said he had 'fried and ate' the other half of the kidney, and it was 'very nise'. A second, similar, letter was received by the doctor who analysed the kidney, and this time it was signed Jack the Ripper (a name which by then had caught hold in the popular press). Both were written in spidery hand-writing, and the spelling and grammar were much worse than in the letter and card sent to the news agency. The letter to the doctor said:

Old boss you was rite it was the left kidney i was going to hoperate again close to your ospitle just as i was going to dror mi nife along of er bloomin throte them cusses of coppers spoilt the game but i guess i will be on the job soon and will send you another bit of innerds.

JACK THE RIPPER

O have you seen the devle with his mikerscope and scalpul a-lookin at a kidney with a slide cocked up.

There were many hoax letters received, but this one, and the one that accompanied the gruesome present of the half kidney, were the only two that the police felt may have been from the real Ripper.

The final murder occurred on the night of the 8th and 9th of November and, unlike the others, it took place in the privacy of the prostitute's own room. Perhaps because he was inside, and the chances of being interrupted were less, the killer had really gone to town and the body was even more mutilated than ever. The victim was twenty-four-year-old Mary Jane Kelly, a pretty girl and much younger than Jack the Ripper's previous choices. Mary rented her own room which she shared either with her regular boyfriend or with another prostitute. She also used it to entertain customers.

She was last known to be alive at 2am, and may well have died between 3.30am and 4am when two neighbours heard a cry of 'Oh, murder!' Mary's home was in a very rough area and nobody took any notice of screams in the night. But the next morning, at 10.45am, when the landlord's assistant called to try to get some rent money from Mary, what he saw through the window of her ground-floor room made him sick. A pane in the window was broken and he was able to put his hand through and pull aside the dirty curtain which was drawn across. On a table in the middle of the room were two lumps of flesh, and on a bed at one side was the rest of the butchered corpse.

Mary's throat had been slashed, both her breasts had been cut off and put on the table, her nose had been removed, her forehead skinned and one leg from thigh to foot had been stripped of flesh. Her stomach had been opened up and organs removed, her liver being found between her feet. One of her hands had been thrust into the hole of her stomach. The body was so badly mutilated that identification was virtually impossible. It was assumed to be Mary's because it was found in her home.

Mary's clothes were still folded neatly on a chair, but in the grate were warm ashes and the remains of some female clothing that had been burned. Who the clothes belonged to – they were not Mary's – and why they were burned is one of the Ripper mysteries. It may simply have been that they were rags that were set on fire to provide the murderer with light for his grisly task. Another unsolved mystery is how he left the room. Neither Mary nor her boyfriend had a key – they had lost it and used to let themselves in and out by putting a hand through the window and releasing the catch. But the room was found locked.

The East End continued to live in fear of Jack the Ripper, but he never struck again. As each killing became more frenzied and gruesome than the previous ones, the only sensible explanation is that something dramatic happened to end his bloodlust. The compulsion to kill was obviously so strong and so frequent that it would have been impossible for him to have simply decided to lie low.

There have been many theories and suspects over the years, and the quest for Jack the Ripper goes on. The most recent suggestion is that he was a Liverpool merchant who came regularly to London on business, fitting in a bit of prostitute killing while he was there. It is as unprovable as any of the other theories

Perhaps the most credible suspect is Montague Druitt, a lawyer and school teacher who committed suicide at the beginning of December. His mother was in a mental home, certified insane, and Druitt's suicide note said he 'felt I was going to be like Mother and the best thing for me was to die'. There is no strong evidence that Druitt was the Ripper, but he was favoured as a possibility by police at the time, and his death fitted into the timetable of killings rather neatly. He would, however, have had to be pretty self-possessed immediately after the murders, as on at least two occasions he was playing cricket (with some flair) within hours of leaving the scene of crime. Although Druitt was obviously depressed enough to kill himself, there was nothing in his behaviour that suggested he might be seriously deranged.

Other suspects included George Chapman, a Pole whose real name was Severin Klosowski, who, thirteen years later, was found guilty of poisoning three women, and Dr Thomas Neill Cream, dubbed the Lambeth Poisoner, who, on the scaffold, allegedly shouted out, 'I am Jack the . . .' It is unlikely that either of them were the

Ripper. Cream was in prison in America when the Ripper was at large. Chapman was in London, he did have some training as a doctor (he had failed to qualify, and worked as a barber), he was in the habit of staying out all night, and he disliked women enough subsequently to poison three of them. But the motive for his murders was money and to get rid of women who were getting in his way – preventing him moving on to other sexual partners. There was no evidence of pathological hatred of women, and to change from slashing and mutilating victims to quietly poisoning them does not add up psychologically. Chapman has remained one of the top favourite suspects largely because the police chief in charge of the Ripper investigation remarked, when Chapman was arrested in 1902, 'You've caught the Ripper then?'

The idea that the Ripper was a doctor was a popular one, and even Queen Victoria's personal physician Sir William Gull has been a contender for the title, his motive being that he was covering up the indiscretions of the Queen's son, the Duke of Clarence in the East End. This is an unlikely theory as the murders were not clean, functional killings.

The Duke of Clarence himself has been put forward, but his programme of royal engagements would not have made it easy for him to butcher prostitutes. More likely is a theory that one of his tutors, a homosexual and woman-hater, was involved, but even this does not stand up to close scrutiny. The desire to link the murders with the Royal family is probably nothing more than an attempt to make it even more interesting than it is already.

Michael Ostrog, a man believed to have been a

Russian doctor and who was frequently detained in lunatic asylums, was another name on the police list at the time, but very little is known about him. He was a conman and a thief, and probably never had any medical training, but he was believed to carry a bag of surgical implements around with him and to have a profound dislike of women. Another doctor, Dr Morgan Davies, was named by a rather strange black magician, Dr Roslyn D'Onston Stephenson, himself a suspect who was twice taken in for questioning. But there is nothing more than rumour and conjecture attached to either of them.

There were plenty of general theories. A female Jack the Ripper perhaps – a midwife with a sideline in procuring abortions. That would explain how the killer was able to pass so easily away from the scenes of the crimes without arousing suspicion, and also it could account for the female clothing burning in Mary Kelly's grate. Or a Jewish kosher slaughterman who would have a good knowledge of the anatomy of animals. Or a butcher, or just about anyone else for that matter. The truth is, as Chief Inspector Walter Dew, one of the policemen involved in the Ripper investigation, wrote in his memoirs fifty years later: 'I am as mystified now as I was then.'

7. The Lambeth Poisoner and the Reading Baby Farmer

Lou Harvey looked years older than her real age of twenty-four. She'd had a hard life. She made her living like hundreds of other girls, walking the streets of London hoping that men would pay them a shilling for quick, joyless sex. Some nights, if Lou was lucky, she found a punter who would take her to a hotel and give her a couple of shillings. It was harder work – she might have to be at it all night. But it was warm and dry, the money was better and she did not have to worry about paying for anywhere else to sleep that night.

The money bought drink, and drink brought companionship, laughter and peace of mind. The prostitutes of London were still reeling, in 1891, from the violence of Jack the Ripper's reign of terror, and many of them needed large doses of Dutch courage to get them out on to the streets.

It was in October 1891, three years after the Ripper's killings stopped as suddenly as they had started, that Lou Harvey met the strange man who claimed he would cure her spots. He seemed like a normal customer, paying her to spend the night with him at a Soho hotel where the rooms were cheap and the landlord knew exactly what the clients were there for. He seemed to be a satisfied customer because he wanted to see Lou again on the following evening. He wasn't attractive – she described him as bald, yet very hairy everywhere else on his body, with a very noticeable squint. But he was well dressed, he had money and he talked with 'an odd accent'. Lou did not recognize it as American.

He told her, on the first night, that he would bring some pills for her the following day to cure her acne. Lou was pleased about that, but even more pleased at the prospect of some easy money. She was not confident that he would turn up – a lot of punters said they were coming back for more, but never did. But there he was, at their rendez-vous on the Embankment, a little bit late but carrying a bunch of roses for her. He took her to the nearest pub, the Northumberland, and bought her a glass of wine. As they left he gave her some figs, telling her to eat them after she had taken the tablets which he then produced from his waistcoat pocket. They were long pills, wrapped in tissue paper.

There was something about his eagerness that worried Lou. She wasn't keen on taking the tablets but, as he was going on about it so much, she pretended to put them in her mouth. He was insistent that she showed him her empty palm to prove that she had taken them; he had not noticed her switch hands behind her back. As they walked on further she surreptitiously threw the pills away behind her. Funnily enough, her customer did not seem to want to stay around after he had seen her swallow his pills, but he did give her 5s for a ticket to the music hall. Lou felt lucky.

She did not know, until a year later, just how lucky. Lou Harper had met the Lambeth poisoner, the man described by the *News of the World* as 'the greatest

monster of iniquity the century has seen'. And it was the
News of the World that finally brought the killer to book.

If Lou had taken the tablets, she would have been the
third victim of the poisoner. Two other girls, both prostitutes, had died agonizing deaths from strychnine poisoning in the ten days before Lou threw the pills away. Both
had been given the poison by a tall man with cross eyes
and a tall silk hat. One of them said his name was Fred.

The first victim was Ellen Donworth, only nineteen
years old. With her dying breath she was able to say that
she had been given some 'white stuff' from a bottle by a
client she had met earlier in the evening at a nearby
hotel. She had met him by appointment; he had written
to her twice, the first time telling her she was going to be
poisoned by a Member of Parliament, Frederick Smith
(one of the W. H. Smith family). The second letter told
her the name of a hotel where they would meet, and
asked her to bring both letters with her. Before she went
she mentioned her odd letters to a police inspector. Ellen
was back on the streets, looking for another customer,
when she collapsed and writhed on the ground in agony.
She died before she could reach hospital.

A week later Matilda Clover, twenty-six died a similar
appalling death. She had been given two tablets by a
client, called Fred, who had visited her in her room in a
brothel. A servant girl working in the house was able to
describe Fred and her description matched that of Ellen
Donworth. Fred had been there before, with Matilda,
and he had written asking her to meet him that night. He
had bought her a present of a pair of boots.

Since Matilda was an alcoholic who drank all day, her
death was initially put down to alcohol poisoning, and

her death throes were thought to be delirium tremens, or the DTs (the wild and frightening hallucinations that go with long-term alcohol abuse. As the *News of the World* later said, 'Her last moments were those of awful agony, but poor, uncared-for, and practically unknown, she passed away and was buried in a pauper's grave.'

After each of these deaths came two more extremely odd letters. When Ellen died the coroner received a letter claiming to be from 'G. O'Brian', a detective, who wanted £300,000 to 'bring the murderer to justice'. Then Frederick Smith MP received a blackmailing letter claiming that incriminating letters had been found in Ellen's possession. The writer of the letter claimed to be a barrister offering legal help, and told Smith to display the letter in the window of his shop in the Strand if he wanted the lawyer to make contact with him. The police advised Smith to do this, but no 'barrister' came forward.

When Matilda died a highly respectable doctor received a letter accusing him of poisoning her, and a similar letter was sent to Countess Russell, claiming that her husband was the poisoner. At this stage, Matilda's death was still attributed to alcoholic poisoning.

For a few months all went quiet, and no streetwalkers were asked to take strange tablets or drink strange drinks. Then, in April 1892, two more girls died. The two, Alice Marsh and Emma Shrivell, lived in the same lodging house and had spent the evening with a man called Fred who said he was a doctor and had bought them wine and tinned salmon.

Afterwards, he had given each of them three long tablets to take. 'Fred' left and, shortly afterwards, both girls were rushed to hospital in agony and died of strychnine poisoning within the hour. Before they died they gave a description of 'Fred': this matched the description of a man seen leaving their building by a policeman.

The double murder really excited public attention. Could Jack the Ripper be on the loose again? The police were baffled: despite all the attempts by the killer to draw attention to himself with his strange letters, and despite having several good descriptions of the cross-eyed man in the tall silk hat, they were no nearer to a solution.

Then came another strange letter and a visit to the police by a man who claimed he knew the killer. The man, an engineer called Haynes, had been told the identity of the murderer by a drinking companion, a chap with a squint and a tall silk hat. His pub friend had been so convincing that young Haynes hot-footed it down to Scotland Yard to accuse a medical student called Harper who, according to the man in the bar, had killed five prostitutes: Ellen, Matilda, Alice and Emma and another girl, a girl called Lou Harvey. But Lou was still very much alive and had not been connected with the inquiry at this stage.

The letter was similar to the others sent after the earlier murders. It was delivered to the father of the young medical student Harper, a doctor living in Barnstaple, Devon. It demanded £1500 to prevent information incriminating young Harper being given to the coroner. Dr Harper handed it to the police.

At this point Matilda's body was exhumed and it was discovered that it was strychnine, not booze, that had killed her. Lou Harvey was tracked down and told of her encounter with the man with the squint and the tall hat, and how she had thrown away the pills designed to kill her. In investigating young Harper the police visited his lodgings, a house in Lambeth Palace Road, and it was while they were there that the policeman who had seen the man leaving Emma's and Alice's home on the night of their murder spotted someone who looked very like him. It was one of the other lodgers, a man who called himself Dr Thomas Neill. A few discreet inquiries, and Scotland Yard were convinced that, although they may not have found the killer, they had probably found the blackmailer. The handwriting on the letter to Dr Harper matched that of Dr Neill, and it was Dr Neill who had persuaded his drinking companion, young Haynes, to go to the police and lay information against Dr Harper's son.

He was arrested and charged with trying to extort money. When the police arrived at his room he said, 'You have got the wrong man!' but they discovered that he had booked a passage to America and was planning to leave England two days later.

It was at this point that the *News of the World* came to the rescue of Scotland Yard. With the sort of investigative journalism that has always singled the paper out, reporters uncovered the true identity and history of the man now known as the Lambeth Poisoner. When the full story was published in the *News of the World* on 3 July 1892 the police – and the rest of Britain – knew that the killer was already in custody; shortly afterwards he was charged with murder.

The *News of the World* revealed that his full name was Dr Thomas Neill Cream – and that he had already killed at least four other women in Canada and America. He had even served a life sentence for murder in the States, and had launched his killing spree among the vice girls of London only months after being freed from the Joliet State Penitentiary.

Cream was a British citizen, born in Glasgow but taken at the age of two to live in Canada where his father was manager of a shipbuilding yard, having learned his craft in the Clyde ship works. Cream was destined to follow him into the yards as a draughtsman, and served an eight-year apprenticeship, but, at the age of twenty-two, he left and went to university in Montreal.

He had already embarked on a career of crime: theft, insurance fraud and even arson. He burned down the lodgings where he was living in Montreal, having left a skeleton that he had bought for medical-research purposes in his own bed – either as a macabre joke or as a serious attempt to fake his own death. He was clever enough to cover his tracks and, although suspicion fell on him, he was never arrested.

While in Montreal he performed an illegal abortion on one of his girlfriends whose father found out and literally forced him, by threatening him with a shotgun, to marry her. A month after the wedding Cream deserted her and soon afterwards turned up in London for the first time, studying for a medical qualification at St Thomas's Hospital. He failed and moved to Edinburgh where he qualified as a surgeon and physician and, as part of his studies, wrote an acclaimed essay on poisons. While he was in Edinburgh his wife died of consumption at her parents' home.

Back in Canada, he set up practice as a doctor in Kingston, Ontario, but had to leave town in a hurry when the body of a young chambermaid, on whom an unsuccesful illegal abortion had been performed, was found in his garden shed. She had died of chloroform poisoning. There was not enough evidence to charge him, because it could not be proved that the pregnant girl had not committed suicide, but the townsfolk felt strongly enough to chase him out of his home.

He surfaced again in another small town, Hamilton, Ontario, and there, the following year, another girl died, again after an attempted abortion. This time Cream was charged with murder, but was discharged because of lack of evidence. Canada was now getting difficult for him; there were too many stories about his medical incompetence, so he left for the States where he settled in Chicago. Astonishingly, he soon became a fashionable and popular doctor.

Within months, another of his patients died, and after her death came the first of Cream's bizarre attempts to draw attention to himself. The woman died after taking medicine prescribed for her by Cream and, although there was no suspicion of foul play at first, Cream sent a letter to the chemist who had made up the prescription, accusing the man of poisoning her. The police had no idea who sent the letter, but started a thorough investigation.

In the meantime Cream had met and fallen in love with a thirty-three-year-old woman, Julia Stort. She was married, but her husband was sixty-one and in ailing health, and she was game for an affair with the doctor who, at thirty-one, was much nearer her own age. Five months after their relationship started, Cream prescribed epilepsy drugs for Julia's husband who died shortly after taking them. The cause of death was attributed to epilepsy and Cream could easily have got away with the murder.

But once again he felt an urgent need to attract attention to the crime. He persuaded the gullible Julia to give him power of attorney to represent her (the legal right to handle her affairs for her) and proceeded to sue the chemist who made up the medicine for her husband. He also wrote to the coroner, demanding that Stort's body be exhumed, but the coroner ignored him. A month later he wrote again and demanded that the tablets found by Stort's bed be given to a dog. This time the coroner agreed and the poor dog died. The body was exhumed and three and a half grains of strychnine were found.

At this point Julia panicked, turned State's evidence and told the police that Cream had tampered with the tablets after they had been supplied by the chemist. She admitted to what the *News of the World* described as their 'immoral relationship'. For a time the police debated whether to exhume the body of the woman patient who had died – and over whose death Cream had tried to blackmail the chemist – but they decided they had enough evidence to proceed. Cream was found guilty and, despite an appeal, sentenced to life imprisonment.

He served only nine years and nine months, and was released in August 1891 on the grounds of ill health; he instantly got better as soon as he was out. On his release he lived for two months with his brother. He collected $16,000 (about £5000) which had been left to him in his father's will, to be held by his brother until he was free, and then set off for England, for what his family hoped would be a fresh start.

Ten days after his ship docked at Liverpool, Ellen

Donworth died. The break in Cream's murder spree, the five months between the deaths of Matilda Clover, Emma Shrivell and Alice Marsh, was spent back in Canada. While he was there, Cream paid to have 500 handbills printed and shipped back to England, but he never distributed them. They said:

ELLEN DONWORTH'S DEATH
To the Guests of the Metropole Hotel

Ladies and Gentlemen,

I hereby notify you that the person who poisoned Ellen Donworth on the 13th last October is today in the employ of the Metropole Hotel and that your lives are in danger as long as you remain in this Hotel.

Yours respectfully,

W. H. Murray

What Cream had against the Metropole was never uncovered. He probably felt he had been slighted in some way. Most of his bizarre crimes were aimed at getting some obscure revenge against individuals or whole groups of people he did not like, for instance, chemists, doctors and prostitutes.

The *News of the World* described its revelations about Cream as 'a startling, strange, extraordinary history, surely!' and it certainly was. Not only did it galvanize the police into charging Cream with the murders of the prostitutes, but it also brought more and more information to light about Cream's behaviour. It seemed that he visited prostitutes constantly, and most of them escaped unscathed. But even when he was under police observation, shortly before his arrest, he tried to persuade another vice girl to take 'an American drink' which he had prepared for her.

Cream was obviously suffering from a deep underlying mental illness, made worse by syphilis which was affecting the functioning of his brain. This probably explains why he made some very silly slip-ups – like including the name of Lou Harvey on the list of prostitutes he claimed young Harper had killed. Not only should he have known that Lou was still alive when he failed to see her death reported in the papers, but he had also come face to face with her since his abortive attempt to kill her. She bumped into him in Piccadilly and he seemed not to recognize her; when she reminded him of who she was he turned on his heel and hurried away.

In between murdering prostitutes he managed to meet and fall in love with a beautiful young woman, Laura Sabbatini, who lived with her mother in Berkhamsted, Hertfordshire. Laura agreed to become engaged to him, although she did not seem to feel any strong affection for him until after his arrest. From then on, she seemed to enjoy the attention she received, especially when she sat in court at the Old Bailey to watch his trial. Cream sent her a constant supply of love letters from prison, and in one of them he made a reference to the fact that she had declared her love for him for the first time since they met. She also played games with him, sometimes accusing him in her letters of not looking at her in court, at other times refusing to return his glances.

Cream was charged under the name Neill with the murder of Matilda Clover, and went into the dock supremely confident that he would be acquitted. The police were ready with three other murder charges, for the other girls, if that had happened. The *News of the World* described it as 'the greatest criminal trial the century has seen', and called Cream an 'atrocious criminal'.

It is questionable whether we have ever seen a man of the character of Dr Neill. Take the charge against him – that of poisoning four girls. True, they were all of the unfortunate class. He met them as other men meet them. But he poisoned them! . . . It cannot even be guessed what motive he had in his fiendish work.

Despite the off-putting squint, Cream was described by the reporter in court as having a pleasing appearance: 'With spectacles on nose and full grown beard, he looked positively benevolent . . . he was well-favoured and comparatively healthy-looking. There was little sign of worry or anxiety.'

Cream was found guilty and sentenced to death, but still clung to the idea that he would be freed. He was hanged at Newgate Prison on 15 November 1892, having written to Laura the day before, saying that 'the last few days have been among the happiest I have spent'. A crowd gathered outside the prison to see the black flag hoisted, the signal that the execution was over. The *News of the World* was there to record the scene:

'Surely there never was such a collection of low-browed men with coarse open mouths and thick necks as was there. In the main it might have been a gathering of possible criminals. Here and there though were faces of intelligence.'

During his time in prison Cream never confessed to the British murders, but would occasionally boast to the warders about having killed many more victims in America. Some time after his death a story went round that, as he stood on the gallows in the few seconds before the trap door was pulled away, Cream said, 'I am Jack the . . .'. He may have been making a last-minute bid to make his mark in the annals of criminal history by claiming the Ripper killings. But, if so, it was as bizarre and naive as some of the letters he wrote after the murders he definitely committed; after all, he was in prison in America when the Ripper was marauding about London.

Today's forensic psychiatrists would have a field day with Cream, the killer who did not see his victims die. Even had he not been safely detained in an American jail, it is doubtful whether he could ever have convinced any-one that he was the Ripper: a homicidal maniac does not change from an overwhelming need to savage and muti-late a human body to remote killing by poisoning.

The girls who were forced to make their livings on the streets ran the risk of meeting a Ripper or a Dr Cream but, on a day-to-day basis, a much more common risk was pregnancy. Contraception was the exception, not the rule, and illegitimate babies were a natural – but expen-sive – consequence of the lifestyle. Back-street abortion-ists flourished, and so did baby farmers, women who looked after unwanted children.

It was not just prostitutes, of course, who had babies: serving girls, daughters of middle-class burghers, and titled ladies all 'fell', married couples had more children than they could accommodate in their crowded hovels, tragic fathers were left holding babies when their wives died. So there was a lucrative market in taking the problem off the hands of the parents. Many unscrupulous women took the hard-earned cash of the poor with promises that the children would be well cared for, only for the babies to die of neglect or grow up in abject conditions. Frequently, the babies died of not-so-natural causes, but getting enough evidence to prosecute was difficult, especially as many of the births had never been registered and the mothers were unwilling to come forward.

Amelia Dyer lived for many years off the proceeds of baby farming. How early in life she realized that the cheapest baby was a dead baby we do not know, but it is likely that, in over twenty years in the business, she killed many of the tots entrusted to her. When justice finally caught up with her, seven tiny corpses were found, they were probably just the tip of the iceberg. Although she admitted her crimes, she herself did not know how many victims she had killed.

The first the police knew about the Reading Baby Farmer, as Mrs Dyer was dubbed by the *News of the World*, was on 30 March 1896 when a Thames bargeman hooked a soggy brown-paper parcel out of the water, to find it contained the body of a fifteen-month-old baby girl, a piece of tape fastened tight around her neck. Whoever had disposed of the body had not been very careful: in the package was the name of Mrs Harding, with an address in Caversham, a village near Reading. By the time the police got to the address 'Mrs Harding' had moved house a couple of times, but they were able to trace her. Neighbours in the streets where she had lived told stories about a bulky carpetbag she seemed to take with her wherever she went, and there were also tales of babies being carried into the house and never seen again.

Eventually the police caught up with Mrs Dyer who was living with an old lady, known as Granny Smith, who was no relation. Tragically, they were just four days too late to save another two children: four-month-old Doris Marmon, the illegitimate daughter of Eleanor Marmon, was handed over to Mrs Dyer just two days after the body was fished out of the river. Eleanor Marmon also handed over £10 to pay for Doris's keep – a huge profit for Mrs Dyer, as two days later Doris was strangled. So, too, was Harry Simmons, a baby boy handed over by a woman whose maid had given birth to him; she paid Mrs Dyer £5. He lasted only a day in Mrs Dyer's care.

When she was arrested the police dragged the Thames around Reading and found both Doris and Harry, and another four babies, making a total of seven. Mrs Dyer said, 'You will know mine by the tape around their necks.' The landlord at the house where she was living identified the bricks, that she had put in the packages to make the babies sink, as bricks that he had been using to support his rabbit hutch.

Two other babies and two small children were found alive in Mrs Dyer's home, and they were returned to their mothers or found foster homes.

Mrs Dyer was fifty-seven, a short, squat woman who weighed 15 stone and had been baby farming around the Bristol area for many years before moving to Reading. She had been admitted to lunatic asylums three times, each time when things started to get hot for her after children had disappeared. She would tell the parents she had handed them over to someone else, and she would then conveniently go mad for a few months. It was while she was in an asylum that she met Granny Smith whom she took to live with her. The old lady helped with the children and told the police that Dyer was 'sometimes' kind to her.

Mrs Dyer's daughter Polly and her feckless husband Arthur were also arrested, but Mrs Dyer made a rambling statement clearing them. Although she was no doubt the murderess, it would have been very difficult for Polly and Arthur not to have realized what was going on, as they had shared a house with Mrs Dyer and Granny Smith for several months. Both Doris Marmon and Harry Simmons had been killed in Polly's home.

Despite twice trying to commit suicide in prison, Amelia Dyer survived to stand trial at the Old Bailey in May 1896. The defence was that she was insane; the jury took only five minutes to decide that she was responsible for her actions and must hang. The execution took place at Newgate Prison on 10 June 1896, and afterwards the *News of the World* gloated over the fact that her body was 'rotting in the quicklime which destroys the inhabitants of the dread cemetery at Newgate'.

Amelia Dyer was the oldest woman to hang since 1843, and no older woman was executed after her. After her death the contents of her cottage in Kensington Road, Reading, were auctioned, and there was much macabre bidding for the beds and bedding that the dead children had no doubt lain on. A child's cradle was bought for 5s, and the sale made a total of £7 15s (£7.75), far more than the goods were worth.

8. 'Last Words of Love'

The dingy basement kitchen was filthy, with greasy pans and unwashed plates everywhere. Friends were expected for dinner, but no food had been prepared. His wife, fat and with dyed red hair, was still in her dressing-gown, her hair in curlers and the smell of whisky on her breath. He wondered if one of her 'gentlemen friends' had been round during the day, making love to her in his house.

Something inside Hawley Harvey Crippen snapped. He had been working hard all day. He was facing money problems, he was madly in love with another woman, and he could not take it any longer. The thought of a lifetime looking at his wife Belle's plump over-made-up face was too much for him. He took out the small packet of deadly poison, hyoscine, which he had told the chemist was for homeopathic remedies. He slipped it back into his pocket and set about preparing the meal for their guests. It would be the last meal Belle would ever eat . . .

The murder of Belle Elmore by her husband, Dr Crippen, is one of the most famous cases in British criminal history, and Crippen has been ranked alongside the most notorious killers of all time. Yet, if he came before the courts today, it would be seen as a low-key domestic murder case, and Crippen would serve no more than the average eleven years of a British life sentence; he would probably be out after eight or nine because he would be the perfect, well-behaved prisoner.

It was not the murder that made Crippen famous. It was the way he was caught – fleeing from justice with his lover disguised as a boy.

Hawley Harvey Crippen, known as Peter to his friends, was an American with a basic medical training that did not qualify him to practise either as a doctor or as a dentist (both of which he did at different times). His training, however, did allow him to put Dr in front of his name. He had an American degree in homeopathic medicine. His family was hard working and religious, and so too was Crippen. But he had a weakness for women and was not a good judge of them.

When he was twenty-five, in 1887, he married a rather dim but pretty Irish girl called Charlotte. Their son Otto was born soon after they married, but three years later Charlotte died and was buried at Salt Lake City, Utah, where the couple were living at the time. Young Otto was sent to Crippen's mother and father in Michigan and grew up happily.

Within two years Crippen had met his second wife, Belle. She was known as Cora Turner when he met her. Even that was not her real name, which was, astonishingly, Kunigunde Mackamotzki. She was the child of a Polish father and a German Jewish mother, an exotic combination that gave her, at seventeen, a pretty face, dark brown eyes, and a small rounded body. That is how she looked when Crippen first met her in New York, and she soon had him dangling from a string.

She was the mistress of a rich businessman who had no intention of ever leaving his wife for her, but paid for her accommodation. She taunted poor Crippen with this, finally telling him that her benefactor was going to run away from his family to be with her. It was a ruse to force the thirty-year-old doctor's hand; he proposed marriage to her. For Belle the match meant security and respectability, and she persuaded her new husband to pay for her to have voice-training lessons. Poor Belle had a small voice and big ambitions; she wanted to be an opera singer.

Crippen was besotted. Belle was an exotic creature who wore brightly coloured stage clothes, she dripped with jewelry and furs (some bought by her new husband, some by her ex-lover). To a patent medical salesman she seemed like a being from another planet, and he worshipped her. Belle lapped it up and a pattern of married life was established in which he waited on her every whim. He knew they would never have children; Belle had had her ovaries removed, possibly as a drastic form of contraception.

The firm Crippen was working for, which sold quack remedies for piles and other common illnesses, and which enjoyed having a 'doctor' as a salesman, sent him to London to be manager of their office there. It was a few months before Belle joined him, and in that time she wrote to say she was giving up opera for the music hall. Crippen replied forbidding her, and shortly afterwards she set sail for London. But while they had been apart Belle had decided that faithful married life was not for her, and she had started seeing other men.

In London she created a scene about her professional career, and Crippen capitulated and allowed her to take to the music hall. She called herself Macka Motski, based on her real maiden name, but failed to take the stage by storm. She changed names again, this time to Belle Elmore, but that was not enough to move her up from the very bottom of the bill. She had a few bookings: a couple of weeks in Oxford as a comedienne, an evening singing at Teddington town hall. Her only chance to tread the boards of a top London stage came when there was a strike of music-hall performers – she was booed for blacklegging.

Still, she fitted into theatrical life well and was very popular with other entertainers. She was treasurer of the Music-Hall Ladies Guild and a leading figure at all their social events.

Crippen went back to Philadelphia, for his company for a few months, and, while he was away, sent money to Belle. But it was never enough for her extravagant tastes and she found ways of making more. To the horror of her husband, she started singing at 'smoking concerts', a polite name for men-only nights where the entertainment was always risqué.

Money was a constant problem for the Crippens. The £3 a week that Crippen was paid by the patent-medicine company was a small wage even in those days, and it stopped completely when the company decided that it did not suit its image for the London manager to be married to a small-time music-hall star.

Belle also started an affair with another stage entertainer, an American called Bruce Miller, who was over in Europe for the Paris exhibition. Miller visited her at home most days, and may even have lived with her while Crippen was away. When he returned, to take a job with a firm of 'ear specialists', Belle confessed her affair and married life, which had not been happy for some time, became even more strained.

The Crippens moved to a semi-detached house in Holloway for which they paid £52 a year in rent. They were so short of cash that they took in paying guests, but it was Crippen who had to get up early to prepare the breakfasts and clean the shoes of their guests, and it was he who prepared the evening meals when he got home from work. Belle had never been prepared to do housework and they lived in squalor. The windows were never cleaned or opened. Belle had two treasured cats who were not allowed outside, so the smell was strong, and it is hardly surprising that the venture with the paying guests did not last long.

When he lost his job Crippen took anything he could in order to earn a living, working as a dentist and as a doctor specializing in women's problems – neither of which he was qualified to do. He found full-time employment with the Yale Tooth Specialists, where he worked in partnership with another dentist; there he met and fell in love with one of the typists, Ethel le Neve.

Ethel was a quiet respectable girl, not very popular with the others in the office because she was always complaining, mainly about her health. But she was a reliable worker. She had been forced to leave home at sixteen – her parents were poor – and go to London to earn a living, a hard and lonely prospect for a young girl. When she met Crippen she was only twenty, but it was four years before they became romantically involved with each other. Ethel lived in lodgings and her landlady was very fond of her, treating her more like a daughter than a paying guest.

But Ethel was not the shrinking violet she was after-wards made out to be. She had changed her name from Neave to le Neve because she thought it sounded more glamorous, and she did not find it hard to develop a taste for furs and jewelry when the chance came . . .

Belle probably knew about Ethel, although Crippen did not flaunt his young lover. When he and Ethel made love it was in hotel bedrooms, usually while Belle was away on one of her infrequent theatrical trips. But Belle and her husband did not share a bedroom, and she had other men in her life. Her American lover Bruce had returned to his wife and family in Chicago, but he and Belle kept up a romantic correspondence and she may have taunted her husband with his name.

She threatened on many occasions to leave Crippen and, if he had let her go, he would perhaps have lived out a quiet and unspectacular life with Ethel. But he was overdrawn at the bank and he knew that, if Belle went, she would take the £600 savings they had (about £40,000 in today's money). At the time of her death Belle had made an arrangement to withdraw the money which, although it was held in a joint account, was at least half hers (it was probably money acquired from her rich ex-lover, or money she made from the 'entertainment' she laid on at the smoking parties. It was certainly far more than she would have made as a bottom-of-the-bill music-hall star).

On the night of her death the Crippens were enter-taining a couple called Martinetti, two retired music-hall acrobats who were friends of Belle's. The Martinettis said later, in court, that it was 'quite a pleasant evening'.

They were the last people, apart from Crippen, to see

Belle alive. According to Crippen, after their friends had gone there was a bitter row, in which a tipsy Belle taunted her husband about her other lovers and accused him of failing to look after their guests properly. (She claimed he should have helped the elderly Mr Martinetti upstairs when he needed to go to the toilet.)

After the row Crippen persuaded Belle to take a nightcap, a drink laced with poison. Death would have come quickly. He later claimed he burned her head, hands and feet to ashes in the kitchen stove, although he may well have disposed of the head in the English Channel when he went on holiday to France. The rest of Belle was buried beneath the brick floor of the coal cellar.

Crippen must have been very confident that he had got away with it, because his behaviour in the days and weeks after the murder was nothing short of foolhardy. He started pawning Belle's jewelry straightaway and, within two days, Ethel moved in to live with him and was seen in public wearing Belle's furs and brooches. Crippen told Belle's friends that his wife had been called back to America because of the illness of a relative, and a few weeks later announced to them that she had suddenly died of pneumonia. When pressed for more details he said that she was in the remote mountains of California and that his son Otto (now grown up and married) was with her when she died.

But he certainly did not pretend to be a grieving widower as he set off with Ethel for a holiday in France. He employed a French maid to move into his home to look after him and Ethel, and he even took Ethel along to one of the social functions of the Guild that Belle belonged to, again with Ethel wearing Belle's jewelry.

Not surprisingly, Belle's friends began asking questions. One of them, an entertainer who had just returned from a tour in America, was particularly persistent because, while he was over there, he had tried to trace Belle. He alerted the police who questioned Crippen for several hours at his dental practice.

Crippen could still have got away with it. He admitted to the police that he had lied about Belle's disappearence; he said she had left him for another man, but that he had covered her tracks to avoid a scandal. He allowed the police to search his home which, despite the French maid, was still in the dirty chaos that Belle had established, and they found nothing. They were prepared to accept his story.

It was only when, returning to make some more routine inquiries, they discovered that Crippen had wound up the dentistry business and left the country with Ethel, that they realized that this was a murder investigation. But it still took them three days to find the remains of Belle, buried in lime, under the coal-cellar floor. Along with a dismembered torso they found some underwear, some hair curlers with dyed hair attached, and a man's pyjama jacket.

By this time the newspapers were full of the story and Crippen's and Ethel's descriptions were published everywhere. Detectives discovered that, before he fled, Crippen had sent the office boy at his firm out to buy clothes for a boy, and they suspected that the slim Miss le Neve might be travelling in disguise.

She was. But the disguise was not good enough to fool the captain of the SS *Montrose*, sailing from Antwerp to Canada. He had a Mr John Robinson and his sixteen-year-old son on board, and there was something very strange about the way the father and son behaved. They held hands a lot and the father looked after the son solicitously. When they played ball on deck, the 'boy' always closed his legs together like a woman would. When a breeze lifted the back of 'Master' Robinson's jacket, the captain saw that the trousers were held together with safety pins. Although Ethel had a boyish figure, the natural curve of her hips obviously did not fit inside boys' trousers. When the captain called to 'Mr Robinson' it took a moment or two for Crippen to respond to the unfamiliar name.

The *Montrose* was fitted with a radio mast and a 'wireless telegraph', a new-fangled invention that fascinated 'Mr Robinson'. He did not realize that it was going to prove vital in his capture, and would help to put his name in the history books. 'Have strong suspicion that Crippen London cellar murderer and accomplice are among saloon passengers . . .' was the beginning of a long cable sent by the captain of the *Montrose* back to the ship's owners in London. The owners alerted Scotland Yard, and Detective Inspector Walter Dew set sail for Canada on a faster boat.

The whole of Britain was riveted by the chase which was carried in detail in the newspapers, with daily updates about the relative position of the two ships. The only people who were unaware of it were the passengers on the *Montrose*. As the ship neared Quebec harbour it was met by a pilot boat; one of the 'pilots' who stepped on board the *Montrose* was Dew who had met Crippen before while questioning him in London. When he recognized the detective, Crippen knew the game was up and was relieved to surrender himself. A note was found in his cabin which suggested he had been planning to commit suicide:

I cannot stand the horror I go through every night any longer, and as I see nothing ahead and the money has come to an end, I have made up my mind to jump overboard tonight. I know I have spoiled your life but I hope some day you can learn to forgive me. Last words of love. Yours, H.

It may have been a genuine suicide plan, or it may have been an elaborate ruse in case the ship was met by the police: Crippen was intending to smuggle himself ashore while Ethel revealed that he had killed himself.

He and Ethel were returned to London on another ship and, during the voyage, they were kept completely separate. Dew found Crippen a reasonable companion and, towards the end of the voyage, he agreed to allow him to see Ethel. They were each taken to their cabin doors and could look at each other, but not speak. Crippen told Dew, 'She's been my only comfort for the past three years.' It was a moving moment.

Ethel was also under arrest, but only as an accessory to murder, and she and Crippen were tried separately. He came before the Old Bailey in October 1910 and, as usual with celebrated cases, the court was packed, everyone trying to catch a glimpse of the 'prim little man in closely buttoned frock coat and gold-rimmed glasses'. He was calm throughout and the *News of the World* wrote: 'It is impossible to build any notion of the man's character from his commonplace, stolid, expressionless appearance, his absolutely imperturbable manner.'

According to the court reporter, there was deathly

silence when Crippen was called upon to plead guilty or not guilty.

People held their breath to catch the first notes of his voice, often an infallible index to character. But as the first words passed his lips and drifted over the court the feeling was one of disappointment. The enigma remained. The voice was as mysterious as the man.

Crippen pleaded not guilty, still maintaining that his wife had gone off with another man and that the remains found under the coal-cellar floor must have been in the house before he moved there. There was a sensation in court when it was learned that Bruce Miller, Belle's American lover, was going to appear as a witness, having been brought over from Chicago where he was now working as an estate agent. Miller admitted sending a card to Belle the previous Christmas with the message 'love and kisses to Brown Eyes', but he denied that they had had an affair. He insisted that the last time he had seen her was six years earlier and that, although he had been very fond of her and they had kissed, because they were both married they had gone no further.

'I thought a great deal of her, but she was a married lady and I let it end at that,' he said. 'I could not be more than a friend, she was a married lady and I was a married man.'

He had seen her, he said, for about five years, while he had business in Europe, but since he returned to America they had kept in touch three or four times a year by letter or card, but that was all. As Miller was living in Chicago with his wife and son, it was obvious that Belle had not run away with him, as Crippen had suggested.

The prosecution was also able to demolish Crippen's assertion that the remains under the floor were not Belle's. A piece of skin with the marks of an operation scar was passed around the court in a soup bowl, to the excitement of the public-gallery spectators. Ladies whipped out lorgnettes to get a better look. Medical experts maintained that the scar was from the abdominal operation that Belle had had.

Much more damning was the proof that the pyjamas found with Belle's remains had been bought by Crippen from Jones Brothers department store in the Holloway Road, and that from the style of manufacture they could not be as old as Crippen was claiming. They had been bought since he and Belle had moved to that house.

The jury was also swayed by evidence of the way in which Crippen and Ethel had behaved immediately after Belle's disappearance. It took them just twenty-seven minutes to decide that he was guilty, and he was sentenced to hang. His last words to the court were, 'I still protest my innocence.'

There was almost as much public interest in Ethel's trial as there had been in her lover's. Again the galleries were crowded, and Winston Churchill was among those who managed to get in to see her charged, under her correct name of Ethel Clara Neave. She was white and drawn, 'the very picture of misery', as the *News of the World* described her.

The jury heard how she had been turned out of her family home at sixteen to earn a living, and how she had been a steady and respectable young lady ever since. Her landlady gave evidence of how she had been given many of Belle's clothes after the murder, but had been told by

Ethel that Belle was in America. It took less time to acquit Ethel than it had to convict Crippen: the jury was out for only fifteen minutes.

Crippen's appeal, on which he placed much hope, failed and he was hanged on 23 November 1910. The prison officers who looked after him in his last days were, like the police who dealt with him, impressed by his polite and considerate behaviour. He spent his last days in the condemned cell reading novels, having three visits a week from Ethel, and writing letters to her.

In a statement he did not admit his own guilt, but was at pains to stress her innocence:

This love was not of a debased or degraded character ... Whatever sin there was – and we broke the law – was my sin, not hers. As I face eternity I say that Ethel le Neve has loved me as few women love men and that she is innocent of any crime. Surely such love as hers for me will be rewarded.

He wrote to Ethel and told her that when he received the news from the Governor of Pentonville Prison that his appeal had failed he kissed her photograph.

'It was some consolation, although in spite of all my greatest efforts it was impossible to keep down a great sob and my heart's agonized cry.'

On the night before his execution he attempted suicide, but was foiled by the carefulness of the prison officers. One of them had heard a noise while Crippen was preparing for bed, a cracking noise. When he handed in his glasses, as he had to every night, they were thoroughly checked and the guards noticed that part of one of the steel arms was missing. They searched his cell and found it concealed in the seam of his pants; he admitted that he had planned to use it to sever an artery during the night.

There are various rumours as to what happened to Ethel after her lover was hanged. One is that she went to Australia, another is that she kept a tearoom in Bournemouth, and a third is that she married a man called Smith who never knew her true identity.

During the pursuit that led to his arrest, and during his trial, Crippen was painted as a depraved monster but, after his execution, public opinion about him changed and he was seen for what he probably was: a hen-pecked and desperately unhappy husband who fell in love with a young woman whose looks and lifestyle were nearer his own.

Poor old Belle had been cheated by marriage as much as he had: she wanted excitement and bright lights but opted for security, which she did not enjoy. They were trapped, both of them, in a joyless relationship which, in the early days of the century, was difficult to end. But did Crippen really set out to murder her? He was unlucky in that his solicitor, a hard-drinking and hard-gambling man, fell out with the most famous barrister of the day, Edward Marshall Hall and, consequently, Hall did not defend Crippen.

If Hall had defended Crippen, he would have run the case differently: records show that his theory was that Crippen was using the poison, hyoscine, in small doses to make Belle sleep, perhaps to divert her from demanding sex (although that sounds unlikely, as the relationship had been very rocky for some time) or to allow him to get out to see Ethel, or even to entertain her in the house. On the night of 1 February, Hall would have argued,

Crippen had inadvertently given Belle too large a dose, and had then seen her death as a chance to start again with his lover.

The police came in for much criticism and Detective Inspector Dew, the man who had made the dramatic transatlantic dash to catch Crippen, resigned from the force. There certainly were mistakes in the handling of the case: if the police had watched Crippen and Ethel they would have been able to arrest them before they left the country; if they had searched the house properly the first time they would have found the body, and to take three days searching a small house anyway was surprising, especially as under the coal-cellar floor should have been an obvious place to look. What's more, it wasn't until the Old Bailey case was in full swing that the prosecution unearthed the evidence about the pyjama jacket.

But, if the police had been more efficient, and Dr Crippen had been arrested before he dressed Ethel as a boy and took her to sea, he would probably never have made it into Madame Tussaud's Chamber of Horrors, and the history books.

9. The Brides in the Bath

The *News of the World* of 3 January 1915 was full of details about the progress of the First World War: Allied Advance in Belgium, Raid on German Fleet, Mud Clogs Rifles – Soldiers Fight with Their Fists, said the headlines. The stories included the report of the legendary Christmas Day in the trenches when the British and German soldiers sang carols together and had a game of football.

But there was a small story tucked away on page nine that caught the eye of a Blackpool landlady, Mrs Crossley, as she took a few minutes' break from her work to read the paper that evening. Bride's Tragic Death. Drowned in Bath on Day after Wedding was the headline, and the story gave details of the inquest on Margaret Lofty, a thirty-eight-year-old clergyman's daughter who drowned in her bath. The death was, the inquest had decided, a terrible accident.

Mrs Crossley called her husband to read the story. For a moment they looked at each other in shocked silence, and then Mr Crossley told his wife that they had to do something. He took out notepaper and pen and sat down to write a letter. He addressed it to The Murder Squad, Scotland Yard, London.

Mr Crossley's letter arrived on the desk of Chief

Inspector Arthur Neil, along with other information from a solicitor in Aylesbury whose client had also read the *News of the World*. Alarm bells rang in the inspector's head – and the hunt for one of the most cold-blooded and ruthless serial killers of the twentieth century was launched. Without the newspaper story, Brides in the Bath killer, George Smith, might have continued his murderous career unchecked and more innocent women would have been lured to their deaths.

When Smith was caught he was known to have killed three women and robbed many more – but the true tally of his victims will never be known. He preyed on lonely spinsters, taking their life savings and, when he could find no other way of getting rid of them, drowning them in their baths.

George Joseph Smith was born into a poor family in the East End of London where he lived with his mother and stepfather. He was only nine when he was sent away to a 'reformatory', effectively a prison for children, where the routine was brutal and harsh with repeated floggings for minor misdemeanours. Smith was sent there for petty thieving and was not released until he was nearly seventeen. The only education he had received was in crime and he took up his career in earnest, being given a succession of short jail sentences for stealing and receiving stolen goods (he persuaded a servant girl to steal from her employers and give the booty to him).

Charming women into doing his dirty work appealed to Smith, and he found it easy. He was tall for the time, at 5'9", with fair hair and very dark eyes which were described as 'compelling' and 'mesmerizing' by women he met. He was not good looking and he could scarcely read and write, but he was a good talker and could pass himself off as a gentleman. He always wore good clothes and could spout romantic poetry to win the hearts of the girls he met. He had that elusive quality, sex appeal.

After a short spell in the army he moved from London to Leicester and, when he was twenty-six, met and married a pretty eighteen-year-old girl, Catherine Thornhill, the daughter of a respectable bootmaker. Her parents were opposed to the marriage, and with good reason; within months Smith had persuaded Catherine to take a series of jobs as a maid and rapidly to leave each one with jewelry and expensive ornaments in her pockets. When he married Catherine he used the name George Love on his wedding certificate, so it may, in fact, have not been his first marriage, simply the first that ever came to light.

Catherine was arrested in Hastings, Sussex, when she tried to pawn some spoons she had stolen. She served twelve months in prison and, when she was released, she identified her husband and turned him over to the law. He got two years in prison and, as soon as he was released, Catherine fled to Canada to get away from him.

It was during Catherine's year in jail that Smith hit upon a con trick that would net him much money over the next few years. He selected a likely looking woman, a spinster or a widow, chatted her up, promised to marry her and then disappeared with her money, her jewelry and sometimes even her clothing. Occasionally, he had to go through with a wedding ceremony to get access to the woman's savings.

His first victim was a middle-aged widow who stood by him during his two years' imprisonment. When he was released he went back to her for just long enough to clean her out of all her valuables, and then he disappeared.

For the next few years Smith worked his way around England, following the same pattern. As soon as he had wormed his way into the woman's affections he would take her out for the day – he was mean enough always to choose a free place of entertainment, like a funfair or a park – then he would make an excuse to leave her for a few minutes. He would then go back to the home they were sharing and disappear with everything he could easily carry away. His victims were touchingly naive, grateful to a man for offering to marry them when spinsterhood was a badge of failure. Some of them were prepared to make over all their savings to him even before the trip to the altar.

As long as Smith kept moving, he could operate very successfully. The reason the list of his victims is incomplete is that many of them were ashamed to go to the police and admit their foolishness; others may simply never have connected their particular conman with the notorious killer that Smith eventually became.

Smith married twice in four weeks in July 1908. His first 'wife' was Florence Wilson, a widow from Worthing, who married him after a three-week whirlwind courtship. He persuaded her to take £30 out of her post office account, which he pocketed, and he then took her to an exhibition at London's White City. He claimed he was going to buy a newspaper, but disappeared back to their digs and parcelled up all Florence's belongings which he later sold. She never saw him again.

By this time Smith had a shop in Bristol where he

traded in antiques, sometimes selling the objects he stole from his 'wives' and 'fiancées'. When he advertised for a housekeeper to look after the shop and flat, he met Edith Pegler, a slim, attractive twenty-eight-year old. Smith fell in love with her, and they married, using his real name, on 30 July. Edith was the one true love of his life, 'the womanly woman with a pure heart', as he later described her from his prison cell. For the next seven years Smith would, in his own twisted way, remain faithful to Edith, always returning to her after his murderous adventures with other women.

During their time together he kept Edith on the move: they lived in Bedford, Luton, Croydon, Southend, Bath, Bristol, Southend again, Barking, Walthamstow, Bristol again, Margate and Tunbridge Wells. Smith explained his absences – sometimes as long as five months – and his piles of cash by saying he was trading in antiques. On one occasion he said he had been to Canada and sold a Chinese picture for £1000, on another that he had been in Spain and had sold antique jewelry for a £200 profit. When he was away he sent Edith postcards, letters and occasionally, money. When she ran out of money she would return to her mother's home in Bristol where Smith would invariably find her.

His next 'marriage' was to Miss Sarah Faulkner, fourteen months after he wed Edith. Miss Faulkner was a clerk from Southampton, with £300 in her savings account and another £100 in government stock. It took her a few days after the wedding to withdraw the money, which she believed her new husband, George Rose as he called himself, needed to set up an antique shop. When she gave him the money they went on a trip to the

National Gallery in Trafalgar Square and Smith left her while he went to the gents. He never returned and, when she reached their lodgings in Clapham, she found he had taken all her jewelry and belongings, worth another £200.

With this total of over £600 he was able to return to Edith and live in style for some months – the average wage for a working man of the time was only £100 per year. But Smith was not clever with money; he invested badly in property and refused to take advice, being paranoid about others ripping him off. By the following summer he was short of cash again, so he kissed Edith a fond farewell and set off on his travels.

He did not need to go very far. A few miles from where he and Edith had been living in Bristol he met Bessie Mundy, a wealthy young lady whose father, now dead, had been a bank manager. Bessie had £2500 invested for her, but it was managed by her uncle and she could not get her hands on it. Her income was £8 a month which did not suit her new 'husband', who called himself Henry Williams and described himself as a picture restorer.

Again, it was a whirlwind romance, and the couple moved to Weymouth – presumably to avoid Smith bumping into Edith. Despite pleas to her uncle for money, Smith had to remain with Bessie for three months before he could get at her cash, and then he only managed to unlock £135. He ran as soon as he had it, leaving Bessie a note saying that he had caught 'a disease which is called the bad disorder', in other words a sexually transmitted disease, from her and that he was having to go to London for treatment. He told her to tell her uncle the money had been stolen.

Poor Bessie had fifteen months to get over the loss of her husband but, obviously, she never did. When she met Smith again by chance, in Weston-super-Mare, she instantly forgave him for deserting her. Bessie was living in a boarding house and her landlady, who was fond of her, advised her to be cautious about returning to her 'husband', But Bessie was smitten and walked out with 'Henry Williams', never to return again, not even to collect her belongings.

Now Smith faced a trickier problem than with any of his previous wives. Bessie was rich, but her money was beyond his reach, until he came up with the plan that would, according to the *News of the World*, turn him into 'a professional murderer who went on from year to year, plying his fell trade'.

He knew that, if Bessie made a will leaving everything to him, when she died her uncle would be unable to prevent him inheriting it. For the sake of appearances he, too, made a will leaving all his property to Bessie; she thought he was being a considerate husband looking after her future. He certainly was planning her future and it was going to be a very short one.

His problem was how to kill Bessie without arousing suspicion, and he hit upon the perfect plan. It meant he had to go out and buy a bath – bathrooms in private houses and lodgings were still uncommon. The bath, made of zinc, cost £2 but Smith managed to beat the price down by 2s 6d (12½p).

The next day he took Bessie to the doctor in Herne Bay, where they were living in lodgings, and said that she had suffered a fit. Bessie claimed she had just had a headache but appeared to accept that, perhaps, she could not remember the fit. Two days later he called the doctor again, saying she had had another one, but when the doctor examined her he could find nothing wrong. That night, at Smith's dictation, Bessie wrote to her uncle describing the bad fits she had had and how her loving and attentive husband had helped her through them.

The next morning Bessie took her fateful bath. She even had to make the endless trips up and down stairs carrying the water in buckets herself, as her 'loving husband' had gone out to buy some fish for her breakfast. Soon after he returned she was dead, naked on her back in the bath, her hair in curlers and a tablet of Knights Castile soap clutched in her right hand. Smith was the only witness and, when the doctor arrived, he said that he believed she must have had another fit. Bessie's suspicious uncle demanded a post-mortem, but the coroner was satisfied with a statement from the grieving husband who cried his way through the inquest. Despite her family contesting the will, Bessie's £2500 was paid to Smith – allowing him to go home to Edith with a bulging wallet.

Once again, the money was invested badly and lasted Smith and Edith only fifteen months. Once again, he needed to find another wealthy lady. And, having got away with murder, he had no qualms about trying it again.

It was in Portsmouth that he met his next victim, a small, fat twenty-five-year-old nurse called Alice Burnham, who was employed looking after an elderly man. Like most of Smith's conquests, poor Alice had never enjoyed much attention from men, and she was instantly infatuated by Smith. Her father, a Buckinghamshire fruit grower, travelled to Portsmouth when his excited daughter cabled him about the wonderful man she had met and intended to marry, and tried his best to talk sense to her. But Alice was determined and Smith married her – using his own name – at the register office in Portsmouth in November 1913. The day before the wedding he took out a £500 insurance policy on his new bride, using the money from her post office savings account to pay the first premium. He then demanded that her father give her all the money he had been keeping for her – £104. When Alice's worried father wrote asking for more details of his new son-in-law's background, Smith sent him a badly written and abusive postcard.

The honeymoon was spent in Blackpool, at the boarding house in Regents Road run by Mr and Mrs Crossley. The Crossleys' home was the second one that Smith inspected for accommodation; he rejected the first because it did not have a bathroom. The next day he took Alice to see a local doctor, but Alice was a good deal brighter than Bessie and he could not pretend to her that she had had a fit. All she could tell the doctor was that she had a headache which he put down to the long journey the couple had made.

Two days after they checked into the Crossleys' house Alice asked the landlady's daughter to prepare a bath for her. She and Smith then went out for a walk in the bracing December air and returned as the Crossley family were sitting down to their evening meal. After a few minutes Mrs Crossley noticed a damp stain on the ceiling, caused by the bath overflowing, and at that moment Smith arrived at the door with some eggs which he claimed he had been out to buy for their breakfast.

According to Mrs Crossley he was dishevelled and out of breath.

He went upstairs to his wife and, within minutes, called for help, saying that he needed a doctor because his wife could not speak to him. She certainly could not; she had been drowned. His behaviour and his comments made Mrs Crossley very suspicious. She was so convinced that he had been involved in some way in his wife's death that she refused to allow him to stay another night under her roof. She told him several times that he was callous. When asked about funeral arrangements for Alice he chose the cheapest, with the comment, 'When they are dead, they are dead.'

'He did not seem sorry at all. He was a very hard-hearted man. His feelings were not those of a husband,' said Mrs Crossley. As he left her house she shouted 'Crippen!' after him.

But there was nothing she could prove and, when the inquest was held, Smith cried all the way through, perhaps as much because he had drunk a whole bottle of whisky as for grief for his 'wife'. The coroner did not ask any searching questions about the death; if he had, he might have discovered that the stout Mrs Smith could only just wedge herself in the narrow bath, so accidental drowning would have been impossible. Smith stayed in Blackpool just long enough to get the funeral arrangements over, three days after Alice's death – less than two months in all since he had married her. Her family were not notified in time for them to be at the funeral and, when her father heard about his daughter's death, he, too, shared Mrs Crossley's suspicions. The insurance company paid out the £500 to Smith.

Smith went back to Edith briefly, but was soon taking another woman as his 'lawful wedded wife', this time a servant girl he met in Bournemouth. Two weeks after first encountering him, Alice Reavil became 'Mrs Oliver James' at Woolwich register office in London. Alice was very lucky; she was not wealthy enough to need to 'take a bath'. Smith simply persuaded her to withdraw all her savings, £78, and then, three days after the wedding, he took her for a tram ride and deserted her. He returned to their lodgings in Battersea and took everything else she owned, including a piano and her clothes.

He already knew he had bigger fish to fry. In June 1914, two months before marrying Alice Reavil, he had met Margaret Lofty, a thirty-eight-year-old spinster whose father, who had been a vicar in Bath, had left her a small inheritance. She earned a living as a companion to wealthy ladies. She had been jilted by her fiancé earlier in the year, and was consequently depressed. Between jobs, she was living with her sister Ethel and her mother in Bath. She did not tell Ethel she had met another man, knowing that Ethel would preach caution, but in the days before her marriage she became 'a brighter and happier woman'. Even so, for Smith it was a lengthy courtship, taking him two months from deserting Alice to taking Margaret out to tea on 15 December 1914. Margaret never returned home, and two days later was married to 'John Lloyd' at the register office in Bath. That same day the newly weds travelled to London and moved into lodgings in Highgate, Smith already having taken out a £700 life-insurance policy on Margaret.

By now, Smith's murderous routine was well established. First, check that the lodgings have a bathroom – in this case it was Margaret who asked the landlady, Miss Louisa Blatch. Second, take new wife to doctor with complaints of unspecified feelings of being unwell. Third, get new wife to write will in his favour. Fourth, get her to write to her family telling them what a wonderful husband she now has. Fifth, persuade her she needs to take a bath . . .

It was on their second evening in Highgate that Miss Blatch, who was ironing in the kitchen, heard the bath being prepared.

'I heard a sound from the bathroom,' she said. 'It was a sound of splashing. Then there was a noise of someone putting wet hands or arms on the side of the bath, and then a sigh, like the sound a child would make.'

The next sound she heard was of the harmonium being played in the downstairs parlour – although Smith had only a rudimentary education, at some point he had learned to play the piano quite well. For ten minutes she heard 'Nearer My God to Thee' being played furiously, followed by the noise of the front door slamming. After another ten minutes the bell rang and it was 'Mr Lloyd'. He said he had forgotten his key.

'Is my wife down yet?' he asked, and showed Miss Blatch a bag of tomatoes he had bought 'for Mrs Lloyd's tea'. He went upstairs and immediately called Miss Blatch. His 'wife's' body, still in the bath, was already cold.

Margaret was buried three days later and, running true to form, Smith would not pay £4 2s 6d for a private grave, but opted for the cheapest possible interment, costing 9s 6d. The inquest on Margaret was held a few days later and the report of it was carried in the *News of the World*. It was that fact alone that led to the end of George Smith's reign as the Brides in the Bath killer. Until then, the deaths of his 'wives' had not been connected. The story read:

Accidental death was the verdict returned at Islington on Margaret Elizabeth Lloyd, 38, who was found dead in a bath at Bismarck-Road, North London, the cause of death being suffocation by drowning. Her husband is a land agent and they were married in Bath on December 17th. They travelled to London the same day and took furnished rooms. The wife complained of pains and saw a doctor who said she was suffering from influenza. It was the second evening of her residence in London that she was found dead. The landlady said the deceased was quite cheerful and happy with her husband, and medical evidence showed that influenza combined with a hot bath might have caused a fainting attack.

When Mrs Crossley, the Blackpool landlady, read about Margaret's 'tragic accident' she was convinced that her erstwhile lodger had struck again. And when Alice Burnham's father, who had a smallholding at Aston Clinton, near Aylesbury, also read the same report, he too was alarmed. He contacted his solicitor in Aylesbury. By the following day, Chief Inspector Neil – nicknamed 'Drooper' Neil because of his round shoulders and his lugubrious expression – was on the case.

Inspector Neil's inquiries started in Highgate and quickly took him to Blackpool; in no time at all he established that the 'bridegroom', in both cases, was the same man. The coincidence of the wives both drowning in their baths was outside all probability. Piecing together the rest of Smith's activities required painstaking research and, in the course of the investigation, Inspector Neil visited forty-five different towns and interviewed over 200 people.

Smith was arrested on 4 February 1915 when he turned up at a solicitor's office in Shepherds Bush which was dealing with Margaret Lofty's will. He was hoping to pick up the £700 from the insurance policy; instead, he walked into the arms of the police. He was originally held on a bigamy charge, while the investigations continued, but that was quickly changed to a murder charge. The bodies of the three women were exhumed, and forensic experts examined them to see if there was any sign of fits or heart failure which could have caused them to drown. There was none.

Chief Inspector Neil was meticulous; he not only tracked down Smith's victims, but also some who got away – one governess, for example, was wooed and won by Smith but became suspicious of him before he got her to the altar and stripped her of her cash. But even Neil admitted that there were likely to be other victims who never came forward, afraid of looking foolish. There may have been other deaths, although with the massive publicity that the case received any unexpected drownings of wives in baths would probably have been uncovered.

It was a nine-day trial which, in those days, was very long. One hundred and twelve people gave evidence and, at one stage, the jury was taken out of the courtroom to see a demonstration of how Smith killed his victims; a nurse in a bathing costume played the role of the 'bride'. Sir Bernard Spilsbury, the first Home Office pathologist, told the court that no woman could accidentally drown in the sort of small bath used by Smith.

It was a lively trial because Smith, who did not give evidence and who pleaded not guilty, interrupted the witnesses. He called Mrs Crossley 'a lunatic', accused the police of bribing witnesses, called other witnesses liars and burst into tears frequently. There were some amusing moments. The court heard how, on his various marriage certificates, Smith was required to fill in the occupation of his father, and this changed from 'detective' and 'insurance agent' to, on one occasion, 'artist, flowers and figures'. The judge commented that what he really meant was 'artist in figures' because, on each occasion, Smith had persuaded his new bride that he was a man of means.

In summing up the judge commented on the war that was raging across the continent, but said that it was right that the courts of England should continue with 'business as usual' despite this 'wholesale destruction'. Although thousands of soldiers were dying in battle it was still important to take time and trouble weighing up 'whether one man should die'.

The jury decided in only twenty minutes that Smith was guilty, and he was sentenced to be hanged. His wife, Edith, left the court weeping; she had said in evidence that Smith had been kind to her and that she was fond of him. She also told Inspector Neil that he advised her 'to have nothing to do with bathrooms, as they were dangerous places. Some women lost their lives through having fainting fits or weak hearts,' he told her. She said that, in all the time she knew him, he only once took a bath himself.

From prison Smith wrote, in his crude handwriting, of his love for Edith being 'immortal'.

'She is the woman I love and hope to meet in heaven,

the womanly woman with a pure heart and clear conscience . . . in spite of it all she loves and forgives me.' He described her as 'noble, honest and Christian' and instructed his solicitor to give all his worldly goods to her. There was nothing to give; what money could be recovered from Smith's investments was used to pay his defence costs and the remainder, a very small amount, went to his victims who were still alive. Even the clothes he was wearing during the trial had been obtained on credit.

The Brides in the Bath killer was hanged at Maidstone jail at 8am on Friday, 13 August. He protested his innocence to the end. There was a large crowd outside the jail waiting for the signal that he was dead, and when the black flag was hoisted a loud cheer went up. Many of the spectators wore the khaki uniforms of servicemen, the rest were well-dressed women, the sort of women that Smith would have naturally targeted in his search for wives.

10. Fatal Attractions

For an hour the killer lurked in the shadows near Ilford Station, watching the late-night travellers returning from theatres and pubs. At last, just after midnight, he spotted them, a married couple walking arm-in-arm out of the station and along the ill-lit road. He fell into step some way behind, hurrying through the pools of light thrown by the sparse street lamps, falling back in the long dark stretches between.

Then, after he had tailed them for a couple of hundred yards, he broke into a run and overtook them, turning as he rushed past to push the woman away. There was a scuffle, the flash of a knife blade, and just as suddenly as he had arrived the attacker was gone.

His victim slumped down against the wall. It was pitch black and the shape of his crumpled body could not be seen without the light of a torch or a match. His hysterical wife, realizing that blood was pouring from her husband's mouth, ran off for help, shouting and sobbing. By the time a doctor arrived, the man, Percy Thompson, was dead.

Three months later, so was his wife, hanged for her part in his murder. On the same day her handsome young lover also went to the gallows.

It was a case of a classic love triangle, described in the

News of the World headline as Enthralling Story of Love and Tragedy. A beautiful older woman, her adoring young lover, but between them lay the shadow of her husband. For fifteen months the two of them had snatched moments of pleasure together, and had poured out all their love and longing in a series of passionate letters. They had vowed to be together, forever, one day; instead, the last time they saw each other was side by side in the dock at the Old Bailey.

The young man, Freddie Bywaters, admitted plunging the knife into Percy Thompson's side. But he denied that Edith, Percy's wife, knew anything about it. To this day her guilt or innocence is in dispute. Were her crazed love letters enough to hang her? Did her hints about poison and killing mean that she was egging Freddie on to commit murder? Or was she a romantic dreamer, a fantasist, a woman who deep down enjoyed having her lover but keeping her marriage intact?

The Thompsons had been married six years when, in 1921, they met Freddie Bywaters. Percy was a thirty-one-year-old shipping clerk and his twenty-seven-year-old wife was manageress of a millinery company. It was unusual in those days for a woman to continue working after marriage, but Edie was very good at her job and earned as much as her husband, £6 a week. She did not want to give up work, nor did she want to have children. She and her husband lived in Ilford and travelled to work in the city of London every day. They owned their own house, but had an elderly couple as lodgers.

Freddie Bywaters had been at school with Edie's brothers, and was also a friend of her sister, Avis. He

Dr Neill Cream, the Lambeth poisoner, who went to the gallows in 1892

Belle Elmore, whose husband Dr Crippen buried her under the floorboards

Detective Inspector Walter Dew escorting Crippen ashore from the liner *Montrose*

Frederick Bywaters, who murdered for the love of an older woman

Edith Thompson and her husband Percy. Was she in on her lover's murder plans?

George Stoner, found guilty in 1935 of battering to death the elderly husband of his beautiful lover

Alma and Francis Rattenbury: her love affair with Stoner cost them both their lives

John Haigh, the acid bath murderer, whose defence was paid for by the *News of the World*

Right Mrs Olive Durand-Deacon: her plastic teeth survived the acid bath

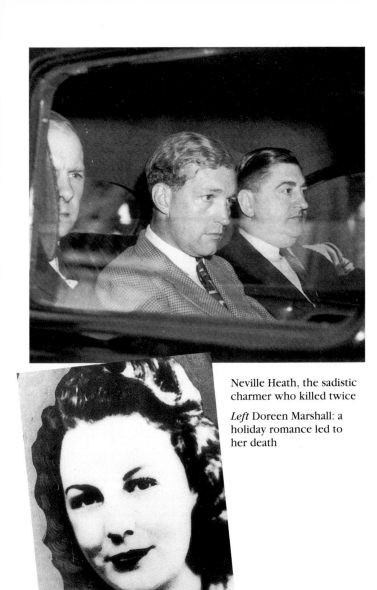

Neville Heath, the sadistic charmer who killed twice

Left Doreen Marshall: a holiday romance led to her death

John Reginald Halliday Christie, who killed his wife and six other women

Norman Rae, the veteran *News of the World* reporter who was on first name terms with a clutch of notorious killers

Dr John Bodkin Adams, the Eastbourne doctor who benefited from the wills of over 100 patients

Mary Bell: the not-so-innocent face of childhood

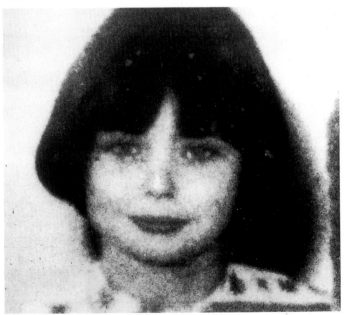

worked as a clerk on a P&O liner, travelling the world. When he was at home he lived with his widowed mother in Norwood, but frequently visited his friends, Edie's brothers and sister.

That is how, in June 1921, he was invited to join Percy and Edie on holiday in the Isle of Wight. Edie's sister was going with them, and they asked Freddie along as a companion for her. By the end of the holiday, though, Freddie had fallen madly in love with the older sister, Edie. He was only eighteen, and it was the first time in his life that he had been deeply smitten. Edie encouraged him and things moved very fast for those days; by the end of the holiday they were kissing and telling each other they were in love.

Edie was a voracious reader, reading newspapers, magazines and popular romantic fiction all the time. Her own defence counsel would later describe her to the Old Bailey jury as

The most extraordinary personality you or I have ever met. She lived a melodrama, an extraordinary life of make-believe and novels. She lived in an atmosphere created by the last impression made upon her mind. She read a book and then imagined herself as one of the characters.

It's probable that she was as much in love with the idea of being in love as anything else. The young Freddie, a good-looking young man with long fair hair and a sensitive face, fitted the bill for Edie's dreams, and was also young enough and impressionable enough to be carried along by her fantasies. After all, life in Ilford was pretty dull: her social life with Percy revolved around visiting relatives, occasional trips to the theatre and – after the threat of losing his wife to another man had persuaded him to take lessons – dancing.

After the holiday on the Isle of Wight Freddie moved in with the Thompsons as a lodger, Percy at first suspecting nothing. But he soon realized that his wife and the young man were fond of each other, and Freddie was asked to leave. He had intervened while Percy and Edie were having a row, and had asked Percy to separate from his wife. Percy refused and would, if Edie is to be believed, continue to refuse until the end of his life.

While Freddie was away on his voyages with his liner, the SS *Morea*, Edie wrote long, rambling love letters, sometimes running to more than twenty pages. She wrote on average every two days, filling Freddie's head with her outpourings of passion and devotion. Freddie kept them all in his sea chest, a mistake that would eventually cost Edie her life.

When Freddie was on leave, the two would meet as often as they could. He would take her to lunch, near the office where she worked. He would meet her again at teatime and he would be patiently waiting for her after work, travelling home to Ilford with her for the pleasure of spending as many moments in her company as possible. Occasionally they would manage to go out in the evening together, booking theatre tickets but, instead, checking into a hotel for a few hours of passionate love-making. Edie was a slim, attractive, very sensual woman, who thrived on the drama of their illicit romance. During the course of their affair, she had to have at least two abortions.

But although there was no doubt of a very real sexual passion between them, Edie also thrived on the months of separation, much more than did poor Freddie. Her love seemed to increase the more she had to express it through letters; he, on the other hand, found another girlfriend while his ship was in Australia, and was even in trouble for failing to get back on board before it sailed from Sydney to Melbourne. He had to rejoin it later. He also wrote letters to her that suggested he would like their relationship to cool to one of friendship, and when he returned from his last leave he did not see Edie for the first two days ashore.

But once he re-met her, all the old fire rekindled, and ten days later he was desperate enough to kill her husband as the couple walked home from a theatre trip.

Although, after their arrest, Edie turned on him, saying she had recognized him as the killer and that she had told him not to do it, Bywaters remained faithful to her until the end of his life. Even after being sentenced to death, he spoke up for her, insisting that she did not know that he was going to commit the murder.

There is quite a bit of evidence that she didn't. In her last letter to him she refers to the fact that they only have three and three quarter years to wait – they had a pact that if, after five years, Percy had not agreed to a separation they would either run away together or commit suicide jointly. There is evidence that Freddie, too, committed the crime on the spur of a desperate moment; he had, in fact, made arrangements for the next few days, including clandestine meetings with Edie.

But the entire thrust of the evidence against Edie was her letters. She had written over seventy to Freddie during their romance, of which thirty-two were produced in court. Those not produced dealt with matters, such as her abortions, which her defence counsel believed would prejudice a 1920s jury very firmly against her. But by today's rather different standards they would have seemed the least damning: Freddie and Edie could not pretend they had not been lovers, but that alone did not make her guilty of murder.

The other letters, those produced, contain plenty of references that could be interpreted as a murder plot against Percy. Edie refers openly to putting glass in his food, and to giving him 'substances', by which she seems to have meant poison. She also seems to incite Freddie, many times, to help her get rid of the obstacle to their happiness. She made lots of references to a book called *Belladonna*, a novel about a murder by poisoning, and she sent Freddie a succession of articles cut out of newspapers about poisoning cases, cuttings with headlines like Poisoned Curate; Women Who Hate Men; Patient Killed by Overdose; Chocolates Poisoned by Drug Injection. There were over fifty cuttings produced in court, but most of them did not have such sinister overtones. There were others like : Battle of Calves and Ankles, a Fashion Story; Do Men Like Red-Haired Women? (Edie's hair was dark auburn); The Ideal Love Letter.

Extracts from the letters leave no doubt that she was dreaming about killing Percy, and may even have tried to:

Darlint, you must do something this time. I am not really impatient, but opportunities come and go, as they have to, because I am helpless, and I think, and think, and think. About 2am he woke me up and asked for water as he felt ill. I got it for him and asked what the matter was and this is what he told me – whether it was to frighten me I don't know, at any rate it didn't. He said a man he knew in town had given him a prescription to drive away insomnia and that he had made it up and taken it to bed with him. He certainly looked ill. I have looked for the prescription everywhere but cannot find it . . .

I am not going to try any more until you come back. He was telling his mother the circumstances of my Sunday morning escapade and he put great stress on the fact of the tea tasting bitter as if something had been put in it. Now I think that whatever else I try at any time again will taste bitter. He will recognize it and be suspicious, and if the quantity is not successful it will injure another chance I may have of trying when you come home . . . He says to his people that he fought and fought with himself to keep conscious. 'I will never die, except naturally, I am like the cat with nine lives,' he said . . . I am going to try glass again occasionally when it it safe.

I used the light bulb three times, the third time he found a piece so I have given up until you come home.

Yes, darlint, you are jealous of him – but I want you to be – he has the right by law to all that you have the right to by nature and love – yes, darling, be jealous, so much that you will do something desperate.

Yesterday I met a woman who has lost three husbands in eleven years, and not through war. Two were drowned and one committed suicide, and some people I know cannot lose one.

Although most of Freddie's replies to her have not survived (she was probably more careful than him, and destroyed them), in the few that are in existence he is as adoring and as obviously besotted with her as she with him. But there are one or two notes of warning; he asked if they could become 'just pals' and, in one letter, he reproached her for her expensive ambitions:

'I want to wish you all that you could wish yourself. I know that these wishes of yours will run into a deuce of a lot of money. Such items as furcoats, cards and champagne will be very prominent on the list.'

In her last letter to him, the day before Percy was murdered, Edie wrote:

'Darlint – do something tomorrow night will you? Something to make you forget. I'll be hurt, I know, but I want you to hurt me, I do really. The bargain now seems so one-sided – so unfair – but how can I alter it?'

This one could have been the most damning of all, as though she were actually egging Freddie on to commit the murder the following night. But the interpretation both she and Freddie put on it is just as feasible: she knew Freddie would be miserable at the thought of her going to the theatre with her husband, so she wanted him to do something to make him forget, like taking her sister out. In fact he spent the evening, until 11pm, at the home of Edie's parents in the company of her sister Avis, and he arranged to take Avis to the cinema the following evening. It was after leaving at 11pm that he walked to Ilford Station and waited there until Edie and Percy arrived home some time after midnight.

As for the other letters: there can be no doubt that Edie was fantasizing about killing Percy. But there was no trace of poison in his stomach, nor any sign of him having swallowed glass, which, even if it had not done serious damage, should have left some scarring of his internal organs. However, the experts could not conclusively rule it out.

When they appeared at the Old Bailey just two months after Percy's death, the great passion that Edie had sustained for Freddie seemed to have evaporated. Her defence was that she knew nothing of the killing, and that all references in the letters were allusions to her wanting to kill herself because she was so unhappily married. She admitted she had tried to make her husband ill, but said she had never intended to kill him. She and Freddie did not even exchange glances. Freddie remained calm throughout the trial, only once looking upset, and that was when his widowed mother, who had never approved of his liaison with Edie, described him as 'one of the best sons a mother could ever have'.

The trial was sensational, people queued all night for places in the public gallery. The *News of the World* described the spectators as 'many fashionably-dressed women who flourished lorgnettes and delicate handkerchiefs' who had fought for places to see Edie Thompson in 'a black velvet hat trimmed with long black feathers' – she did, after all, work for a millinery company.

The prosecution said that 'Mrs Thompson was the dominant partner in the crime. Bywaters's was the hand that struck the blow, but she conceived the crime.'

Freddie admitted committing the murder, but said that he had not intended to kill and that he did it because he felt that Percy was not acting honourably towards Edie who was suffering.

The reason I fought with Thompson was because he never acted like a man towards his wife. He always seemed several degrees lower than a snake. I loved her and I could not see her go on leading that life. I did not intend to kill; I only meant to injure him. I gave him the opportunity of standing up to me like a man, but he would not.

Edie's defence counsel stressed that the court was not there to try her for immorality, and said 'whether it is an amazing passion or an adulterous intercourse – and thank God this court is not a court of morals – it was a great love that existed between two people, whatever else they might name it.'

But the judge summed up very heavily against Edie, saying that 'it is a nonsense about illicit love being great and noble'.

Edie spent her last month in a hysterical state and was taken to the gallows heavily sedated. Freddie remained true to her, although he told his mother that he had never imagined she would turn against him as she had done in the witness box. Because of the way the case was presented – with Freddie as an innocent young man seduced by an older woman who incited him to murder – there was a huge public outcry about him being sentenced to death, and less concern about Edie, even though she was the first woman to be hanged in Britain for fifteen years.

The ultimate enigma of the case is why she and Freddie did not just run away together. By the 1920s, although divorce was still a scandal, it was perfectly possible. Because Edie had her own income, and Freddie was in work, they would have been no worse off financially than she was in being married to Percy. There were no children to fight over. The answer, probably, is that Edie lived in a dream world, a world of high drama and romance, and that she did not awake from that dream until she found herself in police custody for the murder of her husband.

At first sight, Alma Rattenbury has a lot in common with Edie Thompson. They were both respectable married women. They both took younger lovers. They both ended up in the dock at the Old Bailey, sitting next to those lovers, and charged with the murder of their husbands. Yet there was a world of difference between the two women who stood trial twelve years apart.

On paper, Edie Thompson looks the more respectable. Alma was the one with the raffish past; she was already on her third husband. Alma was the one who chose an illiterate seventeen-year-old as her lover, not a young man from her own class. Alma was the one who allowed her lover to have sex with her in the bedroom she shared with her six-year-old son. Yet, in the final analysis, Alma was the one who remained true to her lover, while Edie ditched the young man for whom she had frequently and energetically declared her love. Edie was the one who incited murder; Alma was the one caught up in events beyond her own making.

They both died for their love, but in very different ways.

Alma Rattenbury was born to humble parents in Canada in 1892. She soon proved to be a childhood musical prodigy, earning top money for her family and enabling them to move into higher social circles. By the time she was twenty her violin playing was winning the highest acclaim in Toronto, and her good looks meant that she was able to turn down several marriage proposals. She met and fell in love with a young Englishman called Dorling but, soon after they were married, he was drafted to fight in the First World War. He was sent to France, so Alma took rooms in London and waited for him to return on leave. He never did; he died in the trenches.

Heartbroken, Alma volunteered as a nurse and later became a transport driver in France. It was dangerous work but she was reckless, wanting to be near the place where her husband had died. When war ended she was demobbed to England where she met and married Compton Pakenham, an American university professor. They moved together to Vancouver and Alma had her first son, Christopher. But the marriage was unhappy and they split up soon after the baby was born, Alma going back to live with her mother.

She was thirty-one when she met Francis Rattenbury, a distinguished architect twenty-five years older than her. He lived in a palatial home, having built a thriving practice designing hotels and prestigious buildings, like the Legislative Building of British Columbia. He was also separated from his wife and was entranced by the beautiful Alma who was earning a living by writing popular songs under the name 'Lozanne'. She saw in Francis all the security and comfort that she had been denied in her first two attempts at marriage. In 1925 both she and Francis got their divorces, and they were married six months later. Four years later, with their baby son John and Alma's older son, they came to live in England, Francis going into semi-retirement.

They bought a house, the Villa Madeira, in Bournemouth – the *News of the World* would later dub the case The Villa Madeira Murder. Christopher went away to school and the family settled down to a routine life. Irene Riggs, a local woman, was employed as a companion for Alma and nursemaid for John, and she remained devoted to Alma for the rest of her life. Irene knew, because she lived at the Villa Madeira, that Alma and Francis, known affectionately as 'Rat', were no longer sleeping in the same room, Francis having decided that all he really wanted from his old age was a bottle of whisky a day and a bit of peace. There were occasional rows, mainly because, despite his wealth, he was tight with money, but on the whole he was unconcerned about how his wife spent her time. She shared a bedroom with John and was a devoted mother to both her sons.

But it was a dreary life for a bright, talented woman who was used to being a centre of attention. And it was depressing, looking in the mirror and seeing her beauty begin to ebb away, knowing that she was trapped in a loveless marriage. So when George Percy Stoner came to the Villa Madeira, Alma was ripe for an affair.

George Stoner was seventeen, could scarcely read or write, and was employed by the Rattenburys at £1 a week as a chauffeur and general handyman. He came in September 1934 and, within two months, the part of his duties that he was enjoying most was making love to Mrs Alma Rattenbury, then aged forty-one. He was big and strong, fair-haired with long fair lashes, but not conventionally good-looking. What Alma saw in him is difficult to understand, except that there was a strong physical attraction between them and he was devoted to her. Soon they were making love nightly, either in his room over the stables or in the room she shared with her son.

Her husband, Francis, turned a blind eye. He had told her two years earlier to 'lead her own life', and she admitted to him a month after starting her affair with George that she was now doing just that. He asked no questions, and she was discreet enough not to make her affair too public. She took George with her to London for a weekend the following March, using the excuse that she needed to see a gynaecologist, and they stayed in style at the Royal Garden Hotel. She took her young lover on a shopping expedition to Harrods where she bought him new clothes. Maybe they talked of a future together, although Alma must have realized its impossibility. She had already once tried to break off with George because of the age difference.

However they passed the weekend – and in court the prosecution would talk about 'orgies', but only because they were not married and were sharing a room – the effect on George was profound. When they got back home the boy, now aged eighteen, was unhappy about slipping back into the role of employee. When Alma told him that, the following day, he would be required to drive her and Francis to Bridport and that, while there, she would be forced to share a room with her husband (they were staying with friends and could not ask for separate rooms), George became desperately jealous. He borrowed a mallet from his grandmother's house and that evening beat Francis Rattenbury senseless as he sat in an easy chair.

Having committed the crime George ran, in his pyjamas, to Alma's bedroom. She described the following events:

He seemed agitated. I asked him, 'What is the matter, darling?' and he said he was in trouble but could not tell me what it was. I said, 'You must tell me.' He said I could not bear it, but I told him there was nothing I could not bear. I thought he was in trouble outside, with his mother or something like that. I said I was strong enough to bear anything and he said I was not going to Bridport the next day because he had hurt Rat. It did not penetrate my head until I heard Rat groan. Then my brain came alive. I jumped out of bed and ran downstairs.

In the drawing-room she saw Francis in a chair.

I tried to rub his hands. They were cold. I tried to take his pulse, and shook him to make him speak. Then I saw the blood. I trod on his false teeth. That made me hysterical. I yelled. I took a drink of whisky to save myself from being sick and yelled for Irene. I drank some more whisky neat. I tried to become senseless to blot out the picture.

She said that what happened next was a blank. Irene called a doctor who in turn, called the police, who found Alma drunk and silly – she flirted with officers, tried to kiss one of them, and confessed to the attack on her husband. At this stage Francis was still alive and was transferred to a nursing home where he died the following day.

George and Alma were both arrested and she continued to claim that she was the one who had committed the murder. George also admitted that he had done it; they both tried to protect each other. Her solicitor could not get her to say anything against Stoner. 'I have sunk low,' she said. 'But not that low.' It was only when Alma's defence counsel sent her fourteen-year-old son Christopher into Holloway to beg her to tell the truth, that she did so. The ploy, to play on her maternal instincts, worked, and she explained the full sequence of events. She bitterly regretted making the statement to the police and felt, even though George had wielded the mallet, that she was responsible for her husband's death. After the trial she wrote to a friend, revealing that she was obsessed with the idea that she had let her lover down.

When the couple came up for trial at the Old Bailey in May 1935, George Stoner claimed that he had been under the influence of drugs when he killed Francis; he said he had eaten two eggspoonsful of cocaine in a sandwich. Because tests had not been done on him at the time of the murder it was impossible to know whether this was true or not, but there was evidence that George did buy and use cocaine.

The case lasted five days and, at its conclusion, George was found guilty and Alma was acquitted. But although she was found not guilty of murder, she left the court having heard herself described, even by her own defence counsel, in terrible terms. She was pictured as 'a woman who chose as her paramour a boy of seventeen, almost young enough to be her son . . .' and a woman who 'by her own acts and folly had erected in that young man a Frankenstein of jealousy which he could not control'. The judge, in his summing up, said:

This is a woman so lost to all sense of decency, so entirely without any morals, that she would stop at nothing to gain her end, particularly her sex-mad gratification.

'You cannot possibly have any feeling except disgust for her. But let me say this, that should not make you more ready to convict her of this crime.

His words contrasted strangely with the simple declaration of 'I loved him' when Alma was asked in court why she allowed George into her bedroom, and the way she stretched out her arms to him, before being restrained by two prison officers when he was pronounced guilty.

George himself was portrayed in court as a simple country boy, 'flattered and cajoled . . . impulsive and jealous in his first love . . . under the domination of this woman . . . flung into a vortex of illicit love'. Even Alma's defence lawyer paid tribute to the way George had stood by his mistress throughout the trial, always insisting that he alone was responsible for the murder.

The *News of the World* covered the case in great detail, publishing far more about Alma Rattenbury's background than any other newspaper. The reporter in court, when George Stoner was sentenced to death, wrote:

One thing which will linger in the memory of those who followed this drama of the eternal triangle at the Old Bailey will be the apparent lack of emotion displayed by the boy Stoner. For five days he sat in the corner of the great glass-enclosed dock displaying not the faintest interest in the woman with whom he had been on such terms of intimacy, and whose fate as well as his own was at stake. Even when the death sentence was pronounced he remained absolutely unmoved.

Alma, on the other hand, showed the strain of the trial.

She sat huddled up in her chair, with a wide-brimmed straw hat shading her eyes and the remainder of her face almost buried in a dark chinchilla fur cape, which covered the smart blue costume with blue and white spotted facings, on which was pinned an enormous daisy brooch.

The *News of the World* also described her as 'a mature but comely widow'.

When she left the dock Alma, according to the report, 'tottered forth to freedom with scathing terrible words ringing in her ears'. She was met outside the court by the devoted Irene, with a large bouquet of flowers, and was whisked by cab to a London nursing home.

She did not celebrate her freedom. She was tortured day and night by guilt over George Stoner's fate, and a week after reporting the trial the *News of the World* carried another headline: Chose Death Because She Could not Save Her Lover. Alma had left the nursing home three days after the end of the trial, borrowing £2 from one of the staff, and promising to be back that evening.

She was next seen by a cowman, as she stood with a knife in her hand at the side of a small river in Hampshire. He saw her plunge the knife into her body and fall forward into the river. When she was fished out there were five large and one small stab wounds in her chest. Her lung was punctured in four places and her heart in three, and she was dead before her body hit the water.

There were several poignant suicide notes with her things. They were published in the *News of the World* which described them as follows:

With the eloquence of despair she portrayed her agony of mind at the terrible predicament of the youth whom she loved and who now lies under sentence of death for the murder of her husband.

Just a few hours before her death she wrote:

If only I could help Stoner, I would stay on. But it has been pointed out to me all too vividly that I cannot help him, and that is my death sentence. I had quite made up my mind to finish things should Stoner . . .

The letter was unfinished, as though she found her thoughts too painful to commit to paper.

Another note, again addressed to nobody in particular and scribbled on scrap paper, said:

I want to make it perfectly clear that no-one is responsible for what actions I may take regarding my life. I quite made up my mind in Holloway to finish things if Stoner . . . and it would only be a matter of time and opportunity – and every day, night, minute is only prolonging the appalling agony of my mind.

Just minutes before she killed herself she wrote on the back of an envelope:

Eight o'clock and after so much walking I got here. Oh, to see the swans and the spring flowers, and to smell them. And how singular I should have chosen the spot Stoner said he nearly jumped out of the train one night. It was not intentional, my coming here. I tossed a coin, like Stoner always did, and it came down Christchurch. It is beautiful here. What a lovely world, really. It must be easier to be hanged than to have to do the job oneself, especially under these circumstances of being watched all the time. Pray God nothing stops me tonight. Am within five minutes of Christchurch. God bless my children and look after them.

Another letter, written a couple of hours earlier, told how she had tried to throw herself under a train and under a bus, but there had been too many people around.

Her funeral was enormous. Her shroud and draperies were pink, and so were all the flowers – one of her last requests. Three thousand people crowded into the cemetery at Bournemouth, trampling over other graves, including that of her husband. By contrast, a rather sad bunch of daisies and snapdragons were all that was on his grave.

In the meantime, a petition of over a million signatures had been raised against George Stoner's death sentence, and he was reprieved on the grounds of his age and because he could be deemed to be temporarily insane because of the cocaine.

After Alma's death, her solicitor Lewis Manning gave an exclusive interview to the *News of the World*. This makes a fitting epitaph for her:

Whatever people may say, I am convinced that there was much that was noble in Mrs Rattenbury's character. From the very beginning her one thought has been to protect the boy Stoner. When she realised he had been condemned to death and that she could do no more to save him, life meant nothing to her.

If ever I saw into a woman's soul I saw into Mrs Rattenbury's and I am convinced, as I was from the start, that she had no hand in her husband's murder.

George Stoner served seven years in prison, and after his release returned to live with his parents in Bournemouth. In the 1960s he married his wife Christine, and they have both refused to talk about the case. In 1990 Stoner, then aged seventy-three, was put on probation for two years for committing a gross indecency against a twelve-year-old boy in a public lavatory in Bournemouth.

For months after the Old Bailey trial, coach firms ran fifty shilling (£2.50) trips from London for sightseers to gape at The Villa Madeira. Alma's children returned to Canada, and her faithful companion Irene died only a few years later from cancer.

11. Norman Rae – Crime Reporter

A huge crowd gathered outside Strangeways Prison in Manchester on 12 May 1935, waiting for the black flag to be hoisted, the signal that Dr Buck Ruxton, sentenced to hang for murdering his wife and their maid, was dead. He went calmly and quietly to the gallows. But the crowd outside was not calm and quiet: an anti-death-penalty rally clashed with the other spectators. There was jeering and jostling, and the leader of the rally had to be taken into police custody for her own safety.

In the midst of all the uproar, a man with his collar turned up and a hat pulled down over his face sidled up to *News of the World* chief crime reporter, Norman Rae. He put a letter into Rae's hands, saying that Dr Ruxton had given it to him with instructions to deliver it after his death. The letter was addressed to the paper's editor.

When it was opened a few hours later, in the London offices of the *News of the World* in Bouverie Street, nobody present expected it to be anything more than a protestation of innocence and an attack on the police for the way they had handled him. Ruxton had never, since his arrest, wavered in his claim to be innocent. But the envelope contained what the *News of the World* on the following Sunday described as 'one of the journalistic sensations of the present century'. The note was only five

> *Lancaster.*
> *14. 10. 35.*
>
> I killed Mrs Ruxton in a fit of
> temper because I thought she had
> been with a man. I was Mad at
> the time. Mary Rogerson was present at
> the time. I had to Kill her
>
> *B Ruxton*

THE CONFESSION WHICH RUXTON WROTE ON THE DAY AFTER HIS ARREST SEVEN
MONTHS AGO

lines long, but it was a full confession to the murder:

'I killed Mrs Ruxton in a fit of temper because I thought she had been with a man. I was mad at the time. Mary Rogerson was present at the time. I had to kill her.'

It had been written the day after his arrest, and given to a friend with instructions to store it in a safe. During his trial Ruxton, a GP from Lancaster, asked the friend if he still had it. Despite the weight of evidence against him he was still convinced he would be acquitted, but told his friend:

In the impossible event of a verdict of guilty and if – God forbid – I am to die, I want you to hand the envelope unopened to the editor of the *News of the World*. But remember – it has not to be opened until I am dead.

Did Ruxton do it out of vanity in a bid to make sure his name was across the front page after his death? Probably not. He was an Indian, a Parsee, and as part of his religious beliefs he did not want to die with a lie upon his lips. By confessing at the very end, he freed his soul for the four-day funeral rites that his widowed mother was offering in Bombay, his native city.

His choice of the *News of the World* as a vehicle for his confession was odd: it was work by the reporter Norman Rae which helped land Ruxton in the dock (although the long arm of the law would have inexorably caught up with him eventually).

Ruxton's gruesome crimes came to light when a young woman went for a walk in the picturesque Gardenholme Linn valley just outside Moffat in the Scottish borders. She paused to lean on the parapet of a bridge across a small stream, and her eye was caught by a package wrapped in a bundle of cloth, on the boulders beneath the bridge. She screamed when she saw that the bundle had burst open, and that what looked like a human arm was sticking out of it. She ran back to the hotel where she was staying with her family and returned with her brother. He clambered down, confirmed that it was an arm, and he and his sister dashed to the police station.

Several more parcels were found. They had apparently been tossed into the stream which, until a day or two earlier, had been swollen with rain water. When the level subsided, the grisly bundles were stranded above the water line. The forensic doctors were called in and began the horrific task of piecing together mutilated – and, by that stage, very smelly and maggot-ridden – bits of body. They soon knew they had two corpses on their hands, but they also knew that they were dealing with a clever murderer. Fingertips had been removed from two hands so that fingerprint identification would be impossible, teeth had been pulled out so that dental records could not be used, hair had been removed (almost entirely) and one of the disembodied heads had had its eyes gouged out. The way the bodies had been dismembered, with a knife rather than a saw, suggested that the killer was a butcher or a doctor who knew exactly where to slice through a joint.

At first the scientists thought they were dealing with the bodies of a small elderly man and a woman in her thirties, and they could tell from the well-manicured hands and feet that she was a woman who had the money to look after herself. Within a week, though, the massive police search had turned up even more parcels – thirty were found altogether – and it became obvious that the victims were two women (three female breasts were found).

The hideous parcels yielded some more clues. There was a yellow blouse that had been patched under one arm and was wrapped around one bundle, there was a small child's romper suit around another. And, most important of all, there was a newspaper, the *Sunday Graphic*, wrapped around another. Its importance struck home with Norman Rae, the reporter, before it did with the police. The edition of the paper that had been used carried a special supplement of pictures of the Morecambe Bay carnival, and would have been on sale only within a limited radius of Morecambe, in Lancashire. Only 3700 copies of that edition were printed.

Rae slipped away from the rest of the pack of crime

reporters, sent to Moffat. He covered his disappearance with an excuse about personal problems, and his place was taken by another *News of the World* staffman, John Howie Milligan (whose claim to fame, apart from being northern reporter for the *News of the World*, was that he wrote the comedian Harry Lauder's famous song, 'Roamin' in the Gloamin').

Rae headed off for Morecambe, and there picked up some local gossip about a doctor in nearby Lancaster whose wife had run away from him, taking with her their maid. Rae made a few inquiries and discovered that although the doctor, Dr Buck Ruxton, and his wife Isabella, were a quarrelsome couple who could easily have separated, it was very out of character for the maid, Mary Rogerson, to leave home without telling her parents.

The only time twenty-year-old Mary had been away before was to stay with the Ruxtons on holiday, and she had written home every day. To leave without saying goodbye was a complete mystery, and the girl's father and stepmother were even more alarmed to have been told by Dr Ruxton that Mary had left because she was pregnant. She was 'not that sort of girl' as they later told Norman Rae. He also heard how Mary had a squint in one eye.

Rae got in touch with thirty-six-year-old Ruxton; the doctor was happy to see him. Over the course of the next few days Ruxton was interviewed several times by Rae and Milligan. They built up a dossier on the background of the man who, like Othello, murdered his wife in a fit of frenzied jealousy.

Ruxton was born in Bombay, the son of a wealthy Indian doctor and a French mother. His real name was Bukhtyar Rustomji Ratanji Hakim. He studied medicine at London University, but found the going tough because his English was poor. Unusually for an Indian, he was fluent in French but not in English. He returned to Bombay medical school and then joined the Indian army medical service, with the rank of captain. He married an older Indian woman who was also a Parsee and of whom his family approved. It was probably a partly arranged marriage, done for convenience not love, and when he travelled to Britain again he did not bring his wife with him. The split may have offended his family.

Dr Ruxton was very short of money and not very good at handling what little he had. It was in Edinburgh that he met Isabella, or Belle, who was to become his common-law wife. She was manageress of a tearoom and he spent many hours in there gazing at her. He was good-looking, dark-skinned and reminded Belle of Rudolf Valentino. She was haughty-looking, yet sexy, and to Ruxton – who had an inferiority complex about the colour of his skin – her pale skin was a potent attraction. She was legally married – to a Dutchman – but the marriage, when she was eighteen, lasted for no more than a few months. Her Indian Romeo spent a large amount of his remaining money helping her get a divorce.

Having twice failed to pass his surgeon's fellowship exams in Edinburgh Captain Hakim, as he was then called (he had given himself the first name 'Gabriel'), went to London where he sponged off other Indian families and eventually found work as a locum. Belle joined him and the first of their three children, Elizabeth, was born.

At this point the doctor decided to buy a general practice, and a suitable one became vacant in Lancaster. He may have been financed from India, but money was still tight, and Belle went back to Edinburgh where she supported herself and their baby by working as the manageress of the Woolworth's cafeteria.

Their relationship was always stormy: Ruxton would later say in court that they 'could not live with each other but could not live without each other'. There was a strongly sexual element in their fighting; they always ended up making wild love together after the most vicious rows, and Belle seems at times to have gone out of her way to provoke her husband into a rage, perhaps because they shared a sado-masochistic pleasure in physical violence followed by abandoned sex.

Before moving to Lancaster the doctor changed his name by deed poll to Buck Ruxton. When he had found a house, Belle rejoined him and he set about building up a very prosperous practice. He earned over £3000 a year, a very healthy salary in those days. He was popular with patients who nicknamed him 'The Rajah'. As Norman Rae reported, he was the sort of doctor who never asked how they were going to pay before he treated them (this was in the days before the NHS).

But despite his income, Ruxton lived beyond his means. He had lavish – and bizarre – tastes. He had his house decorated with huge zodiac signs on the walls. He liked bright colours, and painted the house green and yellow on the outside, red and white inside. Even his first car was enamelled white, with bright blue wheels; in the 1930s almost all cars were black. He hated the dark and, at dusk, every light in the house was switched on and stayed on all night. He had a bath every day – considered a tremendous extravagance then – and also changed his clothes completely each day, sending everything to a laundry. His debts mounted and he found himself forced into the hands of moneylenders.

Belle had two more children, Diana Rose and William Gladstone, who was known to his father and the rest of the family as Billie Boy. She and her husband – whom she called Bommie – continued to fight like cat and dog, and on two occasions she complained to the police about him beating her up. Ruxton was summoned to the police station where he was wildly agitated, screaming that his wife had been unfaithful to him and that he was going to kill her. The police sergeant on duty apparently advised him to give the man in question a good hiding instead – not the sort of advice any policeman would admit to handing out today.

Ruxton calmed down abruptly and agreed to give his wife money to go to Edinburgh to stay with her sister. Before she could leave, the couple had one of their passionate reconciliations and Belle stayed. But a month later the police were called to the house, once again finding Ruxton in a towering rage because, he said, his wife was 'going out to meet a man'. He accused Mary the maid of scheming with his wife to deceive him and said, 'Sergeant, I feel like murdering two people in this house.'

On another occasion, when he met Mary's stepmother Jessie, he told her, 'Mary has been working in conjunction with my wife, deceiving me, and sometimes I feel I could choke them both . . . I feel I could gas myself, and would do so but for the poor children.'

Ruxton meticulously kept a diary which recorded the depths and heights of his relationship with 'my beloved Belle'. Whether his observations were accurate – he was obviously gripped by some mania – is hard to tell, but he alleged that on different occasions she tried to chloroform herself, she twice left gas taps switched on in the children's bedroom and she tried to poison his coffee.

Yet there were days when he wrote of his love for her, and he included poems he had composed about her. One entry is about 'Belle kissing my feet' but two days later he records that 'she has thrown a flowerpot at me, a knife and a chair'. On another occasion he says that Belle told him, 'I would rather sleep in the gutter than sleep with you.' She appears to have taunted him with the fact that they were not married.

'When I reminded her that we had taken a solemn oath to live with each other, she laughed,' he wrote. He was worried that she had found out about his Indian wife.

He says she accused him of having an affair with a nurse, and he certainly was convinced that she was having an affair with a twenty-five-year-old solicitor, Bobbie Edmondson, who worked at the Town Hall, immediately opposite the Ruxton house. A week before her death Belle went to Edinburgh with Edmondson and his parents and sister, and they all stayed in a hotel. Ruxton managed to convince himself that Belle and Bobbie were in the same room. When Belle lied to him that she had stayed with her sister – either because she wanted to stave off his frantic jealousy, or because she really was involved with Edmondson – she signed her own death warrant.

The murder of Belle and Mary the maid took place on the night of 14 September 1935, after a violent row about Belle returning home late after a trip to Blackpool. The children were all in bed and apparently slept through the massacre which probably took place in Ruxton's bedroom. It was two weeks before the grisly discovery of parts of the bodies near Moffat (an area that Ruxton had described in his diary four years earlier as 'most glorious and grand scenery'). In that time he made some amateurish efforts to conceal the evidence. He called on his cleaning lady at 6.30am the next day, a Sunday morning, and told her that she was not needed that day because his wife had gone to Edinburgh; he took up and gave away the stair carpet with the help of two patients who were told he was preparing for the decorators; he gave away a blood-stained suit. He also had a series of bonfires in his back garden and, amongst other things, he burned his diary for that year.

When the bodies in Scotland were found – dubbed The Ravine Murders Riddle by the *News of the World* – Ruxton was relieved and delighted when they were identified as a male and a female. He carried on covering his trail. A decorator came in to paint the hall and stairway, and Ruxton tried to persuade the man that he had been booked to do the work some weeks before (he had been booked, but to decorate a different room).

When Norman Rae turned up on Ruxton's doorstep there was already much gossip in the area about his missing wife, and Mary Rogerson's parents had been to the police about her disappearance. Rae talked to over forty of the doctor's patients, and discovered that he had given different stories to several of them for his wife's disappearance.

The police were not far behind Rae. Mary's parents were able to identify the yellow blouse that had been found wrapped around parts of one of the bodies as

Mary's, bought at a jumble sale by her stepmother and patched by her. The romper suit had been given to the Ruxtons for their youngest child.

Ruxton remained at liberty while the police carried out their investigations. He rushed around making disjointed efforts to cover himself. He dashed up to Edinburgh to see his wife's sister, acting the part of the concerned husband who was searching for his missing wife. He even asked the police to issue a statement that the bodies found near Moffat were not his wife and maid, because he said the gossip was ruining his practice.

He was finally arrested on 12 October, almost a month after the murders. An hour before the police came for him he was with the *News of the World* reporter, John Milligan, who described the interview:

He paced rapidly up and down the library floor, nervously fingered an oriental knife (which was never found by the police), ran trembling fingers through tousled hair, and occasionally thumped his forehead with the palm of his hand. Now and again he stopped, swung round, and almost screamed: 'I did not kill my Belle; I tell you she had gone away; she will come back. Tell everybody I am not guilty,' he sobbed. 'Tell them I loved my Belle too much to harm her.'

His distress was very real: as well as fighting to keep himself from the gallows he was probably grieving deeply for the woman he had killed and whom he had undoubtedly loved.

He was tried at Manchester Assizes in March 1936. The trial lasted eleven days and there was a massive amount of evidence against him. The charladies told of stains in the bath, the appalling smell in his bedroom, and even disproved his claim that Mary had been pregnant by testifying that they had found used sanitary towels in her room.

Ruxton was described by J. H. Milligan as a 'restless, impatient figure' in the courtroom. When a model of his house, about the size of a doll's house, was produced in court he craned forward eagerly to see it. When a witness fainted, he gave the police instructions how to treat her. When he was sentenced to death he raised his arm in a stiff salute to the judge, and thanked him 'for the patience and fairness of my trial'. When warders tried to help him from the dock he shrugged them off with the words, 'Don't fuss.'

In prison he veered between being haughty and off-hand with the staff, refusing to use his prison number and insisting on being called by his name, 'pacing his cell like a caged tiger and speaking with a snarl' as the *News of the World* described it, and being friendly and cooperative. He wrote to a friend from the condemned cell:

'Please do speak me fair in death. Try to be good to my children. They are my own flesh and blood. Do something for them. I appeal to you to help my solicitor as much as you can for my children.' After signing his name he wrote the single word, 'Crushed'.

He also wrote to J. H. Milligan, reminding the reporter of 'our interview in my library. Pity! The library is no more. Only the bare walls of that spacious room remain to bear mute testimony of my choice of treasures.' He talked of how he wanted his daughters to be medical graduates and his son to be either a solicitor or a doctor.

'My solicitor has my Isabella's oil painting in life size. It is the talk of the art world. Could you help to get it sold for a fair price to raise an education fund for my children?' he wrote.

Unfortunately for the children, who were being cared for in Lancaster Public Assistance Institution (where their father used to given his medical services free) the painting was not valuable. The insurance policies on Ruxton's life became invalid because he was hanged, and during his trial he was declared bankrupt.

There were many offers from the public to adopt the children.

There was no need for a gallows or a hangman in the case of the murder of Eric Tombe, a young First World War officer who died in April 1922. His body was not found for a year and a half – and by then his murderer had died, shot with his own gun in a fight with a policeman.

The Old Bar Hotel in Scarborough was a genteel establishment where spinster ladies and gentlemen of private means stayed to enjoy the bracing sea air. There were not many holidaymakers about in November 1922 when a man calling himself James Vincent Fitzsimmonds checked in. Fitzsimmonds told other guests he was the son of a Carlisle magistrate.

It was an advert placed by Fitzsimmonds in the local paper that alerted Detective Inspector Walter Abbott; he was asking for financial backers, and the detective suspected he was a conman trying to part investors from their cash. Inspector Abbott went along to the Old Bar Hotel with Detective Nalton, and they met Fitzsimmonds downstairs. After asking him a few questions, Abbott decided to take him to the police station. Fitzsimmonds asked to go up to his room to collect his belongings, and the two cops followed behind.

Detective Inspector Abbott said: 'About half a dozen steps up I noticed his hand go up to his chest and a movement of his elbow. I suspected something immediately. He struggled, I clung to him and he dragged me upstairs.'

On the landing between flights of stairs Abbott and Nalton piled on to Fitzsimmonds and, in the struggle, Fitzsimmonds's gun went off. He collapsed and died immediately.

In his room the police found evidence that led to his true identity. As well as ammunition, a false moustache, a mask and an eyeshade, there were some documents and a cheque book belonging to Eric Tombe. At first they thought it was Tombe whose body was lying in the police mortuary, but a few basic enquiries revealed that Fitzsimmonds's real name was Ernest Dyer. He had been in business with Tombe. They also discovered that Tombe had mysteriously vanished eighteen months earlier.

Dyer, known to his friends as Bill, was, said the *News of the World*, 'a young man whose life would have provided excellent material for a sensational novel'. He was twenty-nine years old, came from a working-class family in Hastings and was the son of a brewer's dray-man. He had started work as a gasfitter's mate but, at seventeen, had sailed to Australia, looking for adventure. He had shipped on a pearl schooner bound for the South Seas and, after a spell as a pearl fisher, had returned to Australia to work as a fruit farmer and an engineer.

When the First World War was declared he joined up immediately, and fought gallantly, winning the DCM at Gallipoli with the Australian army, and then serving in France as a lieutenant with a British regiment, the Royal West Surreys. He was blown up and had to be invalided home, but he recovered from his wounds.

Back in civvy street he married a Scottish girl, Annie Watson, and they set up home in London. Dyer's adventurous spirit had not deserted him, and he took the whole of his army gratuity payment and put it on a horse, Furious, in the 1920 Lincolnshire Handicap. It romped home at 33 to 1, and Dyer picked up £15,000.

He teamed up with an army pal, Eric Tombe, the son of a vicar, from Sydenham. Tombe, like Dyer, was restless and did not want to settle into a routine job, so they pooled their resources and, for £5000, bought a stud farm, The Welcomes, in Kenley, Surrey. They spent another £5000 refurbishing the place, and Dyer and Annie moved in to run it.

It was a big operation. They employed fourteen stable lads and they bought a string of yearlings. Dyer conned clients into believing that he had been a racehorse trainer in Australia and, for a while, it looked as though the business would do well. Friends described him as 'plausible, genial, free and easy'. But Dyer spent money too readily; he entertained lavishly and ran up big debts with local tradesmen, and his wife Annie later described him as having a violent temper. By April 1921 he was in deep trouble.

When the stud farm burned down, Dyer immediately lodged a claim for £12,000 insurance – but the insurance company was suspicious and refused to pay out. Annie and their two children were forced to move into rooms above the stables.

Within a couple of days of the insurance company rejecting his claim, Dyer's business partner, Eric Tombe, who was twenty-nine at the time, disappeared. Tombe lived in a flat in The Haymarket, London. He had trained as a motor engineer but had enough money to live off his private means and, at the time of his disappearance, had £2570 in his bank account.

He was a pleasant young man who enjoyed the company of pretty women; at the time of his death he had two girlfriends on the go, one of whom he was engaged to marry. They were both expecting to meet him in the days after he disappeared, but both were fobbed off by Dyer telling them that Tombe had 'gone overseas'. One of them, highly suspicious of Dyer, went to Tombe's bank and was shown a letter giving Dyer the power to handle

Tombe's bank account, and directing that the money should be sent to Paris. She could see that the signature was a forgery, but the bank manager refused to take her word and continued to send money to France where Dyer was collecting it.

A month after Tombe disappeared, Annie Dyer had not seen her husband for a couple of weeks. But one evening she heard a noise in the grounds of The Welcomes, a noise which she described as the sound of stones being dropped against a drainpipe. She turned her dog loose, but the intruder turned out to be her husband who claimed he was arriving in the dark because he did not wish to be seen in daylight because there were too many people to whom he owed money. The following day he took Annie to France, drew £1350 from Tombe's bank account, and gave Annie a pay-off; they both agreed the marriage was over.

For the next six months Tombe lived on his wits, travelling around Britain and France bouncing cheques and working confidence tricks, until the day on the landing at the Old Bar Hotel in Scarborough when he was killed by a bullet from his own revolver.

The police would have been happy to close the case there. They assumed, because he had Tombe's belongings with him, that Dyer had murdered his partner. But, as the killer was dead, there would be no court case.

But Eric Tombe's parents were very unhappy. Mrs Tombe dreamed about her son nightly, and she had a vivid and recurring dream that his body was at the bottom of a well with stones over it. Eventually, after a great deal of pressure from the Rev. Gordon Tombe, Scotland Yard agreed to search the three cesspits at The Welcomes;

in one of these they found his body, covered with earth and stones.

The body was badly decomposed but it was possible to tell that there were shotgun pellets in the brain, and the skull was fractured – probably from a shotgun being fired at it from close range.

At the inquest, the verdict was that Eric Tombe had been wilfully murdered by Ernest Dyer. The two women in Eric Tombe's life were allowed to give evidence without revealing their names, and they wore heavy veils over their faces. This intrigued the *News of the World* whose headline was Veiled Women's Story of Sinister Farm. The paper described The Welcomes as 'the scene of a devastating fire, a lost fortune and finally murder'.

12. The Acid-Bath Monster

It was fingernails that drew Mrs Olive Durand-Deacon to her death; and it was teeth that convicted her killer, acid-bath murderer John George Haigh. In the sludge that was all that was left of sixty-nine-year-old Mrs Durand-Deacon after Haigh had stuffed her 14-stone body into a vat of sulphuric acid, a set of acrylic false teeth was found. Her dentist was able to identify them.

The plump widow had been lured to her death believing that she was going to make a fortune out of her invention: a new type of false fingernails. She'd designed a paper prototype which she believed was better than the plastic nails already on the market, and Haigh had promised to make them and market them for her. They went together to a workshop he used in Giles Yard, Leopold Road, Crawley, on Friday, 18 February 1949, and while she looked at some designs he shot her in the back of the head.

The motive may simply have been robbery or Haigh may, as he later claimed, have been overcome by a powerful lust to drink blood. After he was hanged six months later he left behind a riddle: was he a slavering vampire, gripped by a mad desire to taste human blood? Or was he a ruthless, mercenary serial killer, who feigned insanity in a bid to cheat the gallows? He had killed at least five people before Olive Durand-Deacon, but they were pre-meditated murders, and each time he made money from the deaths.

Was the money, as he himself said, 'incidental' to his main reason for murder, his 'frantic uncontrollable urge' to drink blood? The killings were well planned and cleverly executed – the 'uncontrollable urge' could obviously be controlled long enough to lure the victims to the right place at the right time. Had he not grown careless with Mrs Durand-Deacon, Haigh's killing career could have gone on and on. It did not bear any of the hallmarks of madness and, when he came to trial, the jury rejected his defence that he was insane.

After shooting Mrs Durand-Deacon he stripped her body of all its valuables: her watch, her jewelry, her expensive Persian lamb coat. He claimed that he stamped the crucifix she wore round her neck into the ground, before slitting her throat with a penknife and gorging himself on her blood. Afterwards he struggled for 'the better part of two hours' to get her body into the vat of acid.

'It is a fatiguing business getting a 14-stone carcass into an oil drum,' he later wrote. 'I am not a strong man.'

It was ten days after Mrs Durand-Deacon's death that John George Haigh was arrested. Careful investigation by the police, tracking down the elderly widow's property which Haigh had been selling, meant they believed they had sufficient evidence to hold him. Haigh was cocky enough to admit that he had killed her, believing, as he told the police, that because there was no body there could be no proof of murder.

'Mrs Durand-Deacon no longer exists. She's disappeared completely and no trace of her can ever be found again. I've destroyed her with acid. You'll find the sludge that remains at Leopold Road. Every trace has gone. How can you prove murder if there's no body?' he said.

He was wrong; there have been other convictions for murder without bodies. But he had made an even more crucial mistake. He had told the police where to start looking for evidence. With the help of brilliant forensic medical work, they were able to prove that plenty of traces of the elderly widow still existed, including the bones of one of her feet and her gallstones. The acid had certainly worked, but it would have needed another couple of weeks completely to eliminate everything, including the acrylic false teeth and a plastic handbag which Haigh had slung into the vat with the body.

If the detectives on duty that night at Chelsea police station were astonished at his admission of guilt, they must have been pole-axed by the rest of the story they heard from the small dapper man they had brought in for questioning. Before they had finished taking his statement, Haigh had admitted murdering another eight people and disposing of their bodies in acid. Although three of the killings may have been entirely imaginary, the other six, including Mrs Durand-Deacon, were definitely Haigh's handiwork.

The disappearance of a plump, elderly widow had led the police to one of the cleverest and most sinister serial killers in British criminal history. But because Haigh pleaded guilty at his trial to the murder of Mrs Durand-Deacon, the only killing he was charged with, the full story of his grisly trail would never have been told had it not been for the *News of the World*.

The newspaper struck an amazing deal with Haigh;

they paid all his legal costs in return for the rights to his bizarre story. The relationship between the murderer and Stafford Somerfield, then the features editor of the *News of the World* and, in later years, its editor, lasted up to, and beyond, Haigh's death. It was Somerfield who took on the macabre task of distributing Haigh's few possessions after he was hanged, including supplying Madame Tussaud's Chamber of Horrors with the suit that his wax-work effigy wears to this day.

John George Haigh was born on 24 July 1909, in Stamford, Lincolnshire, but moved with his parents when very young to the small village of Outwood, near Wakefield. His father, an electrical engineer by profession, was a colliery foreman. He was an only child and had a strange upbringing; his mother and father were deeply religious, members of a sect known as the Exclusive Brethren (commonly referred to as the Plymouth Brethren). They did not believe in any form of organized entertainment, including radio and newspapers. Ironically, at the very end of their lives, they came to rely on Stafford Somerfield and the *News of the World* to keep them in touch with their beloved son.

Haigh later remembered that when he brought home the book, *Treasure Island*, from school his parents attacked his headmaster, saying that it was not a fit book for children to read. When he asked his mother why they did not take a daily newspaper, he was told: 'It's a thing of the world; there is not enough time to read the Bible anyway.' Similarly, his father told him that radio was 'an instrument of the devil; the Antichrist will use it to speak to the world and organize insurrection against God and his saints'. On Sundays the boy was not allowed to walk across fields or to play; he had to spend the day with his Bible.

The young George passed the entrance examination for Wakefield Grammar School, putting him in the top 20 per cent of the population for intelligence. His performance at school was undistinguished apart from his musical aptitude: he played the piano well and his boy soprano voice was good enough to earn him a musical scholarship, under which he got free musical tuition.

Astonishingly, his parents allowed him to join Wakefield Cathedral Choir: the family was living too far away to attend Brethren meetings and they may have thought that any religious activity was acceptable. Haigh occasionally played the organ in the cathedral for minor services. The contrast between the lavish rituals of a Church of England cathedral – one that was so high in its form of worship that it had a reputation for 'being able to show Rome what to do' – and the plain unstructured worship of his parents' ultra-strict sect, may have confused and unbalanced him, although he showed no sign of it at the time.

He later wrote, 'The beauty of the music, the colour, the pageantry and the divine smell of incense all appealed tremendously.'

The intensive Bible study that he was forced to do at home stood him in good stead in school Divinity lessons, for which he won prizes, and in later life he earned small amounts of money writing quasi-religious essays, with titles like 'Loving Words', for magazines.

He learned something else, far more sinister, in childhood: a taste for blood. He later described his bloodlust as having started when he was smacked so hard with a hairbrush that it drew blood.

I thought I should die. I licked the blood off and found it an agreeable sensation. In the utmost secrecy I smacked my own hand with the brush and on more than one occasion, cut my finger. As I surreptitiously and furtively sucked the small wound, a rare mingling of pleasure, surprise and curiosity possessed me. Once acquired, the taste obsessed me, and the recollection of it pursued me down the years. An appetite was unleashed.

I used to sit in the Cathedral in the dark, looking at the bleeding Christ. I remember other incidents from my youth connected with blood. At school I often visited a slaughterhouse where the sight of animals recently killed fascinated and appalled me. I remember also the strange sensation I experienced as a young man when I drew blood as I kissed a girl. But none of these experiences crystallized into a frantic uncontrollable urge until after a motor accident at Three Bridges, Sussex, during the Easter of 1944.

My car collided with a lorry and turned over. I received a cut to the head from which I lost a considerable amount of blood. I did not become unconscious, but broke my way out of the overturned vehicle. Blood poured from my head, down my face and into my mouth. This revived in me the taste.

It was after that date that Haigh embarked on his killing spree, but he was already immersed in a world of petty crime, having served three prison sentences.

When he left school he was apprenticed to a motor engineer. But by the time he was twenty-one he had discovered that 'there were easier ways to make a living than to work long hours in an office', and he began a string of minor frauds, mostly involving insurance companies. He had an agile mind and was probably convicted of fewer crimes than he committed.

His main love, and one that never deserted him, was inventing, and he had some success with his first attempts; when he was twenty-four he and a partner came up with an electrical billboard, a forerunner to the flashing neon signs that are familiar today. One of Haigh's signs was erected in the centre of Leeds, but eventually the company went bust after his partner withdrew his share of the capital.

The following year Haigh married. Beatrice Hamer was a beautiful young girl from Stockport. The marriage was over in a matter of months, he never saw her again, and he never showed the slightest interest in remarrying. Although he was small, he was good looking, with a slight resemblance to Errol Flynn which meant that he could have been surrounded by attentive females. But sex – and women – held no joys for Haigh, although he stressed that he had no homosexual tendencies.

Some women can be amusing and good entertainment, but generally speaking I prefer them at a distance. Ninety-nine per cent are definitely repellent at close quarters. There have been very few intimacies in the past five years [the five years before his arrest], half a dozen topside. I consider intercourse an over-rated pastime.

He was obsessively clean, having a bath and two or three 'complete sponge washes' every day, always wearing gloves in summer to keep his hands clean.

I cannot abide dirty hands (I'm told that my definition of the word dirty would be clean to other people). I cannot abide stickiness on piano or organ keys. I always purchase new books, and will not borrow books if they are not clean. I refuse to handle public-library books.

He spent money on clothes, at the time of his arrest having a dozen 'good' suits in his wardrobe, and writing that 'I loathe unpressed trousers.' He liked red ties and matching socks, insisted on cleaning his own shoes because nobody else did them well enough, had his hair trimmed every fortnight and manicured his own hands 'because I am not satisfied with shop work'.

He served his first prison sentence when he was twenty-five – fifteen months for fraud; he was convicted of arranging hire-purchase advances for non-existent cars. After his release he ran a dry-cleaning company, then left Yorkshire for London where he worked as chauffeur and secretary to William McSwan, the owner of a chain of amusement arcades. He met Donald and Amy McSwan, William's elderly parents, and the family liked him. But steady employment had no charms, and he left the job and travelled round the country operating a share swindle. The law caught up with him and he went to prison for four years in 1937, coming out in the middle years of the war. He worked as a firewatcher in central London and this seems to have had a profound effect on him:

'The ghastly sights after two landmines had wiped out a block of buildings are fixed indelibly in my memory,' he wrote.

Within a year he was back inside, having been caught stealing from bombed houses. By now he had developed a macabre interest in death and the disposal of bodies and, in particular, the effects of acid on flesh and bones. It was in prison that he first experimented with acid; he stole a supply from the tinsmith's shop where he was working and bribed prisoners who had outside jobs on the land, to catch fieldmice for him. He watched the mice die in the acid and timed the length taken to reduce their bodies to sludge. When the tinsmith's shop ran out of acid he experimented by killing the mice with electrical currents, wiring them into the prison-bell system. He damaged the bells but an internal inquiry did not discover the culprit.

On his release he worked as a salesman for an engineering firm in Crawley, Hurstlea Products Ltd. But he hated working for anyone else and left to set up his own company. He parted from Hurstlea on good terms and was a regular visitor to their premises, staying friendly with the manager, a Mr Jones.

Haigh moved into London, living at the Onslow Court Hotel, Queen's Gate, South Kensington, and renting a basement in Gloucester Road as his business base. His 'business' was inventing and, although he was always hoping that he would sell the patent on one of his ideas for a large amount, money was running out. The hotel was quiet and genteel, filled with elderly ladies and one or two retired gentlemen. Haigh was thirty-five and therefore a bit of an odd one out, but he was unfailingly courteous and charming to the resident widows and unmarried gentlewomen.

Four months after the road accident in which he cut his head – and, which he said, unleashed in him the desire to taste blood – he bumped into William McSwan, his previous employer and amusement arcade owner. He became friendly again with the whole family and took on some work mending pintables for the arcades. In September 1944 William went with Haigh to the basement in Gloucester Road and it was here, according to Haigh's own account, that his first murder was committed.

I hit him with either the leg of a table or a piece of piping, I can't be sure which. Then I cut his neck with a penknife. I attempted, unsuccessfully, to drink the blood, and had to run to the sink for a cup in which to catch it. I sat – and I have a strong feeling it was on the body itself – and drank the cup of blood slowly and with immense satisfaction. Eventually I came to, and was appalled by the problem of a corpse on my hands. I experienced no sense of remorse, and left the question of the corpse until the following day and went home to bed.

That night he had one of his recurring dreams in which he was in a forest of crucifixes and a man offered him a cup of blood to drink. On previous occasions the dream faded with him being unable to move and take the drink, but after killing McSwan he was able to 'experience the same satisfaction in drinking it as in actual life'.

The following day he took McSwan's watch, money and other valuables, and then disposed of his body in a stolen waterbutt which he filled with sulphuric acid that he already had for, he later claimed, 'stripping metal'. He claimed that the killing was a spur of the moment decision, fuelled by his lust for blood, and that he did not plan the disposal. He transferred the acid into the waterbutt by bucket, choking frequently on the fumes and needing to go outside for fresh air. A few days later he put the sludge (all that remained of William) down a drain.

He later claimed that he felt no remorse because he was being 'led by a superior force – a superior being who was outside myself, controlling me. That is why I knew no fear and took no trouble to avoid being discovered.'

The truth is that he took considerable trouble to cover his tracks, contacting McSwan's parents and telling them that their son had gone into hiding to avoid being called up for the war – an excuse they accepted because William had discussed doing that. Over the course of the next ten months Haigh wrote letters to them, as if from William, and posted them in Glagow and Edinburgh. Forging was one of his skills: he had earned some popularity at school by forging a master's handwriting.

Haigh's next murder is one of which there is no proof, and may be nothing more than a figment of his imagination; he may well have merged his mad dreams with reality, or he may have included it to help persuade doctors he was insane. His victim was a young, dark-haired woman he met at Hammersmith Broadway and lured back to the basement in Gloucester Road.

'I knew she would have to die. I was in the middle of a dream cycle, and I yearned for the cup,' he wrote. He disposed of her body in exactly the same way as he had that of McSwan.

The following summer he lured both Mr and Mrs McSwan to the basement. This time he was better prepared; he had made himself a mask out of tin to prevent the fumes choking him, and he had a stirrup pump for transferring the acid. He later claimed to have killed them both because he did not get sufficient blood from seventy-year-old Mr McSwan. He also claimed that he did not know that he would gain financially from their

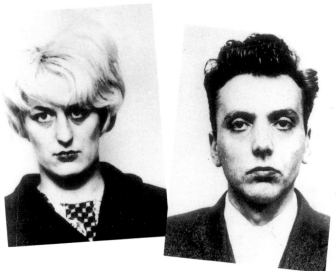

Myra Hindley and Ian Brady, the sadistic Moors Murderers

Hindley's brother-in-law David Smith on the moors he roamed with Ian Brady

Archibald Hall, the butler who served up death

Below Max and Sheila Garvie at a nudist camp: she was convicted of killing him

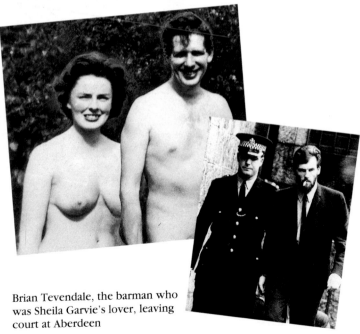

Brian Tevendale, the barman who was Sheila Garvie's lover, leaving court at Aberdeen

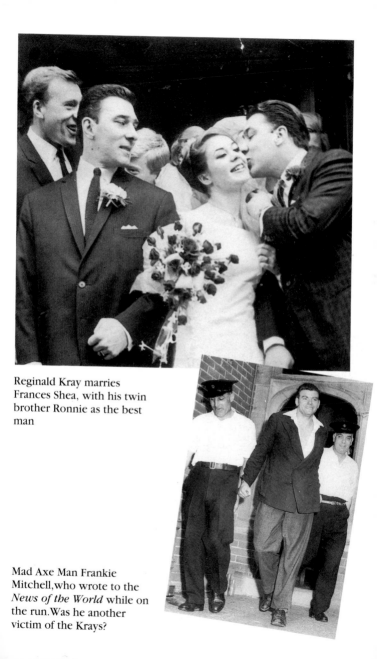

Reginald Kray marries
Frances Shea, with his twin
brother Ronnie as the best
man

Mad Axe Man Frankie
Mitchell, who wrote to the
News of the World while on
the run. Was he another
victim of the Krays?

The Great Train Robbers, l. to r. (*top row*): James Hussey, Charles Wilson, Douglas Goody, James White, Ron Leslie, Bob Welch, (*bottom row*) Roy James, Buster Edwards, Roger Cordrey

Jack Mills, the train driver whose life was shattered

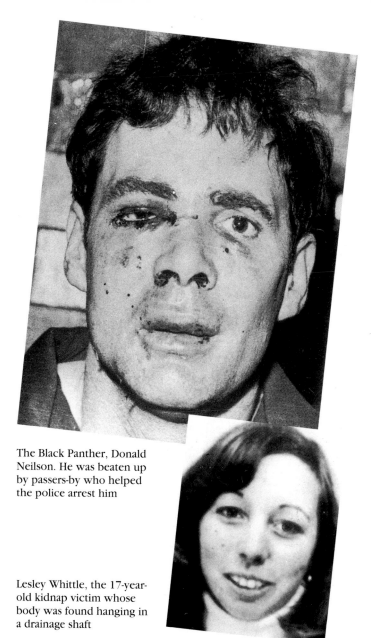

The Black Panther, Donald Neilson. He was beaten up by passers-by who helped the police arrest him

Lesley Whittle, the 17-year-old kidnap victim whose body was found hanging in a drainage shaft

Graham Young: poisoning people gave him a sense of power

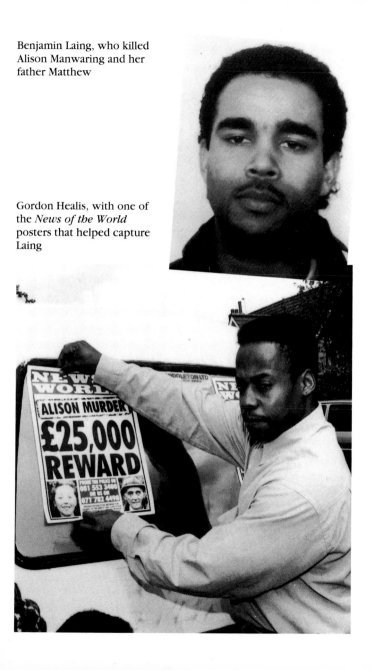

Benjamin Laing, who killed Alison Manwaring and her father Matthew

Gordon Healis, with one of the *News of the World* posters that helped capture Laing

Malcolm Stanfield (*far left*) and his wife Lorraine (*far right*). She had no idea that he wanted her dead

Safely reunited: kidnap victim Stephanie Slater hugs her parents at a police press conference to announce her release

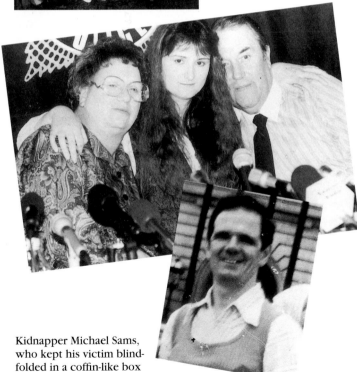

Kidnapper Michael Sams, who kept his victim blindfolded in a coffin-like box

deaths. But gain he did; he passed himself off as their son and sold the property they owned. He made over £4000, the equivalent of about four years' average wages.

Astonishingly, the McSwan family was never reported missing. They had never mixed with their neighbours and had left their native Scotland over thirty years earlier, not keeping in contact with other members of the family.

Two years later he met his next victims, Dr Archibald and Mrs Rosalie Henderson. They were selling a house in which Haigh was interested. The sale did not go ahead but he had charmed them and became a regular dinner companion. Dr Henderson had been invalided out of the Royal Army Medical Corps, and he and his wife were comfortably well off although Haigh later claimed that he believed they were in financial trouble. A few months after Haigh met them they moved to Sussex and, at about the same time, Haigh gave up the basement in Gloucester Road and made his base in the workshop in Crawley. He 'borrowed' it from Hurstlea, the company for whom he had worked. They had vacated it and had no further use for it.

He invited Dr Henderson, with whom he was staying at the Metropole Hotel, Brighton, to the workshop, which he always grandiosely described as his factory, in February 1948. There he cold-bloodedly shot him, again placing the corpse in a vat of acid after his blood-drinking ritual. He drove back to Brighton and told the alarmed Mrs Henderson that her husband had been taken ill. She returned with him and was dispatched in the same way as her husband. This time Haigh netted £7000 in property and assets, by forging Dr Henderson's signature. He also forged complete letters, in Mrs Henderson's handwriting, to her brother in Manchester. They were skilful enough to arouse no suspicion.

He acquired the Henderson's dog, a red setter called Pat. He was genuinely fond of Pat, spending time grooming and exercising the dog. Apart from his parents, with whom he always kept in touch, Pat is the only creature he ever seemed to care for. When the dog started to go blind Haigh found kennels where it would be well looked after, and never failed to pay its bills. Even when he was in the condemned cell he asked about Pat.

The next two 'murders' were as vague as that of the girl he picked up at Hammersmith Broadway. He claimed to have killed a man called Max and a Welsh woman called Mary whom he met in Eastbourne; and in neither case was there any financial gain for him. The lack of detail meant the police could neither confirm nor deny his claim, but he was able to give such precise information about the Hendersons and the McSwans that it seems unlikely that Max and Mary ever existed.

His final victim was Olive Durand-Deacon, one of his fellow residents at the Onslow Court Hotel. She was an intelligent, reasonably wealthy widow who had lived at the hotel for nine years. Haigh, by 1949, had been there four years and the two had become acquaintances; this was not as inevitable as it may sound because many of the ladies in the hotel kept very much to themselves and would not dream of talking to a man without being formally introduced.

Mrs Durand-Deacon was impressed by Haigh's portrayal of himself as a factory owner. She did not know that he was, in fact, substantially in arrears with his hotel bill (not paid for seven weeks) and the manager was beginning to apply pressure. He was always a slow payer, but this was a bigger debt than he usually ran up: nearly £50.

There's no doubt that he made careful preparations for Mrs Durand-Deacon's death. He knew that he would not be able to get his hands on her wealth, but he was desperate and he knew that she walked around every day with a couple of hundred pounds worth of jewelry on her. When she asked him to help develop her false fingernails, she gave him an ideal opportunity to lure her to the workshop. But he did not take her there for another three days, during which time he took delivery of another carboy of acid. His blood lust was under control and, if he did drink from her neck as he claimed – and a blood-stained penknife was found at the workshop – he managed it without making a mess. The only blood the forensic scientists found was a few drops on the wall, consistent with her having been shot near that spot.

He took her Persian lamb coat, her rings, watch, crucifix ('It gave me infinite delight to stamp it into the ground') and the rest of her jewelry, as well as 30s from her purse and her fountain pen. Everything else went into the drum, and the acid was transferred into it with the stirrup pump. Haigh's disposals were getting ever more sophisticated, and he now had rubber gloves, a rubber apron and a gas mask to help him. Then he went to a café round the corner for poached egg on toast.

For the next few days Haigh spent his time pawning her property and solicitously inquiring about her in the dining-room of the Onslow Court. When one of her friends decided to go to the police, Haigh offered to go too. The woman police sergeant who met them took an instant dislike to the oily manner of thirty-nine-year-old Haigh, and a check on his record turned up the fact that he had several criminal convictions. He was immediately under suspicion, but it was a week after the old lady disappeared that the police finally searched the premises in Crawley. They found a receipt for Mrs Durand-Deacon's fur coat, which Haigh had taken to the cleaners, hoping to sell it second-hand for about £50. They tracked down the watch and other jewelry, but they had no idea what had happened to the body until Haigh himself blurted out his story about acid. Before he made his confession, he asked about his chances of being released from Broadmoor.

Forensic scientist Dr (later Professor) Keith Simpson went immediately to Crawley and, in the sludge that Haigh had dumped on littered wasteland outside the 'factory', found a human gallstone. He ordered that the sludge, five wooden boxes containing 475lbs of it, be packed up and crated to his laboratory. In it he found the bones of a left foot, which matched Mrs Durand-Deacon's shoe size, two more gallstones (a typical condition for an elderly, overweight woman), and sufficient fragments of bone joints to show that the victim was female and slightly arthritic. It was the set of plastic false teeth that were the crucial identification evidence.

'Haigh's labours had been in vain. The remains of Mrs Durand-Deacon were identified as surely as if her body had never been given an acid bath,' said Dr Simpson.

While Haigh was under arrest, awaiting trial, the *News of the World* received a small report from a news agency which said that the accused was applying for legal aid as he had no money. The following day Stafford Somerfield checked into a hotel in Lewes, Sussex, near the prison where Haigh was being held, and sent him a message offering to supply lawyers in return for the rights to his memoirs. He received a telegrammed reply:

'Very pleased to accept your offer of solicitors. Haigh.'

He pleaded guilty but insane, and the only defence witness was a psychiatrist who agreed, under pressure, that Haigh understood that what he was doing was wrong under the law. Several other psychiatrists had examined Haigh and come to the conclusion that he was sane. The jury took only fifteen minutes to agree with them.

Haigh's memoirs, published after he was sentenced to death, are a fascinating, handwritten document, carefully preserved in the *News of the World* archives; on reading them it is obvious that he was not 'sane' by the definitions of today. But the jury decision had to be based on whether he understood the actions he was committing, and their verdict under those strictures was probably correct.

Haigh was at pains never to use the word 'murder', preferring 'killing'. He said murder gave 'the impression of cruelty and suffering at the hands of a monster'.

'The word murder is most unpleasant. It makes me wince. It implies a brutal and savage killing done in cold blood and entailing suffering. "Method of disposal" sounds gruesome, but we are only dealing with a carcass by that time.'

He makes a good case for the murders not having been done for money.

Such benefits as did accrue were purely incidental to the prime factor – the desire for blood – and I accepted them as providential and yet another indication that I was being cared for by some supreme force.

There were many other easy ways of making money, even though illegitimately. If it were the object it would have been much more simple to have got rid of my parents and inherited the property. There would have been no questions about that.

He was able to point out the fundamental errors he had made in the murder of Olive Durand-Deacon, errors which, he said, proved that the killing had not been premeditated.

There are so many things I would have done differently if I had sat down and thought out a planned campaign of murder for gain. I shouldn't have ordered the acid in my own name . . . I am quite certain I would not have used the Leopold Road premises where one never knew when somebody was coming into the yard.

He said that, although he took the belongings of his victims, 'I never associated the people with the things. The square box in which the police found the revolver with which I shot Mrs Durand-Deacon was Henderson's. It had on it the initial H, which applied to both of us.'

The final lines of his memoirs betrayed that he knew he was leaving a mystery behind, the mystery of whether he had killed in cold blood or in crazed desire:

As I lay down my pen I am reminded of some lines attributed to one of the great ones of a past age, and it seems apposite to quote them now:

Not till the looms are still and the shuttles cease to fly,
Shall God unroll the canvas and reveal the reasons why.

Stafford Somerfield believed that Haigh was not of sound mind, as he said in a letter to Haigh's old and devastated parents:

'Those of us who were acquainted with your son are now fully convinced that when he committed these deeds he could not have been responsible for them.'

His eighty-year-old father and seventy-eight-year-old mother, both in failing health, were touchingly grateful to the journalist, saying that, as his parents, they knew that 'those deeds were foreign to him'. When their son sent them a visiting order to see him in prison they asked Somerfield to go in their place, as they could not face the journey from Leeds to London.

Somerfield had to convince the authorities that he was visiting as a friend, and not as a journalist, before he was permitted into Wandsworth prison where Haigh was whiling away the hours inventing a device to silence road drills and a method of preventing accidental poisoning by gas. In the last few weeks of his life, the murderer came to rely on the journalist for all sorts of small favours: Somerfield arranged to have Haigh's shoes repaired, he paid for the *Reader's Digest* to be delivered to him, and he passed on reports to Haigh's parents.

Haigh was very concerned about the effect of his arrest and trial on his mother and father, but consoled himself that, because of their religion, 'they thrive on adversity. They believe that whom God loves he chastises.'

After his first visit Stafford Somerfield wrote to the old couple:

Is it any comfort to you to know that his bearing was such that any man, in similar circumstances, would be proud to emulate?

Your son behaved towards me as a perfect gentleman and I did not find the interview a strain or difficult.

Somerfield was allowed to see Haigh again, the day before his execution, on 6 August 1949, two weeks after the killer's fortieth birthday. Again he wrote to the parents after his visit.

Your son said he would be writing to you, but he would like you to know first-hand how he was looking and felt . . . His bearing at the end was magnificent. He showed the greatest possible courage and was, I believe, completely composed. He expressed to me the deepest appreciation of all that had been done for him and the small part that I had been able to play . . . It may be some little comfort to you to know that his last thoughts were of you both and were expressed with kindness and dignity. I believe, as I know you do, that the world did not see the real side of your son. The side you knew, and of which I was permitted to catch a glimpse, was one of great charm and natural affection. The other side can only have been placed there by some evil force of which we are only dimly aware and cannot fully understand.

13. Murder He Wrote

'Neville Heath, the sadist who savaged two women to death, hated my guts. He swore I shopped him. And I did.'

Those words were written by Norman Rae, the *News of the World*'s chief crime reporter through the thirties, forties and fifties, a journalist who was as close to the criminals, whose stories he wrote, as any detective. For thirty years, and more than 2000 cases, Rae covered the big murders, rapes and scandals. His casebook, published in the *News of the World* in the early 1960s, is a fascinating chronicle of the bizarre and gruesome stories he reported.

Rae, who died in 1962 at the age of sixty-six, worked his way up from a one-man paper near Aberdeen where he was born. After serving in the army in the First World War he went back to journalism and, by the early thirties, his byline ('by Norman Rae') was a regular fixture in the *News of the World*.

'My Front Page Murders' was the title of the series the newspaper ran as a tribute to Rae. It opened with the words:

Live with Rae through the spine-chilling INSIDE STORIES of the great crimes. After his action-packed years on the world's greatest Sunday newspaper he gives you now the secrets that no man has ever before recorded. Go behind the scenes with Rae for adventures that are stranger and stronger than a THRILLER. For this is the TRUTH by the man who really knows . . .

One of the killers Rae got to know personally was Neville Heath, hanged for the savage sex murders of Margery Gardner and Doreen Marshall, both of whom had been repeatedly bitten by their killer. Rae argued with his contacts at Scotland Yard over the way the Heath story was handled and, if they had listened to him, Doreen Marshall would not have been murdered.

Heath was a petty criminal, a tall, good-looking young man who liked to swan around postwar London in the uniform of a colonel in the South African Air Force. That is how he first attracted Norman Rae's attention.

'It was a morning in early 1946 in a Fleet Street pub, and Heath, wearing the sand khaki of a lieutenant-colonel of the South African Air Force, was impeccable – except that his medal ribbons were in the wrong order,' Rae wrote.

He went up to Heath and said, 'Excuse me, colonel, but your batman needs a ticking off.' Heath replied, 'Mind your own business.'

'Then for half an hour he glowered across the bar and chuntered about "interfering putty-nosed Scotch bastards". Meaning me. It was such a fuss over a simple thing that I grew suspicious.'

Rae telephoned Scotland Yard and said, 'There's a handsome blond bloke here with crinkly hair who can't be entitled to the medal ribbons he's wearing because he doesn't understand them.'

The Yard told Rae to keep Heath talking. 'But Heath knew what I was up to and vanished.'

Eventually Heath, alias Jimmy Armstrong, was fined £5 for wearing the uniform. But Rae still saw him regularly. Heath loved the pubs of Fleet Street and would hang around, glaring at Rae. Sometimes, however,

I had a pretty girl in tow, maybe a girl reporter talking shop or a witness I had coaxed away from the Old Bailey to interview. Then Heath would interrupt with a brash 'Hiya, baby' for her, and act as though I was an old friend, which I certainly was not, although by now I knew plenty about him.

Margery Gardner knew even more about him, yet she was still willing to go with him to the hotel bedroom where she died on the night of Thursday, 20 June 1946. What Margery knew was that Heath was a sadist who enjoyed inflicting pain on women; that was OK with her, she was into bondage and flagellation herself.

Margery was the daughter of a respectable Sheffield solicitor. She had left home ten years earlier, when she was twenty-two, and had spent her twenties and early thirties drifting through the Bohemian fringe of London society, supporting herself as a fashion artist. She was briefly married and had a child who was being brought up outside London. Margery loved dancing and drinking – probably not in that order – and, when her work dried up, she tried to fund her alcohol habit by exchanging her sketches for drinks in the pubs and clubs of Chelsea. She worked occasionally as a film extra and tried to launch a stage career doing impressions of famous people. She was good for a laugh at parties, not good enough for the professional stage.

She had spent at least one previous night with Heath, at the same hotel where she subsequently died. On that occasion the night porter had to break down the door after a woman was heard screaming. He found Heath in a frenzy, beating Margery black and blue. She was tied to the bed by her feet and hands. Heath had to be forcibly restrained. But Margery persuaded the hotel to drop the affair, saying that she was a married woman and could not face the scandal of a court case. The night porter, realizing he had intruded on a couple of kinky sadomasochists, told the pair of them to clear off.

Heath stayed at the same hotel, the Pembridge Court in Notting Hill Gate, on two more occasions. On the first he had with him a pretty little nineteen-year-old Wren (a member of the Women's Royal Navy Service), whom he had met at a dance and who was completely bowled over by 'Lt-Col' Neville Heath. The girl, Yvonne Symonds, only agreed to spend a night with Heath after he proposed marriage to her, and, perhaps because of her innocence – she was a virgin before that night – she was later able to say in court that he had treated her 'kindly'.

Four nights later, Margery Gardner died in the same room, Room Four, of the same hotel. She had last been seen by friends getting into a taxi, singing, 'I've got a date with my sweetie,' but from her previous experience with Heath she must have had an idea what was in store for her. Not all of it though; she was found the next day savagely beaten, her face and body criss-crossed with seventeen slashing cuts, and with teeth marks all over her naked body. Her breasts had been bitten so hard that her nipples had been almost severed. This time, to prevent the screams disturbing any other staff or residents, Heath had gagged her. Her body was discovered the following afternoon by a chambermaid.

By that time Heath was well away from London. He had travelled to Worthing to visit the girl to whom he had proposed marriage – Yvonne Symonds. He was introduced to her parents at their golf club and the next evening, over dinner, he told Yvonne that he was 'closely connected' with the London murder case, now making headlines. He said he had lent his room at the Pembridge Court Hotel to an old friend, the woman who had been murdered, because she was looking for somewhere to spend the night with a man. Heath implied that she was making money from the arrangement and that he agreed to help her out. He claimed that he had seen her murdered body because, while helping police with their inquiries, he had been taken to see it. He gave his opinion that 'it must have been a madman who did it', and added that it could not possibly have been him because she knew how gentle he had been with her.

In the meantime both Scotland Yard and Norman Rae had matched the description of Neville Heath with that given by the taxi driver who had taken Margery and her killer to the hotel. The police, who also had the evidence of one of his fingerprints on the washbasin in the room, published an appeal for information about his whereabouts.

The police had a picture of Heath – but refused to release it. Rae easily tracked down plenty more pictures of the killer, but Scotland Yard forbade him to print them in the *News of the World.*

I went to the Yard several times and pleaded. Their argument was that they should not be printed in case they prejudiced his trial. My argument was: if we don't print them he may murder again.

AND HE DID.

Twelve days after he killed Mrs Gardner he met Doreen Marshall, a 21 year old Wren convalescing at Bournemouth. He took her to tea, to dinner . . . and to death. All in 12 hours.

Mrs Gardner knew of his perversions. And in my investigations I met a score more women who yielded to him willingly. But Doreen Marshall was an innocent girl. Her father told me that she had been horrified by the reports of Mrs Gardner's death. And if Heath's picture had been published she would not have died. I have always believed that.

After Heath's name was published the parents of his young girlfriend Yvonne became very concerned – and so did Heath. He left Worthing immediately, travelled to Bournemouth and checked into the Tollards Royal Hotel under the name of 'Rupert Brooke'. He posted a letter to Scotland Yard in which he made similar claims to those that he had made to Yvonne: he had loaned his hotel room to Margery and her friend, he had arrived back to find her murdered and, fearing being implicated, had fled.

'I realised I was in a rather invidious position, and rather than notify the police I packed my belongings and left. Since then I have been in several minds whether to come forward or not, but in view of the circumstances I have been afraid to,' he wrote. He said that the police could contact him through an advert in the personal columns of the *Daily Telegraph*. His letter ended with the line, 'I have an instrument with which Mrs Gardner was beaten and am forwarding this to you.' He didn't.

Because no picture was published he managed to stay in Bournemouth without attracting any attention, apart from the hotel staff noticing that he had very few clothes with him. Doreen Marshall had recently left the Wrens and had been ill with flu and measles, so her father had paid for her to have a break by the seaside. She met another girl who introduced her to Heath. Doreen was willing to have dinner with him but, by the end of the evening, appeared to have tired of his company; she ordered a taxi to take her back to her own hotel. Heath countermanded her order, saying that they would walk. He told the porter he would be back in half an hour and Doreen corrected him. 'No – in a quarter of an hour,' she said, apparently not wanting to spend any longer then necessary in his company.

Whatever it was about him that was making her uneasy, her instincts were right. Unfortunately, she wasn't allowed to follow them; she never returned to her hotel. The night porter at Heath's hotel checked his room in the early hours of the morning as Heath had not come in through the main door. He found Heath, alias Group-Captain Brooke, in bed and asleep. He had climbed in through the bedroom window, using a ladder, laughing about it the next day as a joke he had played on the porter. His shoes, left outside his door for cleaning, were caked with sand, and he was probably in such a dishevelled state that he had to avoid using the door.

When Doreen failed to appear the next day the manager of her hotel became worried and contacted the manager of the Tollards Royal where he knew she had gone for dinner. Heath denied that his guest was Doreen Marshall but, later, he agreed to go to the police station to look at a photograph of the missing girl. When he got there he bumped into Doreen's father and sister, and consoled them, saying that he believed she had gone to Exeter with some friends. He admitted his dinner guest had been Doreen but said they had parted at 1.15am at the Pier Pavilion.

An alert policeman noted the resemblance between 'Captain Brooke' and Neville Heath whose picture had, at last, been circulated to all police stations. Heath denied that he was the wanted man, but was arrested.

The police then discovered that he had pawned Doreen's ring and watch, and a left-luggage ticket for Bournemouth Railway Station led to the gruesome discovery of a suitcase containing bloodstained clothing and a riding whip with pieces of human flesh attached. The criss-cross pattern on the whip matched the marks on Margery Gardner's body, and the flesh was later identified as hers.

Heath was taken to London and charged with Margery Gardner's murder.

The same evening that he was charged, Doreen's body was found, hidden in some rhododendron bushes, about a mile from the Tollards Royal Hotel. A young woman found the body: earlier that day she had been walking her dog and had noticed a swarm of flies under a bush. She had later read about the missing girl and went back to the spot with her father. They contacted the police immediately.

Doreen had been brutally beaten up before having her throat slashed. Her hands were badly cut, showing that she had struggled to defend herself against the knife. After death she had been mutilated: one nipple had been bitten off, a knife had carved a Y shape from her breasts down to her vagina, and a piece of wood, probably a branch, had been savagely thrust up her vagina.

The knife Heath used was never found, nor were there any bloodstains on his clothes: the police later decided that he probably stripped naked before attacking Doreen, and then washed himself afterwards in the sea.

Doreen's parents agreed with Norman Rae that, if Heath's picture had been published after Margery Gardner's death, their daughter would never have suffered her appalling murder. Rae, bitterly upset that an innocent girl had died, had to content himself with researching Heath's background; he had a head start over other journalists because he had met Heath and had taken an interest in listening to gossip about him.

Heath was born in Ilford, Essex, during an air-raid in 1917; he was twenty-eight when Rae first encountered him. His father was a barber and the family moved to Wimbledon during his school years. His mother was a large, domineering woman, and Neville Heath, nicknamed Smelly by his school mates, took after her in enjoying bullying smaller children. At the age of eight he thrashed a little girl with the teacher's cane when they were alone in a schoolroom, and more than once he was in trouble for ill-treating animals. At thirteen a master caught him hitting a much smaller boy and predicted: 'You'll be hanged if you don't mend your ways.'

After working as a warehouseman when he first left

school, he joined the Territorial Army and, in 1936, signed up for the RAF and started to train as a pilot. His love affair with uniforms had started and would soon turn into an obsession.

A year later he was arrested for flying a plane under a bridge; he escaped, stole a car and was caught, court-martialled and dismissed from the service in September 1937, eighteen months after joining up. Two months later he came up in court for obtaining credit by fraud at a Nottingham hotel, for posing as 'Lord Dudley' in a London hotel and for trying to obtain a £175 car by false pretences. Eight other offences of fraud and false pretences were taken into consideration.

The following summer he was sent to Borstal for three years for stealing jewelry worth £51 from a friend, again with a clutch of other crimes, mostly stealing cheques and other property, taken into consideration. War saved him from Borstal; he was released to help the war effort. In typically cheeky Heath fashion he later went back to give a talk at the Borstal, on the lines of 'I made good; so can you.'

He joined the RASC. He worked his way up from private to first lieutenant, serving in the Middle East. He was charming and good-looking, and never without a selection of women (often other officers' wives) from which to choose. He entertained lavishly and was very popular. But he was arrested and cashiered for being absent without leave, for fraudulently holding two army paybooks, and for bouncing cheques.

Being returned to England on a troopship he absconded in Durban, South Africa where he passed himself off as a captain. He used the name 'Bruce Lockhart' but, when challenged over his identity, said the name was a cover: he was, he claimed, a member of the British Secret Service on a special mission. Within twenty-four hours of jumping ship he had proposed marriage to a wealthy local girl, and borrowed a large sum of money from her family, before disappearing.

He turned up next in Johannesburg where he joined the South African Air Force, using the name Jimmy Armstrong. He said he had no previous flying experience (despite having qualified as a pilot with the RAF), so his quickness to learn and his aptitude marked him down as a brilliant recruit. He stayed in the SAAF for four years, completing his pilot training and genuinely rising to the rank of captain.

In 1941 he married a beautiful teenage heiress, Elizabeth Rivers, who ran away with him despite her parents' pleas, and, in 1943, their son, Robert, was born. Heath's duties with the SAAF were on transport planes and as an instructor, but when he was seconded to the RAF in 1944 he flew bombing raids over Belgium and Holland. He was based in Oxfordshire and amused himself with the girls from the WRNS camp nearby; at one time he had promised to marry nine different women, all of whom lent him money. He spent all his free time in London and money flowed through his hands on a grand scale. He was shot down in October 1944, but not badly injured.

His marriage was already failing and, when he returned to South Africa, he demanded, and got, a £2000 payment plus the settlement of all his debts from Elizabeth's family, in return for a divorce and an undertaking to leave her alone. She later described him as 'a beautiful dream that turned into a nightmare'. She destroyed all photographs of him and swore that her son would never be told the identity of his father.

Shortly afterwards he was dismissed 'with ignominy' from the SAAF for undisciplined behaviour, claiming a rank to which he was not entitled (he claimed to be a Lieutenant-Colonel even when back at base), and wearing unauthorized decorations. He also came up before the civilian courts for fraud – stolen cheques again – and was deported back to England. He was labelled a 'prohibited immigrant' into South Africa.

He took to the night life of London with enthusiasm, telling friends that his wife and child had been killed in a motor accident in South Africa, and hinting that he had been away on secret but important missions. Some of the people he met in pubs and bars were impressed; Norman Rae was not.

At his trial Heath pleaded not guilty. Realistically, his defence lawyer was hoping to get a verdict of guilty but insane, in which case Heath would not have been hanged. But the jury accepted the evidence of two prison doctors who testified that, although Heath was a sadist, a sexual pervert and a psychopath, he was aware of what he was doing and knew that it was wrong. Fourteen years later his defence solicitor, Joshua Caswell, wrote his memoirs for the *News of the World*. His comment about Heath was:

'He was mad all right. Mad as a hatter. But also unusually intelligent.'

On the final day of the trial Heath did not wear his RAF tie because he was, he said, 'too proud of the RAF to wear it at the last knockings'. He was sentenced to death.

He did not appeal, and expressed no remorse, although he wrote to his parents apologizing for the notoriety he had brought them. Norman Rae, who had disliked Heath from first sight, had the pleasure of writing the report of his trial and death sentence. He started his piece like this:

They have hung another picture on the line in the grisly gallery of human monsters and labelled it 'Smelly'. That was the boyhood name of Neville George Clevely Heath. The portrait reposes in befitting company, though the rotting bones of ghostly neighbours may cry aloud in protest at the affront to their comparative 'respectability'. There is a type of delinquent drafted occasionally into penal settlements with whom the case-hardened old-timer resolutely refuses to associate. The burglar, the blackmailer, the forger, the swindler – these men consider themselves as far removed from the moral pervery as are the poles . . .

I knew Heath well during the months of his final reckless fling in London in an orgy of pseudo-Bohemian 'pleasure'. I knew Heath, too, as the man of business, a charming host, a young officer of gifts with which, properly employed, he could have travelled a long way in any of the Services. But I always suspected Heath the philanderer, the liar and deceiver. Now I can unmask the fake hero, dismissed in disgrace from the Army, the RAF and the SAAF; the thief, confidence trickster, poseur, sadist, practised expert in immorality and, finally, murderer.

Heath was hanged on 26 October 1946. He whiled away his time in the condemned cell playing chess, reading and chatting to his guards, never showing any sign of fear or regret. On the morning of the execution he asked for a whisky as his last request, adding, 'I think I'll have a double.' Joshua Caswell, his defence solicitor, wrote that of all the forty murderers he had represented, 'Heath was the only one who welcomed the hangman's noose.'

What do you do when a poisoner offers you a cup of tea? That was one of the many dilemmas Norman Rae faced in his crime career. The poisoner in question was a frail, sixty-six-year-old widow, mother of four grown-up children, from a council old folks' bungalow in Windy Nook, a suburb of the small town of Felling-on-Tyne.

The headline above Rae's astonishing story said, It was Death to Wed the Widow of Windy Nook. This is what he wrote:

We went into hiding together, Mary Wilson and I, twenty-four hours after the police exhumed two of her husbands. And I knew what the pathologist was going to report. Rat Poison.

She'd had seven hours at the police station protesting her innocence. But I had a hunch that the other two men in her life, the first husband and the lover she cheated him with for 27 years, had also died of rat poison. Inevitably the police would dig them up too, and maybe even before then, they would want to arrest Mary. But I wanted her story first, and I had to have it without other reporters getting near her.

So I took her to a place the police and press would least suspect: a pub almost next door to the police station. I didn't tell the police where we were going but I arranged for a 'go-between' in case Mary was wanted in a hurry. This was December 1957 at Hebburn-on-Tyne, within two miles of where all four men had lived, mated with Mary, died in their agonies, and been buried.

Mary had Room 13. Mine was a bed-sitter next door and the landlord had orders never to barge in unexpectedly, to interfere as little as possible, to try to see that Mary never went out unless she went with me. When we did go out, it was always in my car and we dived in – or out – quickly so that no other reporters could see. Mary's story had to be exclusive.

I made her show me the graves of the first husband and the lover, at Hebburn and Jarrow, because I had to be able to find them again in the dark so that when the police went to open them, I would be there, too. I used an old policeman's trick to ensure that. Each night I would tie a loop of darning wool over every cemetery gate. About eight gates altogether, and nobody could open any one without breaking the loop. In the morning I would remove the wool.

The graves looked desolate and I have a 'streak' (I don't know whether it's morbid or over-sentimental but I'm a great one for putting flowers on graves) so I said to Mary, 'Can't we get some chrysanths or something?'

I got my first inkling of how hard this Merry Widow of Windy Nook could be, Windy Nook being the area where Mary had a clean little lace-curtained six shillings and six pence [32½ p] a week old folks' bungalow. She looked at me watery-eyed from under gingery grey hair and said 'What d'ye wanna waste money on flowers for them so-and-sos for? They're dead aren't they? If you wanna buy any flowers buy 'em for me, or better still, gimme the money.'

She had a thing about money, maybe because most of her 66 years she'd never had any. Her first marriage was to John Knowles – 'I'd been his mother's skivvy' – when she was 23 and he was 30. She and Knowles were together for 43 years, but for most of that time a man called John Russell was her lover. Her story went on something like this:

'Knowles was a bad tempered one and all he left was £27. John Russell left me £70 in his will but when the debts were paid all I got was £6. Then there was my second husband, Oliver Leonard. He wanted to be my lodger but the council wouldn't have it, so we got married, but he was bossy and I'd 'a given owt to be shot of him. He left about £50. My third husband Ernest Wilson said he had £100 and a £50 and my rent was going up so I married him. He didn't give me much trouble.'

Now she said people were gossiping because they were jealous and because she'd tried to be brave and make a couple of light-hearted jokes. Here is a sample of her jokes: the four men died within 26 months and she suggested that the undertaker should give her wholesale rates. And at her third wedding she said the left-over cakes would come in handy for the funeral though she 'might give this one a bit longer'.

Both second and third husbands died within a fortnight of marrying and she made another joke: 'I didn't have to kill them, they were dead already.' But I was convinced she had murdered them and I knew how. She put poison in their tea. And when I woke one morning she was standing by my bed with a cup. I sipped very nervously and she squatted on my bed and said 'Ee, is there summat up with you or summat? I'm staying here till you drink that tea and don't let it get cold neither.' So I drank and I didn't die and we got down to her story again.

One thing she was emphatic about 'Ye know, lad, I'm past wanting owt from a man but a bit of comfort and my keep, like. Security, you know. Even with Russell, we'd had our fun for years, mind, but he was past it. So was I.' Then she tittered and gave me a dig with her elbow that nearly floored me. 'You don't believe me,' she said and obviously she didn't want me to because she gave me another playful punch. 'I bet you Scotch lads are devils.'

By supper time she was calling me Norman and saying 'Ee, you're a luvly lad' and before I went out to tour the cemetery gates (she didn't know about this) she came into my room in a faded pink wrap and said she was fed up listening to the wireless and had I any books? But she didn't like what I offered and said 'Haven't you got a Ruby M. Ayres or summat? I like a bit o' love, don't you?'

Now I find that the older women get the easier their allures are to withstand, and though Mary Wilson could have passed for ten years less than she was, that still didn't make her a Brigitte Bardot. She wasn't my cup of tea, with or without the rat poison in it, and being shut up with her, constantly ducking her crude approaches, was making me irritable. So I telephoned the office for somebody to spell me off before I went mad.

They sent up a young reporter called Johnny Ball, the son of a detective, and sensing the atmosphere he said 'Norman, you'd better watch out. Hell hath no rat poison like a woman scorned.' Next morning Mary's tea tasted decidedly bitter, but it must have been my imagination because I still didn't die.

Now the first instalment of her story was ready, but if she was suddenly arrested after the paper went to press I might get six months for contempt of court, so there was only one way to make sure. I went to the police on Saturday morning and asked direct: 'Are you planning to arrest Mrs Wilson this weekend?'

The answer was no, but there was a definite twinkle in the officer's eye as if something else was planned. So on the way out I lingered. There was definitely something in the air, and that night after I returned, soaked by drenching rain, from my tour of the cemetery gates, I remembered all this. It was

11.30pm, Mary was in bed and I was tempted to go too. I got into pyjamas and then said 'To hell with this' and changed into dry clothes and went out again.

It was 1.15am when I reached Jarrow cemetery, desolate and gloomy in the black night and the driving rain. And the wool across one gate was broken ... I weaved in and out among the trees to where three police cars and a van were parked, and under a tarpaulin, hung on poles like a marquee without walls, policemen were digging by the eerie light of lanterns in the rain.

I watched them bring up the coffin of Mary's lover and open it, then carry it to the van. It was 2am, but my job was not over. I scouted all round the cemetery, checking that no other gate had been opened and no other reporter had come in. Quickly I telephoned my story to London and then drove to Hebburn cemetery. From behind a low wall, with my feet squelching in the wet mud, I watched them bring up John Knowles, the tired old man who had been first to die. Then I telephoned my second story.

When Mary fetched my tea that Sunday morning I was still up and dressed and I told her what had happened. She trembled. She went ghastly white and said 'I'd like to go to Mass, to clear my conscience.' Now, I thought. Now it's coming. The confession I've been trying to get all week. I said very softly 'Clear your conscience of what, Mary?'

'Well, you see ...' she said. 'My conscience is clear, really, but ... er ... but ...'

Before she could get another word out the door burst open and in came the landlord, waving the *News of the World* with my scoop about the exhumations splashed across Page One. 'Have you seen this, Mrs Wilson?' he asked, and I snatched the paper from him. 'This is a private conversation if you don't mind,' I said. 'I know, but look at this . . .' he continued. I took him by the arm and hurried him out. But it was too late.

Mary was calm again and she said 'I don't think I'll bother to go to Mass after all.' I said 'Mary, did you kill them?' and she said 'Norman, as God's my judge, I'm innocent.'

There wasn't much more we could do. Then our go-between rang and said the police would be coming for Mary at about two. They were late. Mary was fidgeting. The strain was awful, and suddenly she was out of the room. I did a double-take and said to Johnny Ball 'Was I seeing things?'

'No,' he gasped. 'The bleach – she's got a bottle of bleach with her.' 'Blimey', I said. 'All we want now is her committing suicide on us,' and we ran to the bathroom, ready to shoulder the door open, but there was no need. There was Mary, with the bleach and a rag, polishing away at the bath.

'This bath's been worrying me all week,' she said, 'I thought I'd best give it a bit of a clean-up, like, before we go.'

At 3.20pm she went off with two detectives and a police-woman and I stood, strangely sad, while the chambermaid stacked up the love stories she'd left behind and stripped the bed like you do after someone's died.

I visited her often before her trial and I was there when she stood silent, frailer than I remembered, and pathetically digni-fied like anybody's old mum in an ancient blue hat and a light grey coat, while the death sentence was passed.

She wrote to me when she was reprieved, five days before she would have been hanged.

Mary Wilson continued to write to Norman Rae, every four weeks, until he died in 1962.

'When she writes gaily of the good old days, she doesn't mean her marrying and murdering days on

Tyneside. She means that sexless "honeymoon" of ours when, as she said at least three times, "Ee Norman, if only I'd met you first." '

Chatting up pretty girls was all part of the job to Norman Rae, but a part he tackled with obvious relish, especially when the girl in question looked more like bosomy fifties film star, Anita Ekberg, than like the elderly widow Mrs Wilson. Here is another story from his My Front Page Murders series:

Sonia Winnickes was beautiful. What you might call Juno-esque, one of those blondes built more like an Ekberg and I couldn't keep my eyes off her, especially where she was most like Ekberg. But she ignored me. She ignored everybody except the man with her, a rumbustious giant who called himself Ronald Chesney and fancied himself as a buccaneer. He looked like one, too, with a gold ring in his ear and a black spade beard that he kept stroking upwards.

Sonia kept looking at him, and every time she looked she went velvety-eyed, and you know what that means. All this was in a Chelsea riverside pub. My next sight of Sonia was in Duren, a little Rhineland city the Allies had knocked about a bit. This time she didn't ignore me. She turned the dogs loose. Two Alsatians, they were most hostile.

In the end though I talked her round, and she gave me her side of all that happened in the months between, which was plenty. It included two murders and a suicide, all done by her friend Chesney.

To my rivals, it looked as though Rae had landed another nice foreign trip, expenses paid. But it wasn't that simple. I came into the story rather earlier in the morning than I liked, on Thursday February 11 1954. Chesney's wife and mother-in-law had been murdered in an old folks' home that the mother-in-law ran in Ealing, West London.

The wife Vera, who was 42 and usually drunk by bedtime was lying in the bath with her nightie up to her waist. She had been smothered, and then finished off by drowning. It might have looked like suicide or an accident, especially with a drunk, but somebody had made a mistake. The bath had been emptied afterwards. Still, it was a clever crime, and quiet.

Downstairs her mother, a wiry 73 year old warhorse who, with no right, called herself Lady Mary Menzies, had been clubbed with a brass coffee pot, strangled with her own stocking and then stuck behind a screen. A crime neither clever nor quiet.

'Flaps' Daws, then a detective chief inspector and later a detective chief superintendent, decided that Vera died first and the old lady was just unlucky: she happened along while the quiet murderer was sneaking out, so he attacked her. And she fought back. Whoever killed her would have scratches galore – and flesh and skin that matched samples taken from under the old lady's nails.

It didn't take long to start suspecting Vera's husband, the same swashbuckling Chesney I had seen in the riverside pub. He was a villain and his record showed that when he was 17 and known as Donald Merrett he shot his mother and got away with a Scottish 'not proven' verdict. He was now 45. But – and it was a big but – Chesney was an international smuggler, known by sight at every port and airport in Britain. He had been to Britain the week before the murders. He came by surprise, bringing Vera a gift he knew she would appreciate: a bottle of gin. They were seen around that night on better terms than neighbours had known for years and he went back through Harwich the next morning. Police and Customs men remembered him going, and his passport was stamped. There was no record of him having entered the country again.

Then, about midnight on the Saturday after the murders, a young West End waiter called on me with a strange story. 'Two years ago' he said, 'I was in Wandsworth Prison and a bloke in my cell offered me £1,000 to do a murder. He wanted me to run over his wife and make it look like an accident. I thought he was joking but after we came out he repeated the proposition, and even showed me where he wanted it done. His name was Ronald Chesney.'

Now why did Chesney want Vera murdered? My waiter knew the answer to that, too. In his palmier days Chesney had settled £8,000 on her, and now he wanted it back, and he wanted a divorce. Vera wouldn't give him either.

We still couldn't figure how a conspicuous character like Chesney could slip in and out of the country unseen, but suddenly that aspect of the problem became less urgent. Because the Tuesday after the *News of the World* ran my story of the murder offer made to the waiter, a man with a copy of it in his pocket shot himself in a park in Cologne. He was smooth-chinned, he wore no ear-ring and his name was John Milner, but we suspected that might be another alias for Chesney. By 5pm we knew it was.

But Chesney had laid an elaborate alibi; he had said that during the 36 hours around the time of the murders in London he was in Amsterdam with Sonia. So why panic into suicide, and why remove his beard? At ten past five on Friday night I was told to fly out to Cologne and find out.

And off I went. At Cologne police headquarters I knew Flaps Daws was inside somewhere but it was a formidable building surrounded by forbidding German police, all armed.

So I dodged away from the rest of the reporters, as I always did, round to the back where I found one friendly policeman, a driver. He pointed out the third floor office that Daws was using and then, very unethically, he gave me a leg up the fire escape.

Once inside I ran straight into Daws who was as surprised at my cheek as I was at my luck. He said 'They have orders downstairs that no reporters can come up. Didn't they tell you?' 'I didn't ask them,' I said and followed him into his office. On the floor were two long boxes that once held bottles of Scotch and I said 'Treating yourself?'

'Have a look inside,' a German detective said and in the boxes were two arms with scratches galore – and fingerprints of course. Chesney's. Later on when Flaps told the Customs men what was in those boxes they didn't believe him so they looked, too!

Meantime my story was taking shape, and I pressed on. Chesney had bought his *News of the World* in Cologne – the price 30 pfennigs was still pencilled on it – and the story had shaken him. It didn't name him and it didn't give his reasons for wanting Vera dead, but to a guilty man it was sticking out a mile that we knew everything. He told Sonia Winnickes, who was with him, that he must go to London and clear his name. So why didn't he?

The only person who might answer that was Sonia, and she had gone into hiding. Where? The police looked blank, but one a little kindlier than the rest followed me out and said 'If you go to Duren about twenty miles from here you might find something.' I did.

I engaged a German photographer with a car. I went to Duren and I found Sonia's father, a thin-faced greengrocer with a shabby shop and no wish to help me at all. 'Ches the

Englander' had caused her enough worry, he said, and now he was dead she should be spared any more. So I fetched a bottle of hock and asked him again. Halfway through our second bottle I was holding a picture of him in uniform, taken off the sideboard, and we were swopping stories about the Kaiser's war. Before we finished the third bottle he gave me Sonia's address and a note to her.

Presenting the note was more difficult, because she was in an old villa, well back from the road, with padlocks and chains festooning the high iron gates. When I just touched them two Alsatians appeared, advancing purposefully and snarling horribly. We shouted, the dogs barked, and eventually an old gardener shuffled out. After 25 minutes' haggling he escorted me in, to the coldest reception I ever had.

Sonia had been crying. Now for some reason she wore a fur coat while she drank tea with her mother and four other gloomy women, while two small boys zigzagged between them, playing tag. It was like a paper-chase at a funeral. Everybody read my note except Sonia, who wasn't interested. At last one of the women handed me a cup of tea and one of the zigzagging boys promptly spilled it all over me. I mopped my jacket, patted the boy's head with the other hand and told the embarrassed mother it was alright. I knew what boys were because I had two of my own. And look, here was their picture.

The picture was solemnly passed around. I had never stooped to such corn for a story before but I wanted Sonia's – and quickly. It was now 9pm and back home the first editions were already running.

I told Sonia how thrilled my boys were at Daddy going to Germany, and how disappointed they would be if Daddy didn't have a story about her in the next day's paper; to say nothing of Daddy's Editor. Finally, Sonia volunteered her first piece of information, which was that her ever-loving Ches had robbed her of £40 and touched her for her last £85 to go to London and she was broke.

I took the hint and said something might be arranged. And now Sonia really began to talk. First, why had he been so keen to go to London? Well, Sonia had found out that he had been taking out a waitress – on Sonia's money – and they had quarrelled about it. She said it was all over and he pleaded, offering to marry her. He had been promising to marry her for five years and always Vera stood in the way but now, to show how sorry he was, he would go to London and definitely get free from Vera.

As we know, he did.

And Sonia shattered his 36-hour alibi. He had even tried to confuse her into believing that he had been with her at the vital time. He had tapped that front page of the *News of the World* and said 'They can't pin this on me because I was in Holland with you at the time.'

But he wasn't. They did go to Amsterdam together, but they parted on the Tuesday, and the murders happened the following night.

Sonia's five years with Chesney had been tempestuous, full of passion and full of quarrels. He took her to London three times, introduced her to Vera – and when money ran short he tried to put her on the streets. Sonia and I talked until 11.30pm, then while the photographer drove twenty miles to Bonn to wire his pictures I had to find a telephone and settle down to ninety minutes dictating my story.

By this time it was well into Sunday, so I caught up on Saturday's lunch and at noon Sonia and I settled down to the second instalment of her history. The last piece of the jigsaw fell into place. Months before, Chesney had met a man in

London who looked like him without a beard, so he got a copy of this man's birth certificate from Somerset House, then a passport in his name, duly 'witnessed' by a doctor. It was a long-laid plan. Just before he took an air ticket to murder, he shaved. That explains why a man known all over by his beard was able to get in and out of Britain without it.

Sonia loved him. The day he was buried I took her to lay flowers on his grave. She chose them. 'Red roses for undying love and daffodils to herald the spring' she said. It was a lovely thought. It might have been even lovelier if she had offered a couple of marks towards them instead of expecting me to pay the lot.

After all, she was his mistress, not mine. Worse luck.

One of Rae's most sensational cases was that of Herbert Leonard Mills, known as Len, who murdered a forty-eight-year-old woman – and then confessed to the *News of the World* reporter. I Share a Room with a Strangler was the sensational headline over Rae's story about the case:

There was Nottingham, famous for its girls. And there was I in its best hotel, sharing a suite with a strangler. He had killed once and I knew he was capable of killing again just to get into the headlines, because he was that kind of killer: cocky, cold and greedy.

A document that could hang him was under my pillow and there was only one way he could get it back. Come to that, if he decided to bolt, there was only one way he could get out and that was past my bed. So he could kill two birds – and one reporter – with one stone if he wished. I went to sleep.

This was Herbert Leonard Mills. I called him Len. He called me Norman, for we were buddies. But I wouldn't have trusted him an inch. I had suspected for six weeks that he had killed

Mabel Tattershaw, a hard-up drab of 48 who died because she made one last snatch at romance with a kid of 19. And she happened to pick this kid who was obsessed with the idea of committing the 'perfect crime', and was prepared to gamble on it.

I think I sensed his guilt in the first minute of our conversation and that was on the telephone at 11.30am on Thursday August 9th 1951. I had already taken twenty calls that morning: tip-offs for stories that might 'make' (be good enough for the paper) and tips for horses that could never win. Then this calm, clear voice, not an unpleasant voice at all, came on from Nottingham asking 'What would you pay for the exclusive story and pictures of a murder?'

I was feeling bright that morning so I said 'Is this a murder you have done or one you are going to do?' 'It's one I discovered yesterday. A woman strangled in a wood outside Nottingham.'

'How do you know she was strangled?'

'I just do. You come to Nottingham and I'll show you. You can take pictures and then tell the police and get the credit for discovering her yourself.'

'You mean you haven't told the police?'

'Not likely. I want some money out of this.'

I scribbled a note to Victor Wyeth, sitting next to me. 'Tell Nottingham Police to intercept this call.' I kept Mills talking until a girl cut in: 'Sorry caller, your time is up.' Mills said plaintively that he had no more money and I said 'Give me the number and I'll call you back. Don't go away.' Then the line went dead. Blast!

I tried to call back and was told: 'Sorry, there's a delay, the trunk lines are awfully busy.' Blast again! Still, we got back, and I kept Mills talking and talking and again the girl cut in: 'Sorry, you'll have to break off now, the trunk lines are terribly busy.' Twice that happened and Mills was getting peevish. 'Here,' he said, 'Why all the chat? You'll get the story when I see your money, so are you coming up or not?'

Eventually, thankfully, I heard the kiosk door open and a man said 'We are CID officers.' Then someone took the phone from Mills and said 'Thank you, *News of the World*. We'll contact you later.' They did, and by then they'd found a woman exactly where Mills said, so I dropped the story I was on – an unexciting epic on measles statistics – and was in Nottingham by the first train, expecting to find Mills at the police station.

But they had questioned him and let him go. They told me where to find him: in a cafe, and how to recognise him: a pale youth with light blue eyes and a limp. I let him talk at me for a couple of hours about his discovery and about his passions, which were poetry, race horses, and easy money. He would never work. That was for mugs.

A year before he had stolen £50 and run it up to £3000 by backing odds-on favourites, and then lost it all and another £1000 which he never paid because, he smirked 'I pleaded the Gaming Act and I knew they couldn't touch me anyway, being under 21.'

Now if he could raise £1000 he guaranteed to be rich in a year. How would he raise it? 'Well, maybe there'll be another body and if I find it I reckon it'd be worth £1000 to a newspaper for the story of the coincidence.'

I said 'If you find another body the police might think it's more than coincidence.'

'Ah, the police,' he said. 'They won't solve this murder and they certainly wouldn't solve a second one.' 'Why are you so sure?' I asked, 'I hope you didn't touch anything?'

'Certainly not, except her beads, which were on the grass. It

was finding them that made me look down, and there she was
in a little valley – but I've told the police about them and that's
alright.'

'So you didn't go near the body?'

'No, I tell you. I'd gone there to write a sonnet, so after I
found her I sat down to think what to do, and I read a bit. I
read Shelley's "Ode to Death" – another coincidence, eh? –
then I came away.'

'This was yesterday morning?'

'That's right.'

'And without going near her, how can you be sure she was
strangled? The police don't seem to think so.'

'Those police! Look, I'll lay you ten to one she was strangled
and 100 to one they never find the killer.'

I booked a room for him on the promise that he kept away
from other reporters. I phoned the office that we had 'a right
hot customer we ought to keep tabs on' and that I was bringing him to London to write his own story. He loved that idea.

I told Superintendent Peter Ellington, head of Nottingham
CID, where Mills would be if they wanted him, and on the
train the next morning I tossed my talkative friend the morning papers. They said Mrs Tattershaw's face was bruised and
she had been battered to death.

Mills scoffed. 'They're crazy. There was no bruising, just a
few scratches where he dragged her along afterwards.'

'Oh,' I said, making it sound casual, 'You don't think she
was killed where she was found?'

'Definitely not, and she wasn't beaten to death either. That
takes a bit of doing with a strong woman like that, but strangling's easy.' When I looked up he was smiling at his outspread
fingers and, seeing me, he said: 'Do you think these small
hands of mine could strangle a woman?'

I didn't answer. I left him with colleagues in London and went back to Nottingham to pin down the facts, which were these: Mabel Tattershaw played footy footy in a cinema with a youth on Thursday August 2nd. She dressed up in her pitiful best to meet him the next night. And she was never seen again.

A News of the World man delivered Mills back to my hotel in Nottingham on Saturday night, too late for the other Sunday newspapers to get at him, and now he said he had some evidence. 'Vital and sensational' he said.

When I told him he had better give it to the police he said he was not giving, but selling. He said the police weren't very kind to him over the £50 he stole 'so to hell with them.' Next day he produced his evidence. It was sensational all right. He said 'You know the police still say her face was bruised and blackened and I say it wasn't. Do you know why? It's because I must have seen her straight after the murder, before her face showed bruises. You see it wasn't Wednesday I found her. It was the Sunday before.'

I told the police, but when the inquest opened Mills three times repeated that he had found her on Wednesday. And when the pathologist said it was strangulation he gave me a cheeky thumbs up across the court. Afterwards, I said how clever he was, guessing straight away at what the police took days to establish, and he basked in this praise, so I piled it on.

'I bet there's a lot more you could tell them, Len,' I said, and he replied:

'You can say that again. And do you know something? I've got a feeling I'm going to find another body.'

That jolted me, and when I'm jolted I joke while I play for time. So I said 'Well, remember ours is a Sunday newspaper, so be sure you find your bodies on a Saturday night in future.' Then it happened. Saturday night I was in the office when a newsflash came from Nottingham. Another woman found dead. I was shedding blue lights. I could see myself in the dock for inciting this idiot to murder and I didn't relax until 1am when I got hold of the Nottingham CID chief. The new death was a suicide.

But the first thing Mills said when we met the next Friday, after he had telephoned me to come up, was 'I bet you thought that was me.'

'Well, you did say you'd find a body on a Saturday,' I said.

'Ah, but I didn't know this one was there,' he said.

'Surely you didn't know Mrs Tattershaw's body was there until you found it?'

He looked uneasy. 'Norman' he said, 'You think I murdered her, don't you?'

I said 'I think three things. Either you saw it happen, you know who did it, or . . .'

'Or what, Norman?'

'Or you murdered her.' And I left him for an hour to think that over. When I got back I ordered an orangeade for him – that was all he ever drank – and a pint for myself. I sat and sipped, looking at him coldly while he chain-smoked nervously. He got more fidgety. All of a sudden he was interested in Broadmoor: had I been there, what was it like? Yes, I'd been there, twice.

'Can you have a bet in Broadmoor?' he asked, and I said, 'I expect so. They're allowed money, and they bet in prisons, so why not in Broadmoor.'

Then he wanted to know if I had met Haigh, the acid bath killer, and Heath, the sadist. Yes, I had met them both. Why were they caught, he wanted to know. Because they made mistakes, I told him. They left clues.

'But there's no clues here,' he said.

I said 'Haven't you seen the evening papers? They've found two light hairs on Mrs Tattershaw's coat.'

'They couldn't,' he blurted out, 'because I put my coat over her coat before I . . .'

'Len,' I cut in, 'You realise what you were just about to say?'

'I think it's about time I told you the truth,' he said.

'So do I,' I said, and I fetched a few sheets of hotel note-paper, headed The Black Boy Hotel, Nottingham, and a carbon, and while the denizens of Nottingham chatted around us in the lounge Leonard Mills wrote for nearly two hours. That was the document that lay under my pillow that night and next morning I delivered it, together with Herbert Leonard Mills, to Superintendent Ellington of the CID.

As it happened, it was just nice timing for our first edition, and it was the only time a murderer's statement in court has contained the words 'And now having been warned by Mr Rae of the *News of the World* I have determined to make this statement which I realise involves a charge of murder. I now confess . . .'

I regret to say that Mills didn't have any bets in Broadmoor after all. He was so sure – ready to bet on it to the end – that they wouldn't hang a man under 21.

But they did.

The carbon copy of the confession, which Norman Rae kept when he handed the top copy to the police, is now carefully filed away for posterity in the *News of the World* archives.

Mills described how he met Mrs Tattershaw in the cinema, and got talking to her when she came and sat next to him. She asked him to meet her again the following day. He realized that this gave him an opportunity to do something that he had been dreaming about: to commit the perfect murder. He was a little bit worried when he met her that, as they walked together towards the murder spot in the wood, he had been seen by an old schoolfriend of his, but he hoped that he had not been recognized. Mills said he was 'quite proud of my achievement. I have been most successful, no motive, no clues. Why, if I had not reported finding the body I would not have been connected in any manner whatsoever.' And if he had not been persuaded to confess to Norman Rae he might never have been convicted: the police had their suspicions, but they had very little evidence.

14. Rae's Last Case

A thick rasher of gammon, two fried eggs, baked beans and some chips, with thick bread and butter and a cup of tea. That's the meal that almost bought the *News of the World* it's scoop of the century: an exclusive interview with mass-killer Reginald Christie while he was on the run from the police.

Unfortunately for Norman Rae, the paper's celebrated chief crime reporter, the killer was scared off the arranged rendez-vous by the chance arrival of two policemen. Rae had, as usual, been on the famous 10 Rillington Place murder story from the very beginning. He knew Christie – and Christie knew him. When the murderer was desperate, he turned to the journalist Rae. This is Rae's story of how he nearly netted the biggest story of his eventful life as a reporter:

John Reginald Halliday Christie, the bald bigot who half-gassed his girls then strangled them and kept their corpses in a cupboard, was on the run. Every policeman in London was hunting him. And he rang me up.

It was twenty past eleven on Saturday night, just right for a scoop no other Sunday paper would have time to catch up on, and this looked like the scoop of a lifetime. 'You recognise my voice?' he said. Now, once you've heard it you could never forget that gravelly grating of his.

(Christie had been gassed in the First World War, and his voice had never fully recovered.)

I said 'Of course. It's Christie!' And I waved frantically for somebody to start tracing the call. Christie said 'I can't stand it any more. They're hunting me like a dog and I'm tired out. I'm cold and wet and I've nothing to change into. I've nowhere to turn, nowhere to go and I'm hungry. Starving hungry.'

I said 'So?'

'Mr Rae, look. Get me a meal and a smoke and just let me sit somewhere warm and cosy for a bit. Then you can do what the hell you like with me. Write a story about me. Anything.'

And that's when Christie put in his order for his fry-up. It was arranged that he would meet Rae next to some bushes opposite Wood Green town hall clock, in north London, and Rae promised that he would not alert the police. He told Christie he would have another reporter with him, driving the car.

'I was picturing the thrill of it. When I'd fed Christie and let him warm through I would ring Scotland Yard and say casually 'By the way, if you're looking for Christie, I'll bring him along.'

We parked opposite the town hall as arranged, well out of the way of any lamplight. I opened the door and we waited. Suddenly there was a rustle in the bushes and a man came forward slowly, hesitantly. Then it happened. I was too fed up to even inquire why – whether there had been a Saturday night fight at the local dance hall, or whether it was just an ordinary policeman's meet on the beat. But two policemen approached, one from either side. I saw them and swore. Christie saw them and fled. Just a scurry in the bushes and he was gone.

We drove on for a few yards and returned when the policemen had gone, but Christie never came back. That Sunday, March 29 1953, he tramped back to Rillington Place, where sightseers were making a grisly holiday of the whole business. He was not spotted and recognised, even by people who had known him for years. On Tuesday morning he was arrested on the towpath at Putney, just leaning on the railings, too hungry to run and too weary to care.

For Norman Rae, Christie was the one that got away. But the veteran crime reporter had already had plenty of contact with the meek little clerk who lured a series of women to their deaths, knocking them unconscious with whiffs of gas from the kitchen cooker and then strangling them in a sexual frenzy, keeping clippings from their pubic hair as souvenirs. At least five women died this way. Christie also murdered his wife and may have been the killer of Beryl Evans and her fourteen-month-old baby daughter Geraldine. Beryl's husband, Timothy Evans, was hanged for the murder of Beryl and the baby; controversy has raged ever since as to whether or not he did it, or whether they were two more victims of the strange, bespectacled teetotaller who lived in the flat downstairs.

Christie was tried for the murder of his wife Ethel, the only killing that did not have a sexual motive. This was a deliberate choice by the prosecution because they wanted to establish that he was sane enough to hang, and that not all his murders had been carried out in crazed lust. The Old Bailey jury decided that he should go to the gallows and he was hanged in Pentonville Prison on 15 July 1953.

Christie lived at the house in Rillington Place for fifteen years, and all seven women were killed on the premises. His first victim was a twenty-one-year-old Austrian girl, Ruth Fuerst, who was working in a munitions factory. Christie, who was forty-five in 1943, was working as a special constable in the War Reserve Police. He met Ruth while making inquiries about a theft, and he invited the tall, striking girl back to his home on two or three occasions. His wife Ethel had returned to her native Sheffield to avoid the bombing raids on London, and Christie had the flat – three rooms on the ground floor of the three-storey house – to himself.

In his confession he claimed he strangled her because he received a telegram to say his wife was returning home, and Ruth was putting pressure on him to run away with her. The confession came almost ten years after her death, and when her skeleton was unearthed from the garden of 10 Rillington Place it was impossible to tell how she was killed. But as strangling was definitely Christie's choice with his other victims, it's likely that is how Ruth met her end.

It was after he had committed his first murder (but more than nine years before his arrest) that Christie first met Norman Rae, at Paddington police station. One of Rae's detective friends said to the reporter:

'See that War Reserve constable over there? Somebody gave him a helluva bashing, broken ribs, the lot.'

'Trying to stop a rough house?' Rae asked.

'Not him. He was mucking around with a War Reserve

policewoman and somebody wrote and told her old man. He got compassionate leave from the army to settle things, and he settled Constable Christie all right. This is his first day back, but I don't think he'll be here long.'

He wasn't. He had to leave the War Reserve Police over the matter. The woman involved was divorced by her husband, but her association with Christie also ended – in later years she must have looked on that as a lucky escape.

Christie's second victim was Muriel Eady who worked with him at the radio company where he was a clerk. Muriel and her boyfriend used to visit the Christies socially but, one day, Muriel went to Rillington Place on her own while Ethel Christie was away on holiday. Christie said in his confession that he had promised to help her get rid of her catarrh. He persuaded her to inhale a concoction he mixed, which included Friar's Balsam, and while she had a scarf over her head he fed gas into the jar from which she was inhaling. When she was unconscious he strangled her. Her body, too, was later retrieved from the garden. Her death, in October 1944, was just over a year after the murder of Ruth Fuerst.

Christie's killing spree stopped for a few years. In 1948 a young couple, Timothy and Beryl Evans, moved into the flat on the top floor of 10 Rillington Place – an old man occupied the flat on the middle floor. The young couple, whose baby daughter Geraldine was born a few months after they moved in, got to know the Christies well. The Evans's marriage was a stormy one; on one occasion Tim Evans left home with a blonde friend of theirs for a couple of nights, but returned to his wife. Another time he threatened to throw Beryl out of a window.

Beryl was pregnant, but did not want another baby. Christie offered to help her procure an abortion, telling her and her husband that he had been training as a doctor before the war. He warned them of a risk, but, according to Tim Evans, although he, himself, was opposed to it Beryl wanted to go ahead.

What happened next is still the subject of discussion and controversy. One thing is certain: Beryl and baby Geraldine died. Whether Evans killed them or Christie killed them is the point of debate. Evans initially confessed, but later said that Christie told him his wife died during the abortion, and that Geraldine was given to a couple from Acton to look after. Tim Evans was a simple young man, scarcely able to read and write, but not an innocent. His mixed-up, contradictory and lying statements after his arrest made it difficult at the time – and even more difficult today – to discover the truth of what actually happened to his young family.

When the bodies of Beryl and Geraldine were discovered, in Christie's locked wash-house at the back of 10 Rillington Place, Norman Rae covered the story for the *News of the World.*

I saw a lot of Christie around this time. He was upset because he said Evans had let down the tone of the place. It was bad enough having negroes living all around Notting Hill he said (he was insanely bigoted about negroes) but fancy having a man charged with murder in the same house. It was terrible, he said.

Then while he was waiting to give evidence at Evans' trial at the Old Bailey, I told him that Evans had withdrawn his confession and was now accusing him of the murder. He sagged against the wall, overcome with indignation. How dare anyone suggest such a thing about him. 'Me, who's been a policeman,' he said. He told me he had always been most respectable.

He didn't mention that he had already murdered two women whose bodies he first concealed in that wash-house, then transferred to the garden where their disjointed bones were now mingling with the bones his dog dragged in.

While Timothy Evans was being sentenced to death a wild sobbing startled the court. It was John Reginald Halliday Christie, and when I saw him afterwards he was still sobbing, so I bought him a cup of tea and told him not to upset himself!

Evans went to the gallows on 9 March 1950 still protesting his innocence and blaming Christie.

Christie and his wife Ethel continued to live in the ground-floor flat, but Christie's health – mental and physical – was in decline. To the deep annoyance of the Christies the house was bought by a Jamaican, Charles Brown, and the two flats upstairs were rented out to West Indian families. The Christies complained several times to a local legal centre (set up for the poor who could not afford lawyers) about the noise from their neighbours.

Ethel was taking sleeping tablets and sedatives, and Christie, who was no longer able to work, was in such a bad way that he was advised by his doctor to go into a mental hospital. He said he could not leave Ethel. A few months later, though, he left her permanently – he murdered her. He later claimed that she had taken an overdose of her sleeping tablets, but no traces were found in her body. He may have killed her because she knew too much about the murder of Beryl Evans and baby Geraldine, and her mental state was such that he could no longer trust her not to talk.

Whatever the motive, after nineteen years of what appears to have been a reasonably close marriage, he murdered her and buried her under the kitchen floorboards. He then disintegrated mentally, selling off all the furniture and living with his dog and cat in one room, sleeping on a mattress.

In the next ten weeks he murdered three more women, all prostitutes, who were lured back to his flat, gassed, and then strangled. He had sexual relations with all of them, either before or after their deaths, and he kept samples of their pubic hair in a tobacco tin. Their bodies were stored in a coal cupboard off the kitchen, and Christie was seen by neighbours regularly dousing the whole of the ground floor of the flat with disinfectant. Despite these rudimentary precautions against the smell arousing suspicion, he made little real attempt to cover his tracks. From the carefully executed and disguised murders of Ruth Fuerst and Muriel Eady, he had descended to a final orgy of killing.

Norman Rae ran into him, by chance, during these last grisly days of his life at 10 Rillington Place.

I tried to get him to come for a beer with me, but he wouldn't drink; he preferred to talk about his pet hate, his neighbours. He told me he was thinking of getting out of his home after 15 years living there, because, he said, of the smell of the neighbours.

He insisted I go back with him to the house and smell it for myself. I could smell nothing. I realised afterwards of course why he wanted me to go there: he wanted me as a guinea pig, to test whether the corpses that were rotting there could be smelt.

On Friday, 13 March 1953, Christie sublet his flat to an Irish couple, taking three months' rent in advance. He took his dog to the vet and had it put down, and he shambled off with all his possessions in one suitcase. That night he turned up at a hostel for down and outs.

When his landlord discovered the flat had been sublet he evicted the Irish couple who had spent one night there. Three days later one of the Jamaicans, who lived upstairs, started to clear the mess from the downstairs flat so that it could be re-let. He knocked on a kitchen wall that had recently been wallpapered over. It sounded hollow. He pulled off some of the paper and, with the help of a torch, could see through a gap in the boards of the coal-house door; he saw the naked back of a woman.

The four bodies were soon found, three in the cupboard and one under the floorboards. When the police started to dig in the garden Norman Rae watched them, from the window of a neighbouring flat, while they uncovered Christie's first two victims. They had the corpses, they knew who the murderer was, but the police did not have Christie.

Neither did the *News of the World*, after the untimely arrival of the police outside Wood Green Town Hall. But it was six days from the bodies being found to Christie being arrested. When he was taken to Putney police station a newspaper cutting was found in his wallet: it was Norman Rae's report of the evidence he had given at Timothy Evans's trial.

Christie confessed to all the killings, including Beryl Evans, but he denied knowing anything about the death of the baby. He was tried at the Old Bailey in June 1953, charged with the murder of his wife, and the jury took just eighty-five minutes to find him guilty. He was sentenced to death.

The *News of the World* immediately published The Casebook of John Christie, the story of his life from birth to the condemned cell. 'He Started Just Like Any Other Innocent Babe' said the headline:

It was 1898 and spring was in the air as Mrs Mary Christie set out from the house on the hill, overlooking Halifax to register the birth of her sixth child. Proudly she walked through the streets of stone houses and into the office of Registrar George Lingard. 'Another one, eh, Mrs Christie?' said the registrar, for everyone knew the daughter of one of the town's most respected citizens, who owned a large bootmaking business. 'What name is it this time?'

'John Reginald Halliday Christie' said the happy mother – Halliday after grandfather the wellknown bootmaker.

Mercifully she died before the world knew she had registered the birth of a monster who was destined to shamble across the pages of criminal history and leave a dark stain as the Ripper of Rillington Place . . .

Christie's father, a frightening, bearded man who was nicknamed Mephistopheles by the local children, worked as a carpet designer at a large carpet mill. The family was reasonably well off and eminently respectable. Reg, as he was known, was a lonely boy who left school at fifteen and started a series of different jobs, being sacked from the first two for petty pilfering. He had his first encounter with a girl when he was seventeen; she took the initiative and persuaded him to go with her down a local lover's lane. When he was unable to rise to the occasion she nicknamed him Reggie-no-dick, a name which rankled with him and may well have laid the foundations of his sexual problems.

He served in the trenches of the First World War at the age of nineteen, and was gassed twice, being blinded for two months and losing his voice for several weeks. He had never been strong and the gassing may well have contributed to the ill health that dogged him for the rest of his life. When he was just twenty-one he married Ethel, but it was a shaky union.

Christie changed jobs every few weeks, and eleven months after their wedding day he was sent to prison for three months for stealing postal orders. Two years later he was bound over for obtaining money by false pretences and given a year's probation for violence.

At this point the marriage broke up for nine years. Christie's family was appalled by his lawlessness, and he abandoned Ethel and moved to London where he lived in lodgings and continued to move from job to job and petty crime to petty crime. After nine months in prison for stealing he seemed to settle down and held a clerical job for five years, but this ended when he was again sentenced to prison for hitting Maud Cole, a woman he met on a coach trip to Margate and with whom he was living. He hit her with her son's cricket bat, causing a 5″-long wound. They had been rowing about the fact that she was supporting him.

Four years later he went to prison again, for stealing a car. This time, and for no obvious reason, Ethel, who had been working as a typist in Sheffield, decided to visit him, and after he came out of jail they set up home together. Her influence seemed to steady him and, for ten years, he avoided all trouble. It was not a passionate marriage; Christie admitted that they had sex a few times after first being reunited, but eventually all physical contact ceased. Ethel, who married in the hope of having children, must have been resigned, by this time, to a childless marriage. The couple moved to Rillington Place in 1938 and it was five years later that the first murder occurred.

Neighbours in the area had mixed views about Christie, but uniformly said they would never have suspected him of being capable of such appalling crimes. To some of them he was the ultra-respectable clerk who thought himself rather superior; to others he was an officious nuisance who used his position as a War Reserve policeman to poke his nose into everybody else's affairs.

Norman Rae, who met him during this period, later wrote: 'I confess he didn't give that cold shudder between the shoulders – what I call "crime reporter's instinct" – that I have got from other people with murder in their blood.'

Christie, aged fifty-four, was hanged on 15 July 1953 in the same prison, Pentonville, and by the same hangman, Albert Pierrepoint, as Timothy Evans. In 1966 Evans was granted a posthumous pardon, and his body was removed from inside the prison walls (where all hanged prisoners were buried) to consecrated ground. Norman Rae had died four years before; but the veteran crime reporter was convinced that Christie did *not* kill Beryl Evans. He wrote:

Christie had no conscience about murder at all. But he did not murder Beryl Evans. He may have known something about it. He may have helped Timothy Evans to get rid of her body, and their child's body, too. He probably did. But before Christie's trial and after, I searched and questioned all over London and South Wales where Timothy Evans came from, and I am sure of one thing.

At an inquiry to decide whether Timothy Evans had been wrongly convicted a barrister asked 'Is it conceivable that there were two stranglers living in one house?' And the answer is: there were.

Doctor Arrested at Eastbourne was the *News of the World* headline on 25 November 1956, marking the start of one of the strangest cases in British criminal history. Dr John Bodkin Adams was either a compassionate man who believed in easing the suffering of his dying patients, or a serial killer who made a fortune from the wills of the old ladies he bumped off. When he came to trial at the Old Bailey in April the following year, the jury decided he was not guilty of the murder of one of those patients. He was a free man.

Although he was struck off the medical register for four years, he was later reinstated and the old ladies of Eastbourne continued to flock to his surgery. When he died he left a small fortune – not surprising, since he had been a beneficiary in 132 wills, picking up two Rolls Royces, antiques, jewelry, silver and £45,000.

The rumour around Eastbourne was that, before his trial, he went on his rounds with a bottle of painkiller in one hand and a will form in the other: I'll ease your pain if you'll ease my bank balance was the deal he was rumoured to strike with his doting patients.

Gertrude Hullett, a wealthy widow who lived in a mansion on Beachy Head, was one of his patients. She became addicted to barbiturates while 'Dr John' – as the plump, bespectacled bachelor Irish GP was known locally – was treating her for a nervous breakdown. She died in July 1956 and Adams certified her death as due to cerebral haemorrhage. Rumours were in full swing because there had been a succession of deaths from which the doctor had benefited. Although the British newspapers did not dare print them; for fear of libel, the French magazine, *Paris Match*, had no such compunctions. Was it safe to go into a nursing home in Eastbourne, the magazine asked?

Pushed into action by the publicity, and by Mrs Hullett's friends who were concerned when they discovered that her Rolls Royce was earmarked for the doctor, the local police called for an autopsy. The conclusion was that she had died from barbiturate poisoning, but the inquest decided that she had committed suicide.

The police asked for – and got – permission to exhume two other bodies of elderly female patients who had died while in Dr Adams's care. One of the bodies was too far decomposed to be of any use but the other was that of Mrs Edith Alice Morrell, the widow of a wealthy food importer. She had suffered a stroke, was partly paralysed and had severe arthritis; Dr Adams prescribed heroin and morphine to control her pain. She made several wills, changing her mind at frequent intervals about who would inherit what. Before her death Dr Adams contacted her solicitor himself, telling the lawyer that she wanted to leave a chest of antique silver and a Rolls Royce to him. The solicitor refused to change the will until instructed to do so by Mrs Morrell herself; she soon did so. Before her death she changed it again, cutting the doctor out completely. Despite that, when she finally died her family allowed the doctor to have an antique cupboard, the silver and the car.

After a lengthy and painstaking inquiry the police finally charged Dr Adams with the murder of Mrs Morrell. He apparently said, at one stage during his interviews, that 'easing the passing of a dying person is not all that wicked. She wanted to die – that cannot be murder.'

It was obvious it was going to be a difficult case to prove. The victim had been dead for six years, she was eighty-one years old when she died, and after her stroke other medical experts had estimated that she had between six and twelve months to live, yet she had survived for two and a half years under Dr Adams.

The main witnesses at the trial were four nurses who had attended to the old lady, and their memories of the timings and amounts of drugs did not tally with the record books produced in court. Their evidence was challenged by Adams's defence lawyer and he was acquitted on 10 April 1957. The *News of the World* estimated that more than a million words about the case had been 'telephoned, cabled or radioed all over the world'.

Dr Adams returned to Eastbourne, and lived comfortably and without courting publicity. His reception in the town was mixed. He was either a saint or a sinner, although the true answer was probably somewhere in between. He was greedy and wanted a share of the financial wealth and security that his rich old patients enjoyed, but if he aided them towards their deaths it was only when they were in great pain and looking forward to a release from it.

When he died in 1983, aged eighty-four, he left £400,000. More than twenty women were named as beneficiaries, for sums ranging from £500 to £5000, for 'their loyal support given to me in my time of trouble'.

15. Monstrous Women

As the new teacher was being shown around the school she saw a six-year-old girl lying stiff under one of the desks in a classroom.

'That's Mary Bell,' she was told. 'You'll get to know her soon enough.'

Five years later, in 1968, the whole of the country got to know Mary Bell when she became the most famous child killer in British history.

The disturbed little girl who used to crawl under the desks and pull at the hairs on the teacher's legs to get herself noticed eventually found a way to attract the attention she craved.

At first, it was very hard for the police to believe: two little boys were dead and the killer was a small, very pretty eleven-year-old girl.

It was so hard for them to believe that it resulted in Mary Bell nearly getting away with the perfect crime: the first killing was put down as an accident. It was only after the death of the second child, two months later, that they were forced to face the terrible fact that sweet little Mary was a killer.

The first victim was four-year-old Martin Brown whose body was found in an upstairs room in a derelict house on the Scotswood Road council estate in

Newcastle, near where Mary Bell lived, on a Saturday afternoon in May. There were no signs of injury on his body, and an empty pill bottle lay nearby – the death was put down to a tragic accident.

Two boys found the body and called two workmen into the house. One of the workmen tried to give the kiss of life to the little boy, but it was too late. While they were waiting for the emergency services to arrive, two young girls came into the house. One was Mary, eleven the next day, and the other was her best friend, Norma Bell, who was thirteen. Despite sharing a surname, the girls were not related, but lived next door to one another. And despite the fact that Norma was older and much bigger than Mary, it was Mary, a pretty dark-haired little girl with bright blue eyes, who was the leader.

The girls seemed to know about the body and had to be sent away as they tried to go upstairs. But that alone was not enough to raise suspicions – it was just the first in a series of macabre events over the next few days. Two days later there was a break-in at Woodlands Crescent Day Nursery, close to Mary Bell's home.

It looked at first like a straightforward case of childish vandalism: slates had been pulled from the nursery roof and cleaning materials were strewn about. But what made it much more than vandalism was the discovery of four notes, scrawled in childish handwriting and badly spelled:

'I murder so that I may come back,' 'Fuch of, we murder, watch out Fanny and Faggot,' 'We did murder Martain brown fuckof you Bastard,' and 'You'd better look out there are murders about by Fanny and Auld Faggot.'

But even when the nursery was broken into again, four days later, and Mary and Norma were caught on the premises and admitted the previous break-in, the significance of the notes was not appreciated.

There were children and their parents living around the Bell home who knew that Mary Bell was a strange child with a strong sadistic streak, but not even they suspected her of killing Martin. Just two weeks before Martin's death another little boy, a three-year-old, suffered severe injuries after falling from the top of an air-raid shelter while playing with Mary and Norma.

The following day the mothers of three girls aged eight, six and five complained to the police that Mary Bell had attacked their daughters and squeezed their throats. Mary and her pal, Norma, who was with her, were given a ticking off by the police. The day after Martin's death, Mary again had her hands around the throat of another child; this time it was Norma's eleven-year-old sister Susan, and Mary only released her grip when Susan's father hit her on the shoulder.

Three days later Mary called at Martin's home and asked to see him. Martin's mother, deeply upset, tried to explain to the pretty little girl on the doorstep that her son was dead. Mary replied, 'I know, I want to see him in his coffin.'

At school she drew a picture of the scene of Martin's death, complete with dead body and a bottle labelled TABLETS in capital letters, in the exercise book in which her teacher encouraged her to write 'news'. She also started spreading rumours that her friend Norma had killed Martin. When Norma's parents heard the rumours, Mary went round and apologized. A couple of weeks later, a fourteen-year-old boy came across Mary and her best friend Norma having a savage fight, with Mary screaming, kicking and pulling the bigger girl's hair. When Mary screamed, 'I am a murderer,' the boy, who knew her as a kid who told lies, laughed openly. Mary then pointed at the derelict house where Martin had been found and said, 'That's where I killed Brown.'

But, despite all these desperate attempts to link herself with Martin's death, it was not until the second killing that Mary's claims began to be taken seriously. Two months after Martin died, three-year-old Brian Howe, another child from the same area of the council estate, disappeared. A search was launched, but without success until Mary Bell suggested to Brian's fourteen-year-old sister that her little brother might be playing among some concrete blocks on an area of waste land known to the local kids as the Tin Lizzie.

At eleven o'clock that evening, Brian's body was found in the place that Mary had suggested. The body was crudely covered with grass and weeds. Brian had been strangled and there were superficial cuts on his belly and puncture marks on his legs. Lying nearby was a pair of scissors with a broken blade. A post-mortem showed that death had been quick. There were bruise marks around the little boy's neck and the small cuts on his body had been done after his death – they were almost in the shape of the initials M. and N.

But the most horrifying piece of information that the doctor passed to the police was that the fingermarks on the dead boy's neck could not have been done by an adult hand, and that the amount of pressure needed to kill such a small child was not great. The killer was evidently another child. During the next twenty-four hours 1200 Newcastle children were given questionnaires to fill in about where they had been during the vital last few hours of Brian's life.

Gradually, the numbers of suspect children were whittled down until there were only two names remaining: Mary and Norma Bell. Both accused each other of committing the crime, but it did not take the police, led by Chief Inspector James Dobson of Newcastle CID, long to realize that Mary was the leader of the two girls.

Under questioning, she showed a streetwise sophistication – whereas Norma was a tearful and distressed child. It was Mary who said:

'I'll send for some solicitors, they will get me out. This is being brainwashed.' On another occasion, when the phone in the interview room rang, she asked, 'Is this place bugged?'

When told she was going to be charged with Brian's murder, she said, 'That sounds fine by me.'

By this time questions were also being asked about Martin's death. Handwriting experts proved that Mary and Norma had written the notes found in the nursery school. But Norma's mother said that her daughter had been with her, watching her do the ironing, at the crucial time.

Both girls denied having anything to do with Martin's death. Norma at first told a series of lies about the death of Brian, but eventually told the police that she had seen her friend Mary strangle him, and that afterwards they had been twice to see the body and Mary had marked it with a razor blade and the scissors that had been found. Norma told the police where the razor blade was hidden.

Mary told the reverse story, putting the blame on Norma. But she also skilfully tried to implicate a local boy who, luckily, could prove that he had been out with his family on the day that Brian died. It was four-and-a-half months before the two girls stood trial, accused of the two murders. Mary was held in remand homes, with other girls in trouble with the law, where she enjoyed a perverted celebrity status. She ran away twice but was quickly recaptured.

At the eleven-day trial, held the fortnight before Christmas 1968, Norma was found not guilty of both charges and was set free. In court, she was so upset that on one occasion the trial had to be halted.

Mary was found guilty of the manslaughter of the two small boys – not murder, because the jury believed that she was suffering from diminished responsibility at the time of the killings. She, too, cried during the trial – but those watching her believed it was more from anger and exhaustion than from pity for her victims.

She was given a life sentence; this posed enormous problems for the Home Office. There was nowhere suitable to keep an eleven-year-old girl; other girls of that age who come before the courts have invariably been involved in petty crime, not killing.

Eventually, it was decided to send her to an approved school for boys in Lancashire where she was held until she was seventeen and old enough to go to an adult women's prison. A handful of other girls were introduced to the school, but they were invariably older than Mary.

She wasn't an easy child to deal with. Less than eighteen months after being sent to the approved school she accused one of the masters of indecently assaulting her; this proved in court to have been a malicious and untrue accusation.

When she was twenty she absconded from Moor Court Prison where she had been sent to help her prepare for eventual release. She was on the run for five days, during which time she had a brief relationship with a man nine years older than her. They met when she thumbed a lift to Blackpool.

Exclusive: I Loved Mary Bell was the headline on the *News of the World* story, in which twenty-nine-year-old Clive Shirtcliffe told of meeting Mary and another girl as they hitchhiked away from the prison in Staffordshire. Shirtcliffe and a friend took Mary to Blackpool. They described the reaction of the twenty-year-old girl to her first taste of freedom in nine years.

We passed a lake, with little white yachts sailing on it. Mary shouted we must stop. She stood on a stone wall drinking in the scene . . . We bought an ice cream and she ate it as if she had never had anything like it before . . . At a [motorway] service area she was like a sleeping princess who had just been woken up after 100 years. She couldn't drag her eyes away from the things in the shop. The crowds of people frightened her . . . She was unusual for a girl who had been in prison. We were swearing, and she asked us not to.

After visiting Blackpool, where she spent her first night with Shirtcliffe in a boarding-house bedroom and lost her virginity, Mary and the two men went to Birmingham and Derby. With her hair dyed auburn and some borrowed clothes she hoped to avoid being recognized, but the newspapers were full of the story of her escape and it was only a matter of time before she was picked up. Clive Shirtcliffe and his friend were later given suspended jail sentences for harbouring her.

Mary Bell's mother told the *News of the World*, in another exclusive, that her daughter had intended to stay free for six months, holding down a job, to prove that she was a suitable case for release.

It was another three years before the authorities agreed with her. She was freed just before her twenty-third birthday, a stunningly pretty girl who had spent all her adolescence in custody. She had been prepared for life on the outside of the prison walls by six months of working in a café in York, returning to Askham Grange Prison every evening.

Since her release in 1980 she has given birth to a daughter. The child was made a ward of court – a move that Mary supported because it means that the High Court could ban any information being published about the little girl's name or where she lives.

Mary still maintains that she had nothing to do with the death of Martin Brown, and that Brian Howe's death was an accident. What is possible is that neither of these little boys would have died if Mary Bell's own early life had been different.

She was born when her mother, Betty, was seventeen and unmarried. Betty had a history of psychiatric problems, but had always discharged herself from hospital after only brief stays.

Betty came from a stable and loving background: Mary's grandmother and aunts and uncles were respectable and caring people. But from childhood Betty had been odd, refusing to eat with the rest of the family.

Her food had to be left on the floor in a corner behind a chair. Later on she would eat standing up, but only if the rest of the family pretended not to see her.

When she married Billy Bell and had another two children she still never sat down to a meal with them, although she prepared meals for them. Mary, known to the family as May, spent her childhood being ferried backwards and forwards to hospital, more than once for having swallowed pills of her mother's (on one occasion she proclaimed loudly to everyone at the hospital that her mother had fed them to her).

She was also shuttled around the family; whenever Betty could not cope she was left with aunts and uncles. There were times when she was more with relatives than she was with her mother – and there were other occasions when she was dumped with people who were not in the family. She was two and a half when she was left with one couple who wanted to adopt her. But her mother reclaimed her a few days later. Mary remembers the incident; her hair had to be cut off because she had lice.

On another occasion she was 'given' by her mother to a woman whom she met at an adoption agency. The woman had been turned down as an adoptive mother, because of her age, and was leaving the agency in tears when Betty marched in with three-and-a-half-year-old Mary. When Betty heard the woman's story she handed Mary over to her. It was only when Mary's grandmother and aunt insisted that Betty find her daughter, under threat of calling the police, that the mother went out and brought back the child.

By the time Mary started infants school she was already showing obvious signs of being deeply disturbed.

She would lie rigid on the floor under her desk, she would tell endless lies, she would kick, pinch or hit the other children.

'Mary was always drawing attention to herself. She seemed to have a need to be noticed – perhaps punished, too,' said one of her teachers.

'If she couldn't get my attention any other way she would sit under the desk and pull the hairs on my legs. I remember letting her do it – I was so determined not to give in to her craving for attention.'

At home she had tantrums and screamed for her own way. Her parents' marriage was not happy – both of them went away from home for days at a time, leaving the other one to look after the children. Mary learned to fight on the streets of the council estate where they lived, and she learned to be cunning and crafty, shifting the blame on to other children for things she had done.

Looking back, it's clear that she needed much help at this stage of her life; perhaps, if she had had it, she would not have needed to draw attention to herself in the appalling way that she did. And she would not have become one of Britain's most notorious female prisoners.

It was 8.20 in the morning. The housing estate was waking up. Children were dawdling towards school, workers were queueing at bus stops, doors were opening to take in the milk that had been left on the step.

A bread man, wearing a white overall and carrying a large basket of wrapped sliced loaves, knocked at the back door of 16 Wardle Brook Avenue, Hattersley, near Manchester – and came face to face with the only woman whose name would eclipse Mary Bell's in the annals of twentieth-century female crime.

She was a smartly dressed woman with blonde hair neatly backcombed and lashings of thick eye makeup. There must be some mistake, she thought, taking in the white coat and the basket of loaves. They didn't have bread delivered.

'Is your husband in?' asked the bread man.

'I haven't got a husband,' said the woman.

'I am a police superintendent and I have reason to believe there is a man in this house,' said the 'bread man', opening the white coat to show his uniform.

For a moment, and only for a moment, Myra Hindley was flustered.

'There is no man here,' she said. But as soon as she realized that Superintendent Bob Talbot was not going to be easily fobbed off, she ushered him into the house and said, 'He's in the other room.'

Superintendent Talbot walked through to the living-room where Ian Brady, naked except for a vest, lay on the divan settee, writing a note with a green biro. Bob Talbot, only promoted to superintendent five weeks earlier and due to start a fortnight's holiday that day, Thursday, 7 October 1965, said the words that opened the most infamous case in British criminal history:

'I have received a report that an act of violence took place in this house last night and we are investigating it.'

The report had come from seventeen-year-old David Smith, Myra Hindley's brother-in-law. Smith had been present at the house in Wardle Brook Avenue, the night before, when another seventeen-year-old, apprentice Edward Evans, had been savagely beaten to death. Evans was the last of the victims of the Moors murderers; Smith, devastated by what he had witnessed, rang the police early the next morning.

He warned them that Brady and Hindley had guns; that is why Bob Talbot chose to approach the house disguised as a bread man. He didn't want any crazed gunman taking potshots at him. But, once inside number 16, it was hard to believe that these two young people were dangerous killers. The young woman was dressed for work, her boyfriend was writing a note to his boss explaining that he had sprained his ankle and would not be in the office that day.

The house was clean and well kept. A budgie swung contentedly on its perch. Myra told Superintendent Talbot that her Gran was in bed upstairs. It all seemed so normal . . .

But when Bob Talbot and another detective searched the house they found it was very far from normal. One of the bedrooms was locked and Myra Hindley told him that she kept her guns in there. She said the key was at her office. The Superintendent told Myra to get her coat, the police would take her to work by car to pick up the key.

She said, 'It's not convenient, I don't want to go.'

When Talbot insisted she looked at Brady and said, 'Well, you had better tell him.'

Brady stood up and said, 'There was a row last night. It's in the back bedroom.'

He turned to Myra and said, 'Give them the keys.'

When they unlocked the door the policemen found the lifeless, battered body of Edward Evans, neatly trussed in polythene and a grey blanket. Even then, it could have ended there. A very straightforward case: a couple of young men have too much to drink, a violent row erupts, it gets out of hand, one of them gets killed. That's the story Ian Brady told Superintendent Talbot.

It might have been enough for some policemen. But there were one or two things that Talbot did not like: the expert way the corpse had been tied up, the loaded guns, the stories David Smith was telling of Brady bragging of burying bodies on the moors.

For some reason Bob Talbot could not explain, the scruffy teenager with a record for violence was more believable than this tidy young couple with their neat house, their car, their smart clothes. The youth, married to Myra's sister Maureen, was at the Hyde Road police station telling chilling tales of Brady's fascination with Hitler, the writings of the Marquis de Sade, his philosophies about death, crime, punishment . . .

Brady was arrested and taken to the same police station, the police making sure that he did not see Smith, the boy he had hoped to train as his apprentice in murder. Myra Hindley was not cautioned, she did not have to go anywhere. But she wanted to stay near Ian. So she picked up her dog, Poppet, and went to the police station where she drank tea all day and demanded dog food which the police, obligingly, provided.

Detective Policewoman Margaret Campion was called back from another job to question Myra. She knew within minutes of sitting across the table from the bleached blonde that this was one of the toughest nuts she had ever had to crack.

And the experienced woman detective would not crack her. It was to be more than twenty years before

Myra Hindley would tell the truth about the Moors Murders.

'I didn't do it. Ian didn't do it. I am saying nothing. Ask Ian. Whatever Ian has done, I have done,' were the words that WPC Campion, and all the other policemen and women who tried to question her, heard from Myra. Ian Brady would trip himself up, reveal things inadvertently, be provoked into speaking without thinking. But not Myra. The detectives on the case soon realized she was a formidable opponent.

The house at Wardle Brook Avenue was searched and 170 photographs, many of them views of the moors north of Manchester, were found. Myra's seventy-seven-year-old granny was taken to stay with friends. The old lady had heard Edward Evans's last screams but had been told by her granddaughter that she'd dropped a tape-recorder on her foot and shouted out in pain. To her dying day, old Mrs Maybury never spoke about that night.

The car was also searched and yielded three sheets of paper, neatly folded and written in Ian Brady's meticulous handwriting. There were columns of abbreviations and lists, some obvious and some obscure. GN meant gun, HAT meant hatchet, Pro P meant Pro Plus, a mild stimulant that could be bought over the counter. Others, like TICK and PB and WH, were harder to decipher.

He said the sheets were written after the murder, as part of a disposal plan for the body. But the police did not believe him. Among other things removed from the house was an old exercise book, found inside a locked wardrobe. It seemed to contain nothing but scribbles and doodles: there were many names jotted all over the place:

Ian Brady, John Sloan, Jim Idiot, Alec Guineas, John Kilbride, J. Thompson, John Gilbert . . .

As Bob Talbot glanced through the names, one leapt out at him: John Kilbride. A neighbouring police force, Lancashire, had covered the area with posters of a grinning, cheeky-faced twelve-year-old who had disappeared without trace almost two years before: John Kilbride. On its own, it was not evidence. But the scribbled name added weight to David Smith's story about bodies buried on the moors. And if John Kilbride was up there, what about other youngsters who had gone missing from the area: sixteen-year-old Pauline Reade, twelve-year-old Keith Bennett, ten-year-old Lesley Ann Downey?

For five days after Ian Brady was arrested, Myra Hindley was still free. She was not allowed back to the house, which was sealed off, but she was able to go into the office where she and Brady both worked and where they had met nearly five years earlier. She collected their wages and burned an envelope of documents that Brady had hidden there.

Then, on 11 October 1965, Myra Hindley was arrested and charged with being an accessory to the murder of Edward Evans. She would never be free again.

Already, the police were searching the moors, trying to identify Ian Brady's endless scenic photographs. They took David Smith and his wife Maureen up there, to help them remember where they had been on drives with Brady and Hindley. But it was hopeless; the moors are vast, and David and Maureen were unable to be sure.

But then the police had an unexpected bonus. Pat Hodges was a bright twelve-year-old who lived two doors away from Myra in Wardle Brook Avenue. She had become a favourite friend of theirs; even Ian, who was usually impolite to any visitors, tolerated having her around the house.

Pat had been taken out with them on car rides, sometimes late at night. To the moors. And Pat was able to remember the route they had regularly taken. Sitting in the back of a police car with a policewoman, she directed the driver to the Ashton to Huddersfield road, telling him to stop at exactly the spot where Myra Hindley had parked while Brady carried out his gruesome burials – and where she, Pat, had been taken for picnics.

When the army of police diggers moved to that area, it was not long before they found two bodies: Lesley Ann Downey and John Kilbride. Nearly twenty-two years later, Pauline Reade's body was also found close to the spot where young Pat had been given sandwiches and glasses of wine.

While the police were getting results on Saddleworth Moor, Detective Chief Inspector John Tyrrell, of Manchester police, was getting results elsewhere.

Number 16 Wardle Brook Avenue had been thoroughly searched several times. The garden had been dug up. The houses where Hindley's parents and Brady's mother and stepfather lived had also been taken apart.

But John Tyrrell wouldn't let it go at that. He knew from Brady's lists that they were up against a meticulous mind. He went back to the house in Hattersley and started looking again. Painstakingly and systematically, he inspected all the books on the shelves until he came to a small white prayer book that had been given to Myra by an aunt and uncle when she converted to Roman Catholicism at the age of sixteen.

There were two initials on Brady's list still unexplained: PB. Prayer book. Rolled very tightly and slipped inside the spine of the book Inspector Tyrrell found a small piece of paper: a left-luggage ticket. It was a piece of detection work that later earned him praise in court.

The day before Edward Evans was murdered Brady had parcelled together in two suitcases all his Nazi propaganda, pornography and the Marquis de Sade's ravings. They were loaded into the back of Myra's van and for 2s (10p) deposited at Manchester Central Station left-luggage office. Hiding the left-luggage ticket in a prayer book was one of his twisted jokes.

When the police recovered the suitcases, they were brought to Superintendent Bob Talbot's desk. Inside were the books (as expected) and also a black wig, a length of rubber hose covered with lead, some bullets, a notebook containing lists of names of books and notes about sexual perversions, and a cosh with the word Eureka written on it.

There were a couple of tapes and a tin containing some photographs. The detective expected them to be more views of Saddleworth Moor.

But when he turned the first one over, he was sickened.

It was a picture of a little girl, naked except for her brown-buckled shoes and striped socks, and with a scarf tied across her mouth: little Lesley Ann Downey, the girl who had disappeared in Manchester after visiting a fair last Boxing Day. There were nine pictures altogether. It was such a staggering find that, for a moment, Bob Talbot forgot about the tapes. When he remembered, he wasn't expecting them to improve on the evidence the suitcase had already yielded.

And, at first, they did not. There was Brady's voice chanting, 'Sieg Heil, Sieg Heil' – nasty, but not illegal. There was some marching music and an extract from the Goons show. Then he came to the last track on the tape. Bob Talbot could hear quite clearly two voices that he had come to know well: the voice of the woman who had opened the door to Talbot, the bread man, just ten days earlier. And the voice of the man who had been lying on the divan in the sitting-room that morning. There was a third voice – the voice of a young girl, a voice that would be formally identified in court by Mrs Ann Downey as the voice of her daughter, Lesley Ann.

Alone in his office, Superintendent Talbot was the first person to listen to the tape recording that would become the most infamous exhibit ever brought into a British court of law, a tape recording of the suffering and torture of a young child just minutes away from death. As the voices faded, the tape carried on with a recording of the Christmas carol 'The Little Drummer Boy'. Bob Talbot, and all those who heard that tape, would never again be able to listen to that song without choking back tears.

Without that tape, Myra Hindley might have persuaded a jury that she was the innocent dupe of an evil man, an unwitting or unwilling accomplice. The tape, more than anything else, put her firmly in the dock as an equal partner to Brady. When she was shown the photographs and the tape was played to her, Myra Hindley almost cracked. She lowered her head, clutched her handkerchief and whispered, 'I am ashamed.'

It was the only time the police, who questioned her relentlessly, ever saw a chink in her armour. And it lasted only a few seconds. Then she returned to her stoical refusal to say anything, other than 'Ian didn't do it, I didn't do it.'

She said something else, though, when the police told her that her dog Poppet had died under anaesthetic. A vet had been called in to examine the dog's teeth to establish its age because, on some of the photographs taken by Brady on the moors, the dog was a tiny puppy. Its age was a way of dating the pictures and establishing whether they had been taken before, or after, the murders of the children. Unknown to anyone, the dog had a kidney complaint and did not survive the anaesthetic.

'Murderers!' Myra Hindley screamed at the police – a strange accusation from the woman who would, six months later, be sentenced to life imprisonment for the murders of Edward Evans and Lesley Ann Downey, and of harbouring Ian Brady after the murder of John Kilbride.

When the case came to court, it was dubbed the Murder Trial of the Century by the *News of the World*. Myra Hindley's hair had been carefully rinsed lilac-blue before the start of the trial, a colour that would be washed out by the end of the three weeks. She listened to the charges against her with blue hair and heard her sentence with bleached, yellow hair.

The most dramatic day was when the jury, the press and the spectators in the public gallery heard the tape for the first time. A BBC sound engineer, who had previously been working on the 'Pinky and Perky' show, had eliminated as much background noise as possible. As the pathetic voice of the dead child was heard in the hushed room, three women in the public gallery covered their ears. When the sixteen minutes of tape was over, there was stunned silence, even among the case-hardened lawyers and court staff.

David Smith's wife, Maureen, was heavily pregnant when she gave evidence. The most startling fact that she revealed was that her husband, David, was in the pay of a newspaper, the *News of the World*. The paper had been paying him between £10 and £20 a week, was paying their hotel bills and had taken the pair of them to France for a holiday (six months before the trial their combined wages had been £12.50 a week). The paper had spent weeks winning the trust of the two frightened youngsters. There were no legal restrictions in those days on interviewing witnesses and, in total, the paper paid Smith £1000, £600 of it in small amounts and £400 after the trial was over.

The paper was attacked in court for having 'bought up' the chief prosecution witness. It had, the judge said, handed the defence 'a stick with which to beat' Smith and his wife. But the defence could not make too much of Smith's relationship with the *News of the World*: the original statement the youth had made to the police before Brady and Hindley were arrested – and long before he had met anybody from the paper – had been an even stronger condemnation of the murderers than the evidence he later gave. Myra Hindley, in particular, was much more heavily implicated in the killing of Edward Evans in Smith's first statement.

Questions were subsequently asked in parliament about the way newspapers could do deals with witnesses, and the payment to David Smith was the last time it happened – legally.

For a time after their imprisonment Brady and

Hindley maintained their relationship, exchanging letters and campaigning to be allowed to see each other (as they would have been allowed to do had they been married). But within a few months of arriving in Holloway Myra Hindley embarked on the first of many lesbian relationships, and her dependence on Brady waned. Her prison career has been chequered; there was a controversy about a prison governor taking her for walks on Hampstead Heath, and, more seriously, a planned escape attempt when she was involved in a relationship with a prison officer.

She has made the best of prison educational opportunities and has an Open University degree. She has reverted to her Roman Catholic religion and has gathered around her a group of campaigners who fight for her release. In 1987 she finally confessed to her part in the murders. Detective Chief Superintendent Peter Topping, head of CID at Greater Manchester Police, had already reopened the search of the moors, and the body of Pauline Reade, one of the victims she and Brady were never charged with murdering, was found. The body of Keith Bennett has never been discovered, much to the anguish of his family, but in her confession Hindley admitted that he was another of their victims. It was to Peter Topping she confessed, claiming that she did so out of remorse. Cynics believe it was a calculated decision to help her win freedom.

Brady is now held in a secure psychiatric hospital in Liverpool. His health, both mental and physical, has deteriorated badly. Hindley, in contrast, is fit and well, and still believes that one day she will be released.

It looked like a bad car smash. The red Mini had careered off the road and hit a tree. The two people inside were both hurt, and there was blood spattered all over the interior. The man, a nurse called Raymond Cook, was not badly injured. But his wife, June, a schoolteacher, died soon after being rushed to hospital.

Something did not add up. The car was damaged, but not wrecked. It had obviously not been travelling fast when it hit the tree. So how did June suffer such terrible injuries?

It could easily have been statistically recorded as another fatal car crash. But the police started asking questions, and doctors started looking critically at June Cook's injuries, and before long it was clear that the Red Mini case was not an accident at all. It was a murder. June Cook had been bludgeoned to death with a blunt instrument before the car hit the tree.

The 'accident' in 1967 sparked a police inquiry that ended with two men and a woman being sentenced to life for murdering June Cook. The woman was Kim Newell who would meet both Hindley and Bell in the thirteen years she served in jail. But before the police could interview her about her part in the murder, *News of the World* reporter, Charles Sandell, had beaten them to it. When he was later asked by Detective Superintendent Ian Forbes, the head of the police team investigating the car crash near Henley-on-Thames, whether he thought Kim Newell knew anything about the matter, Sandell replied that he thought she did. He passed on to the police that Newell said she had nothing to hide and would welcome a visit from them.

Kim Newell was a very pretty twenty-four-year-old

who had been having an affair with Raymond Cook whom she had met at the hospital where they both worked. The pair enlisted the aid of an old boyfriend of Newell's, a tree-feller and illegal abortionist called Eric Jones, and the trio planned June Cook's death. They wanted her out of the way so that Raymond Cook could inherit her property. Their first plan, to stage a drowning accident, had to be called off because Cook needed time to persuade his wife to make her will in his favour; their marriage was unhappy and her current will left everything to their two young children. When he had persuaded June to be reconciled, the second plan was drawn up.

On the day of the murder Raymond Cook took his wife out to dinner. As they drove home he spotted a man flagging them down at the side of the road. The man, Jones, claimed to be having problems with his car and Cook offered him a lift to a garage. Once inside the Mini, Jones and Cook overpowered and killed June, and then staged the 'accident'.

Kim Newell was heavily pregnant with Cook's baby when she appeared in the dock alongside her lover and Jones. Midway through the thirteen-day trial Jones changed his plea to guilty, and gave evidence against the other two. All three were sentenced to life, and Kim Newell gave birth to her son in Holloway prison.

When she came out, aged thirty-seven, she told the story of her life to the *News of the World*, including how she had met and fallen in love with a prison maintenance worker. Their affair, which started three years before her release, was carried on with the help of other prisoners and, she claimed, the connivance of some staff at Moor

Court, an open prison. She and her lover, who was five years younger than her, were able to make love most days.

When she was released he was waiting for her, having divorced his wife. A month after she came out of prison they were married. Kim Newell died of cancer in 1990; she was aged forty-seven.

16. The Butler Did It

The silver-grey Ford Cortina – with its bizarre cargo – sped north up the M1 on a cold December night in 1977.

In the front seats were two murderers. In the back was a drugged eighty-two-year-old retired Member of Parliament. Sitting next to him was a fifty-one-year-old woman, dressed in a wig and a mink coat belonging to the old man's wife.

And in the boot was the body of his wife . . .

Within ten days, both the back-seat passengers would also be dead, caught up in a grotesque chain of murders that began almost by accident.

The old man was Walter Scott-Elliott, an ex-Labour MP with a large personal fortune which included houses in France and Italy, as well as a flat in fashionable Sloane Street in London. He had bank accounts in different countries, antiques, paintings, jewelry.

In the driving seat was his butler, Archibald – known as Roy – Hall. Hall had been working for the elderly Scott-Elliott and his wife, Dorothy, for less than a month, but they had already come to regard him as the perfect butler: efficient, courteous, always willing to help.

What they didn't know about fifty-three-year-old Hall, who used the surname Fontaine, was that he had a long criminal history stretching back over the past thirty-six years. He had already committed his first murder and got away undetected.

Hall was born in Glasgow, the son of a post office clerk. He was always different from the kids he grew up with, developing from an early age a taste for the finer things of life – and a line in dishonesty to finance them.

In his early teens he was collecting for the Red Cross – and passing on only a fraction of the money. From the age of seventeen onwards he was in and out of prison for theft and housebreaking. By the time he was twenty-seven he had realized that, with his well-groomed appearance and the smooth accent he had cultivated, with only a trace of his Glasgow origins left in it, he could pass for one of the gentry.

He had already started to find work as a butler but envied his employers their life of wealth and luxury. While working for one family who were on holiday abroad, he used their invitation to a royal garden party in Edinburgh, hiring a dress suit, driving their Bentley and hobnobbing with ease with local bigwigs.

On another occasion he darkened his skin with walnut juice, checked into a posh hotel as an Arab sheikh and arranged for samples from jewelers' shops to be brought to his room. While the shop owners waited outside he took the jewels into the bathroom and escaped through another door, leaving his Arab robes behind. He became a good actor, posing as a lord and running up large bills in hotels. He was even invited to a civic reception by the mayor of Torquay who thought he was a wealthy American from the deep south.

Prison played a large part in his life but, in between

sentences, he was always able to find work as a butler. He was bisexual, having relationships with both men and women. He befriended one young pregnant Irish girl and they worked together, as a housekeeper and butler; he was delighted with the baby girl whom he unofficially adopted as his daughter. He was briefly married, but the relationship ended when, soon afterwards, he was back in jail; he lived for some time with a widow who later told the *News of the World* that 'he was so passionate that no woman would ever have dreamed he was gay'.

It was in 1977 that his murdering spree began. His first victim was another petty criminal, a man called David Wright, whom Hall had met in prison. Hall was working as a butler on a wealthy estate in Scotland and Wright came to stay with him.

Wright wanted to steal jewelry from the big house where Hall was working but Hall, having spent fifteen of the past twenty years in prison, was trying to stay out of trouble. When Wright insisted, Hall took him rabbit-shooting, but it was Wright who was the target, not the rabbits.

He buried his friend's body in a stream and covered the grave with rocks. For the next few months he took every opportunity to return to the spot and add more rocks; when the police eventually found the body they admitted that, if Hall had not given them explicit disections, it would never have been discovered.

Hall's urge to stay out of trouble was short-lived. When his employer found out about his criminal record he was fired. He moved to London where he became butler to Walter Scott-Elliott and his wife, Dorothy, who was crippled with arthritis. Their obvious wealth was too much of a temptation. Hall had renewed a five-year relationship with another Irish woman, Mary Coggle, fifty-one, who was known as Belfast Mary. The pair had also struck up a friendship with a petty criminal, thirty-nine-year-old Michael Kitto, who soon became Hall's homosexual lover.

Hall proposed that Kitto should help him burgle the Scott-Elliotts. The plan was for Kitto to break into the flat so that it would look like an ordinary burglary. On 8 December 1977 the two men went drinking. They returned to the flat for Hall to give Kitto a tour of the rooms, to help him when he broke in.

Hall believed that Mrs Scott-Elliott was away in a nursing home for a few days, and he knew that her husband relied on sleeping pills and slept very heavily. To his surprise, when he opened the door to her bedroom, he found that Mrs Scott-Elliott was there. She challenged him and, in a panic, the two men leaped on her and held a pillow over her face until she stopped breathing.

Hall, scared by what he had done, arranged her body in bed as if she was sleeping. Her husband had been roused by the commotion and called out from another room; Hall told him that Mrs Scott-Elliott had had a nightmare. The next morning he told Mr Scott-Elliott that his wife had gone out shopping. The old man went to his club for lunch, and Hall and Kitto enlisted Mary Coggle's help.

When the old man returned they drugged him with his sleeping pills and he became so befuddled that he did not realize that his 'wife' was Mary Coggle wearing Dorothy's clothes and one of her wigs.

That evening he was bundled into the back seat of a

hired car next to Mary, who was wearing Dorothy's mink coat, while the real Dorothy's body was hidden in the boot.

The strange carload set off north. They spent that night at a cottage in Cumberland that Hall had previously rented. The original plan was to dispose of the body in that area, but Hall decided it would be better to press on into Scotland where the law meant there was a chance of obtaining a 'Not Proven' verdict if things went wrong.

They drove north again, with Scott-Elliott heavily drugged in the back seat. Dorothy Scott-Elliott's body was dumped in an isolated stream in a remote part of Perthshire, the body being covered with bracken and leaves.

Without any clear plan, the murderers drove back to Cumbria where they left Mary Coggle looking after Mr Scott-Elliott. Hall and Kitto drove to London and ransacked the Sloane Street flat. They changed their hire car to a red Granada and went back to Cumbria, offloading some of the stolen antiques on to an unsuspecting dealer in Staffordshire.

Again, after picking up Coggle and old Mr Scott-Elliott, they drove up to Scotland again, this time to rid themselves of the burden of the old man. They stayed overnight at a hotel in Blair Atholl, Perthshire, where the old man took all his meals in his room. The hotel staff remember the two younger men as well dressed and talkative, and the woman as blonde and brassy. The following morning the bill was paid by a cheque signed by Mr Scott-Elliott who had to be held by the two other men and propelled to the reception desk.

But, despite his muddled and drugged state, the old man's breeding showed through and he courteously thanked the staff for a 'very nice stay'. Later that day, in a lonely spot in Invernesshire, the eighty-two-year-old man was partially strangled and finally beaten to death with a spade that Hall and Kitto then used to bury him in a shallow grave.

Next, it was Mary Coggle's turn. She wanted to keep the mink coat that she had now been wearing for over a week, but Hall was convinced this would give them away. Mary tried to persuade him by lying naked on the coat in front of the fire in the hotel room they shared in Edinburgh that night. Hall agreed to let her keep the coat – but the next day, back at the rented cottage in Cumbria, he again told her it had to be burnt.

Mary began to shout abuse at him, so Hall picked up a poker and knocked her out. He then put a plastic bag over her head and asphyxiated her. Again, Hall and Kitto drove over the border into Scotland with a body in the boot. But this time they did not drive as far; Mary was dumped in a stream under a bridge on the Glasgow to Carlisle Road, dressed in men's clothing and with her hands and feet tied.

Their carelessness with the disposal of her body meant that she was the first victim to be found; her corpse was discovered on Christmas Day, but was not identified for several days.

Although the Scott-Elliotts had been away from London for ten days, no alarm had been raised, and Hall and Kitto were able to spend their last Christmas of freedom in high style. They visited Hall's family and gave everyone expensive presents. Hall's brother, Donald, got more than a present. Seventeen years younger than Hall, the two brothers had never been close. Donald Hall had a series of convictions behind him for sexual assaults on little girls, and was only released from prison after serving three years for burglary on 10 January 1978.

He had less than a week to live.

Despite a deep-seated dislike of Donald – he described him as a cheap little crook with perverted tastes – Hall took his brother back with him and Kitto to the rented cottage in Cumbria. Donald Hall was curious about the source of Hall's and Kitto's money, and his questions made the two murderers nervous. They saw that he was a weak character who could not be relied upon to keep quiet. They had now found an answer to any problem in their lives: murder. It was Donald's own boasting, that he knew the perfect way to tie someone up, that was his undoing. As he demonstrated, he became a sitting target for his brother and Kitto, who chloroformed him and then drowned him in the bath. Yet again, Hall and Kitto set out on a familiar journey – north to Scotland with a body in the boot.

It was the middle of January and the weather was atrocious, with snow falling heavily. They knew that the ground would be too hard to dig a grave, so they checked in for the night at the Blenheim House Hotel, North Berwick. But the hotelier was suspicious because the two men had no luggage. They were drinking freely and charging the bar bill to their room numbers; this made him fear that they were conmen who would skip away without paying their bill.

While they were having dinner he rang the police, and gave them the make and registration number of the

Granada. Hall had changed the plates on the car so, when the police crosschecked with the vehicle-licensing computer, it was obvious there was something wrong.

The butler and his accomplice were just settling back with large brandies at the end of their meal when two policemen came in to question them about the false number plates and the fake tax disc on the window of the car. The two men were taken to the police station for questioning, although the police had no idea that this was anything more serious than a car-theft case.

As a result, Hall was allowed to go to the toilet unaccompanied. He climbed out of the window and hailed a taxi; he was on his way to Dunbar when he was caught at a police road-block. By this time the body in the boot had been discovered, and both Kitto and Hall made full confessions to the whole series of murders.

On remand waiting for trial, Hall tried to kill himself with a drugs overdose. After being sentenced to life imprisonment, both he and Kitto received extra sentences on further charges of murder and manslaughter. In Hall's case, the judge recommended that he should not be eligible for parole. In a remarkable jail interview for the *News of the World*, Hall vowed that he would kill Kitto:

He grassed me up and I'll never forgive him for that. I have a lot of friends in prison and I'll make sure I get him. I'd planned to kill him anyway, after the other murders. I thought that if he was out of the way there wouldn't be trouble from anyone. But I was wrong. The whole thing was a mess from start to finish.

He and Kitto had so distrusted each other that they

had had a pact while on their murderous rampage: if one of them had the gun, the other would look after the cartridges.

Hall tried to kill himself again when, eighteen months into his sentence, he went on a prolonged hunger strike, saying that he intended to starve himself to death. His weight dropped from 13 stone to 6 stone. But he took just enough food and drink to survive, and eventually started to eat normally again. In 1984 he repeated his hunger strike and his weight again dropped to less than 7 stone, but he recovered.

He is now over seventy, one of Britain's longest serving prisoners. He has maintained his meticulous appearance and is still nicknamed the Butler by other inmates.

'On an old wartime airfield a car was left parked beside a small two-seater plane. And its discovery sparked off a mystery that has baffled police for the past two months . . .' said the *News of the World* on 14 July 1968. The story was about a missing farmer, thirty-five-year-old Max Garvie, who lived with his wife and three children on a 400-acre farm at Auchinblae, Kincardineshire.

Four months later, the mystery was solved when – in one of the most sensational and kinky court cases in Scottish legal history – Garvie's wife Sheila, her young lover Brian Tevendale, and Tevendale's friend, Alan Peters, stood side by side in the dock at Aberdeen, accused of killing Max Garvie. The story itself was not so unusual: unhappy wife takes younger lover and then helps him bump off rich husband. The twist was in the nature of the man they killed, an outwardly respectable family man.

Max Garvie's character was summed up in a description that appeared in the missing persons' section of the Scottish *Police Gazette*, during the months before his body was found in a disused quarry tunnel.

Spends freely, heavy spirits drinker, often consumes tranquillisers and Pro-Plus tablets when drinking. Is fond of female company but has strong homosexual tendencies and is often in the company of young men. A man of considerable wealth and until four years ago completely rational. Of late has become very impulsive, probably brought about by addiction to drink. Has threatened suicide on at least one occasion. Deals in pornographic material and is an active member of nudist camps and an enthusiastic flyer. May have gone abroad.

It was enough to give any wife a motive for murder.

Max Garvie was a handsome young man who married Sheila Watson, a pretty secretary who had worked as an assistant housekeeper at Balmoral. Within the first two years of their marriage they had two daughters, and appeared to be a happy and loving couple. Farming was Max's main interest and he worked hard.

But after seven or eight years of normal married life, he began to change. He developed a passion for nudism and took Sheila with him on nudist holidays. They went to Corsica to a nudist holiday centre when she was three months pregnant with her third child, a son, born in 1964. She later said she did not want to go, but did it to please her husband. Max became obsessed with nudism and even founded his own nudist centre at a cottage he owned near Aberdeen. It was known locally as Kinky Cottage. He spent a fortune having trees planted around it for privacy, and Sheila performed the official opening ceremony. To Max's annoyance she refused to do it naked.

Max also founded a flying club. He used his own plane to fly around Britain and to Holland and Germany – he may have used it to bring pornographic material back into Britain. At her trial Sheila Garvie revealed how, at this stage of his life, he was filling his bookcases with sex manuals; his farming books and magazines were tossed unopened into the bin. She also claimed she had a problem with his 'abnormal' sexual demands which caused her, at one point, to be admitted to a mental hospital.

He took nude photos of her – fifty-seven in all – and she was later horrified to find he had shown these to the man who acted as navigator in his plane; he let her know this by saying, 'I have seen more of you than you think.' The Garvies had a blazing row and Sheila told him that she believed the pictures had been for his eyes only.

Max developed a passion for politics and became heavily embroiled in his local branch of the Scottish Nationalist Party. There he met twenty-two-year-old barman, Brian Tevendale, on an outing to Bannockburn. They had a few drinks together and Garvie invited him to go flying the following day. Soon afterwards, Tevendale visited the farm for a weekend.

'We went out on the Saturday night, drinking. We had a few drinks when we returned home to the farm and I went to bed. A short time later Sheila was pushed through the door and the door was shut. She said she had been told to spend the night in there – or else.'

Garvie was titillated by the idea of his wife making love with another man. He did everything he could to throw the two of them together, even laying on the soft lights and sweet music to get them into the mood. Sheila later said that he believed that making love to another man would make her a better lover for him. Indeed, she and Brian did become lovers. On some evenings Garvie would toss a coin to see which of the two men should sleep with Sheila first, and when he lost twice on the run he insisted on being in the room with them.

Tevendale was spending all his weekends at the farm and the neighbours were beginning to gossip. They had more to gossip about when a tall slim blonde joined the weekend parties: Brian Tevendale's sister, Trudie. Trudie was married to a policeman, Alf Birse, but she was happy enough to join in her brother's strange arrangement with the Garvies. She met them when Brian brought them to her house, and when she saw Brian embracing Sheila Garvie she turned to Max Garvie and asked if he minded seeing his wife with another man. Max laughed and told her that he wanted to see Sheila enjoying herself, and he liked seeing them together.

Before long, Max was embracing thirty-one-year-old Trudie and the foursome had been established. After the trial the *News of the World* published The Secret Diaries of Trudie Birse. She wrote:

I daydream back to those wonderful times when the foursome was new, when every experience with Max was new, when the foursome owned the world. I return particularly to the memory of a weekend when we raced pell mell from Aberdeen to Edinburgh in Max's great bronze Jaguar, stopping at pubs and hotels along the way.

They spent that night in two different hotels, Trudie and Max booked in as Mr and Mrs Garvie and Brian and

Sheila as Mr and Mrs Tevendale. But Trudie also wrote of a violent side to Max, remembering one occasion when he beat Sheila so badly that she had to wear a surgical collar.

Giving evidence at the trial of her brother and his lover, Trudie revealed that Max told her Sheila was frigid and didn't respond to his lovemaking. He asked Trudie to question Sheila and Brian about their lovemaking, and report back to him. He also said that he had told Sheila he had had more pleasure from Trudie in two weeks than he had had from her in their whole married life. Yet Trudie also told the court that, after intercourse with her, Max would send her to a spare room to sleep so that he could have sex with Sheila which, she said, Sheila hated.

On one occasion Max even laid on a girl for Trudie's husband, Alf, the policeman, and for one night the four-some became a sixsome.

Garvie also told Trudie that he loved her brother, Brian, perhaps more than he loved Sheila. According to Tevendale, on the one occasion that Garvie made homo-sexual advances to him he repulsed him. But the two were close drinking friends and Tevendale told the court how Garvie would fly his plane while drunk, 'shooting up' the traffic. He also told the court that Max wanted to have anal sex with Sheila and threatened that he would break her neck if she did not agree.

Inevitably, the whole situation started to turn sour, and two meetings were held to discuss the future of the foursome. At the second meeting Garvie laid down the law; he and Trudie were not going to see each other any more and Sheila must not see Brian Tevendale. But, by this time, the barman and the farmer's wife were in love and they refused to split up. Sheila told the group that Max had used them all for his own selfish ends, and he could not expect her to give up her lover just like that. Max Garvie was furious and threatened to shoot his wife 'between the eyes'. When Sheila and Brian Tevendale ran away to Bradford, he pursued them and brought them back.

On 14 May 1968 Max Garvie attended an SNP meeting and was never seen alive again. After three days his sister reported him missing. One of his cars was found at the airfield where his plane was kept, but the plane was still there. Neighbours reported seeing another plane take off from the field and, for some time, it was thought that Max Garvie had gone with a friend, perhaps on one of his runs to the continent for pornographic material.

It was Sheila Garvie's mother who reported her daughter and her lover to the police for murder. Sheila's mother did not approve of the affair with Tevendale and she had promised Max Garvie that, if anything happened to him, she would make sure that Tevendale did not bring up his children. When Sheila admitted to her that Max was dead, and that Tevendale knew something about it, she decided the best course of action was to go to the police. It is doubtful that she expected her daughter to be charged with the murder.

What happened at the farm on the night of Max's death? Two different stories were told in court. According to Brian Tevendale, he arrived after Max's death, summoned by a phone call from Sheila. She said Max had threatened her with a rifle, insisting that she allow him anal sex; she had grabbed the gun, there was a struggle and Max Garvie was killed. Tevendale admitted that he and his friend, motor mechanic Alan Peters, wrapped up and disposed of the body.

Sheila's version of events tallied much more closely with that of Alan Peters. She admitted letting the two men into the house, but then said she went to her own room. Peters claimed that Tevendale hit Garvie with a rifle butt and then shot him, through a pillow, while Sheila stood outside the half-open door. Peters said he only helped with the disposal of the body. Trudie, who had certainly not been there, was able to tell the court the version that her brother had told her before his arrest; it was similar to the story told by Peters and Sheila Garvie, except for one critical difference. In Tevendale's version it was Peters who struck Garvie with a steel bar before he, Tevendale, shot him.

Both prosecution and defence lawyers enjoyed themselves at the trial, letting rip with their epithets for Sheila Garvie. She was 'Lady Macbeth', 'Lady Chatterley', 'the brain' behind the murder, 'as hard as nails'. Max Garvie, it was claimed, was 'destroyed by a Frankenstein of his own making'. The jury decided that she and Brian Tevendale were both guilty, but they returned a 'Not Proven' verdict (only possible under Scottish law) on Alan Peters.

The decision to parade through the court all the facts about her husband's kinky sex life may have cost Sheila Garvie dear; it might have been the swinging sixties in London, but the Highlands of Scotland were horrified by the goings-on at the farm, goings-on in which she had, at least in part, willingly participated.

Sheila Garvie served ten years in jail on a life sentence. She has married twice since her release, and has worked as a social worker. In 1988 one of her daughters, Wendy, was sentenced at Bristol Crown Court to be detained in a mental hospital for an attack on the home of her ex-lover. She was eleven years old when her mother's trial rocked the nation.

17. Kings of Crime

'Where's all the birds, where's all the booze?'

The cocky little man with the hat pushed jauntily on to the back of his head had been invited to a party. A party meant birds and booze. He crashed down the stairs to the basement flat expecting to find plenty of both laid on; instead, he came face to face with his executioners.

Jack 'the Hat' McVitie knew all the men in the living-room of the dismal Stoke Newington basement flat. He thought some of them were his friends. But two of them, the two he recognized instantly, he knew were not feeling friendly towards him: the Kray twins. It didn't take more than a second or two for him to size up the situation; this was no warning, no beating-up to make him toe the twins' line. He could see it clearly in Ronnie Kray's bulging eyes and swollen, red face.

But it was not Ronnie who was going to kill him. It was Reggie, working on Ronnie's orders, trying to prove that he was as hard and violent as his domineering brother. For a few seconds it looked as though Jack the Hat was going to live to tell the tale; Reggie's gun jammed as he tried to shoot the little conman. He tried a second time, but again the gun did not go off. Jack the Hat made a dash for the window, breaking it and thrusting his head and shoulders through in a desperate bid to escape. He was pulled back and Ronnie Kray held him from behind, in a bearhug. Reggie Kray plunged a knife into his face and, egged on by Ronnie's ranting, 'Don't stop Reg, kill him, kill him. Finish him off for good,' the knife was thrust repeatedly into McVitie's stomach.

Jack 'the Hat' McVitie was dead. In life, he had been an irritant to the Krays, an unreliable small time criminal on the fringe of their East End empire, a renegade who would refuse to kowtow to them. In death, he was to be a far more serious problem; it was for the murder of Jack the Hat and the murder of George Cornell, another London gangster, that, they would stand trial at the Old Bailey. They were sentenced to life imprisonment, with a recommendation from the judge that they should serve a minimum of thirty years.

The Kray twins' trial, in 1969, was, to that date, the longest and most expensive ever run at the Old Bailey. It was also one of the most fascinating. The story of the Krays is a story of violence, madness, murder and glamour. Identical twins, they were doomed from birth to mirror each other's actions; when one of them took to murder, the other had to follow suit.

Ronnie and Reggie: The Terror Twins was the *News of the World* headline on 'the first full inside story of Britain's most vicious gangsters'. It told of their rise to power in the East End and their reign of terror over the small time crooks and hoodlums; it told of the madness that plagued Ronnie Kray all his life (and has resulted in him serving much of his sentence in Broadmoor). It told of the deaths of Jack the Hat and George Cornell, gunned down by Ronnie in the Blind Beggar pub; of the mysterious disappearance of the 'Mad Axeman' Frankie

Mitchell, sprung from Dartmoor by his 'friends' the Krays and killed when they could think of nothing else to do with him; of the henchmen who were attracted by the glamour of their power and then found themselves trapped in the twins' out-of-control spiral of violence. It told of the tragic suicide of Reggie's young wife, the beautiful girl who had little choice but to marry the gangster boss who had chosen her.

Reggie and Ronnie Kray were born in the East End in 1933; Reggie was the older by an hour. Their father was a second-hand clothes and jewelry dealer, a wanderer who disappeared for days, travelling the countryside and coming back with a bag full of gold and silver to sell. He made good money and, despite his gambling and beer drinking, the twins, their older brother, Charlie, and their mother, Violet, were better off than many of their neighbours. Charlie was an easygoing child; the twins were different. From early childhood they fought, often with each other, desperate all-out fighting until one or the other was forced to surrender. But, despite the constant rivalry between them, it was when they turned on others that they were at their most fearsome.

At the age of seventeen they made their first appearance at the Old Bailey, charged with assault on a younger boy who had been beaten up with bicycle chains. They were acquitted because of a lack of witnesses. Already the people of the East End had wised up; one girl who had seen the attack was told that her pretty face would be permanently scarred if she did not have a sudden attack of amnesia. It was not a good idea to appear as a witness against the Krays; this fact helped them more than any other in their criminal career. In the same year they became professional boxers, lightweights, and had some success. Ronnie was vicious and fearless, but Reggie was the one who showed signs of real talent.

Boxing did not channel their violence and they continued to get into trouble with the police. From the age of fourteen Ronnie hit his father whenever he felt like it; the old man now kept away from the family home in Vallance Road, Bethnal Green, more than ever. They adored their mother and she was able to shut her eyes to their true natures until her death in 1982, going to her grave believing 'they were good boys, really'.

The twins were called up for national service but decided, within the first day, that they were not going to do it. They spent two years on the run or in military prisons, their violent attacks on officers and military policemen adding to their reputation as hard men. When they returned to civvy street they did so on their own terms because the word was out that they were too mean to tangle with. They based themselves at a rundown billiard hall, The Regal, and surrounded themselves with other East End toughs; the gang was nicknamed the Firm and Ronnie was known as the Colonel. Ronnie was already the acknowledged leader and everyone around him – including Reggie – lived in fear of his mad rages. Weapons were no problem for the Firm and they soon built up an arsenal of guns and knives. They earned big money by 'protecting' the local pubs and clubs, the owners paying the Krays to keep trouble away. Those who did not pay got trouble alright: Kray trouble.

They avoided jail sentences by buying up or threatening witnesses, or by confusing witnesses because they were identical twins. But there was one violent incident that Ronnie could not cover up. At a pub called the Britannia he viciously slashed a boy called Terry Martin with a bayonet and, despite every effort to buy the boy's silence, Ronnie was tried and sentenced to three years in jail.

Reggie took over running the empire and proved to be very good at it. He opened a club, The Double R (R for Ronnie and R for Reggie), and ran it efficiently. He was still violent, but his attacks were calculated and aimed at those who were thwarting him in business. He avenged himself on Terry Martin by arranging for the Martin family's drinking club to be burned to the ground. When he heard that a gunman was out to get him, Reggie arranged for the man to be supplied with a doctored gun; when he attempted to shoot Reggie the gun exploded and the man spent a month in hospital. The twins' older brother, Charlie, joined Reggie in the business, and the Double R became a favourite spot with villains and celebrities. Both the Krays sought glamour and a cover of respectability, and Reggie, with Ronnie out of the way, was able to deliver both.

In prison Ronnie made friends with Frank Mitchell, a giant of a young man with a low IQ. Mitchell was child-like, affectionate, devoted to Ronnie, but he was also wild and uncontrollable when faced with authority. He spent more of his life behind bars than he did free, and he was so strong and fearless that the prison officers steered clear of him.

But when Ronnie was transferred away from Wandsworth Prison, close to all his London friends and relatives, to Camp Hill jail on the Isle of Wight, he began to suffer schizophrenic delusions. He was eventually transferred to a mental hospital in Surrey and his condition was stabilized with drugs. He was convinced that, because he was no longer within the prison system with a date set for his release, he would spend the rest of his life in hospital. Desperate, he arranged with Reggie to change places with him during visiting hours, and Ronnie was spirited away to a caravan in the countryside. Under regulations then existing, if a prisoner who was certified insane was free for more than six weeks he could be returned to prison to finish his sentence, and that is what happened to Ronnie. After six weeks he gave himself up, and less than a year later he was out to take over as head of the Firm.

Violence escalated, a lot of it meaningless. Ronnie's mental illness now ran the firm, and when Reggie was sentenced to eighteen months in prison for a protection racket there was no check on Ronnie. He loved showbiz glamour, rubbing shoulders with film stars like Stanley Baker and Barbara Windsor, singers like Frank Sinatra and Judy Garland, and boxers like Rocky Marciano, as well as American mafia bigshots. He now openly flaunted his homosexuality, surrounding himself with young, pretty boys with long eyelashes, and holding parties for them at which he would sit and drink, watching them dancing. He ran the business empire into the ground, making many enemies, and taking strange and unsuccessful financial risks at the fashionable Knightsbridge nightclub, Esmeralda's Barn, that the Krays had forced the owner to hand over at a ridiculously low price.

When Reggie came out of prison, at the age of twenty-seven, he fell in love with a sixteen-year-old schoolgirl, Frances Shea. She was pretty, innocent and

earnest, terribly in awe of Reggie. He was shy and gentle
with her, never forcing a sexual relationship on her but,
instead, writing romantic poetry. Reggie idealized
Frances; his own sexuality was not as clearly defined as his
brother's, and he longed to settle down in a 'normal'
heterosexual relationship. But there could be nothing
normal about being involved with a Kray, as Frances
found to her cost. Reggie wooed her for five years until,
at the age of twenty-one, she gave in to his request to
marry him. Her parents did not approve, but the
wedding was a huge social event with fleets of Rolls
Royces ferrying the guests and trendy photographer
David Bailey taking the pictures.

The honeymoon in Greece was not a success, and nor
was life at home. Reggie was out all day, but would not
allow Frances to work or even to take driving lessons; he
was jealous of her getting too close to a driving instructor.
In the evenings, Reggie would either leave her on her
own in the flat below the one where Ronnie entertained
his boys, or he would take her to sit with the other
womenfolk – the wives and girlfriends of other members
of the Firm – in clubs and pubs around the East End.
Ronnie loathed Frances and the fact that she had come
between him and his twin, although outwardly he kept
up a polite facade. After eight weeks Frances went home
to her parents. For the next year she and Reggie saw each
other on and off, and Frances also saw a psychiatrist – the
same one who was treating Ronnie.

The Firm's violence was beginning to get out of hand.
An old friend who made a joke about Ronnie putting on
weight ended up needing seventy stitches in his face.
Despite the fact that a crowded bar of people saw Ronnie

take him into the gents, and despite the fact that the victim was conscious throughout the attack, when the police made inquiries they were told that nobody had seen anything. A young man was branded on the face with a red-hot knife-sharpener which Ronnie held in a gas flame. He was even capable of inflicting physical harm on himself; when somebody asked him how he would take the pain he put others through, Ronnie took out a knife and cut his own hand so deeply he needed hospital treatment.

Ronnie was obsessed with the idea of killing somebody, and top of his list of enemies were the rival Richardson gang. When he heard that one of the gang, George Cornell, had called him 'a big poove', he wanted blood. He bought two Browning machine-guns and even tried to buy limpet mines. He and Reggie both took to wearing bullet-proof vests.

In the end Ronnie did not use the machine-gun. He and one of the Firm, a tall young Scot called Ian Barrie, found Cornell sitting on a bar stool at the Blind Beggar pub. Barrie fired two shots into the ceiling to send the barmaid and other witnesses scurrying, and then Ronnie shot Cornell through the head. When the police arrived, nobody had seen a thing. Although the whole of the East End knew who had done it, the police could not nail it on Ronnie Kray. At an identity parade the barmaid failed to pick out Ronnie. She had, she told the police, a poor memory for faces.

Ronnie's dreams and delusions were getting wilder, his mood swings more unpredictable, and everyone lived in fear of him. His next decision was prompted by a need to feel popular; he decided to spring Frankie Mitchell, 'the

Mad Axeman' from Dartmoor. Mitchell had earned his nickname after brandishing an axe at an elderly couple while on the run from a hospital for the criminally insane. He was being held indefinitely in prison and was desperate for a release date. The Krays visited him, sent him presents and arranged for him to have other visitors. The staff at Dartmoor found him amenable and he was given privileges, including much freedom when out on the moors with working parties. The decision by Ronnie to get his friend out was later said in court to be because the Firm needed a strong man for their team but, in fact, they had more than enough strong men around them. The springing of the Mad Axeman was more likely prompted by Ronnie courting popularity with his underground contacts.

Getting Frankie off the moor was easy enough. By the time the police had caught up with the news he was eating fish and chips in a flat in Barking. The owner of the flat was a man who kept a bookstall, and who was sufficiently in fear of the Krays to do as he was told. From his hideout, and with the help of the flat owner and the Krays' henchmen, Frankie Mitchell made a couple of desperate pleas for what he wanted: a date for release from prison. 'I am not a sex maniac or a murderer,' he wrote to the Home Office, but his pleas went unheeded. Poor old Frankie had a much more miserable time being a guest of the Krays than he did being held at Her Majesty's pleasure. He was cooped up in the flat for days, the only improvements over prison life being a constant supply of booze and the services of a girl to whom the Krays paid £100. Mad Frankie fell touchingly in love with her and, on Christmas Eve 1966, they exchanged cards with sentimental messages scrawled inside; Frankie gave the girl a prison comb, his only possession.

By then the Krays had been harbouring Frankie for twelve days and they did not know what to do with him. His presence had become an embarrassment and a threat. That evening they sent a car to pick him up. He stepped outside the flat. Those left behind heard a noise, like a car backfiring, and Frankie Mitchell disappeared off the face of the earth. When, two years later, the Krays were tried for murdering him, they were acquitted; there was no body and, to this day, the Mad Axeman is officially still on the run. There are at least two other Kray associates who disappeared as completely as did Frankie.

Reggie's private life was very unhappy. Frances's depression worsened, and, fourteen months after her wedding day, she took an overdose and killed herself. The Krays stage-managed her funeral, just as they had her wedding, with another fleet of Rolls Royces. There were hundreds of wreaths; it would have been bad form for anyone who had dealings with the Krays not to have sent one. Reggie sent three and wrote a sentimental poem about Frances. But behind the public show of grief, Frances's family blamed the Krays for the loss of their daughter's life. When Reggie insisted that she be buried in her wedding dress, they did a deal with the undertaker to make sure her corpse wore stockings and an under-skirt, so that as little of her flesh as possible touched the hated dress, the symbol of the great unhappiness that had come into the life of their beautiful daughter. Frances's death had a profound effect on Reggie, otherwise the calmer of the twins. He became bitter and angry, he drank excessively, he blamed all his misfortunes on

Frances's family. He even had her brother brought to
him; he fully intended to kill the boy but was so struck by
the resemblance between the two of them that, instead,
he broke down in tears.

Reggie descended into the kind of senseless drunken
violence that had always been his brother's stock in trade,
shooting one man through the leg in a drunken fury
because he believed the man had slagged off his dead
wife. He became almost as unpredictable as Ronnie, and
more and more dependent on his brother's leadership.

When Ronnie began to taunt him with the fact that he
had never killed anyone, Reggie was forced to respond.
Ronnie's feverish obsession with death now pivoted on a
secret Nigerian society he had read about – the Leopard
Men. Members were initiated by killing an enemy of the
group; Ronnie dreamed that, eventually, all members of
the Firm would be blooded in a similar way. But, first, he
had to goad his brother Reggie into joining him as a
murderer. He, Ronnie, had killed George Cornell.
Although others had 'disappeared' around the Krays,
Cornell was the only one to have died directly at the
hands of a twin. Until Jack 'the Hat' McVitie annoyed
them . . .

The police had monitored the Kray gang from its early
days, but had been thwarted in every attempt to charge
them with their most serious crimes because of lack of
evidence. But by the time they killed Jack the Hat they
were getting careless; they were running out of steam,
Ronnie was perilously close to needing to be institution-
alized and Reggie was still distracted with grief for
his strange, idealized love of Frances. The cracks were
beginning to appear around them, and Detective

Superintendent Leonard 'Nipper' Read was amassing much information, if not a lot of evidence.

The reason the Krays killed McVitie was that he had failed to carry out a 'hit' for them, for which he had been paid. Now the man who had been the intended target of the hit was prepared to give evidence about frauds in which he had been involved with the twins.

The Krays' 'accountant', a Jewish banker with a stutter called Alan Cooper, was one of the first witnesses that Read won over. Cooper had been involved in helping Ronnie try to pull off three arranged 'hits', none of which had worked. When Cooper was arrested after sending a courier to Glasgow to buy dynamite, he passed on sufficient information for Read to begin to feel he was on the scent.

At dawn on 9 May 1968 the police swooped on the council flat in Shoreditch where the Krays' mother, Violet, was living. They found both the twins there: Ronnie in bed with a pretty boy and Reggie in bed with a pretty girl. Read had enough to hold them; he then embarked on a systematic attempt to break down East End resistance. With the Krays behind bars, everyone who knew anything about their activities was approached. Slowly and steadily, more and more came forward to give evidence. Members of the Firm were 'turned' with promises of substantially reduced sentences. Others, like the barmaid at the Blind Beggar, responded to their consciences.

The trial lasted forty days, – the Krays denying everything. They remained loyal to each other all the way through; Reggie Kray might, arguably, have received a lighter sentence if he had been prepared to tell the truth about his brother's domination over him. Ultimately, they were found guilty of the Cornell and McVitie murders, but acquitted (at a separate trial) of murdering Frankie Mitchell. They were thirty-four years old when they were sent to prison, with a thirty-year minimum recommendation, in 1969.

Since then, there have been orchestrated campaigns to free Reggie. Ronnie, in Broadmoor (where he has, pre-posterously, married), accepts that for him a life sentence will mean life. But Reggie, well into middle age, is por-trayed as a victim of the legal system, a gangland killer who only inflicted violence and death on other under-world hoods. His sentence has been compared to that of other murderers who, on average, serve eleven years of a life sentence.

The twins' mother died in 1982 and their father six months later. They are regularly visited by their brother, Charlie, and they also occasionally meet when Reggie is allowed to have lunch with Ronnie at Broadmoor.

Some *News of the World* stories run and run . . . and run. The Great Train Robbery is one of them. On 8 August 1963 a gang of hardened criminals held up a mail train and got away with over £2 million (worth over £20 mil-lion thirty years later); it was the biggest crime of its kind ever, and it was carried out with such ruthless profession-alism that the thieves became folk heroes despite the fact that the train driver, Jack Mills, was seriously injured and died prematurely, never having been able to shake off the physical and mental effects of the attack.

When the eleven members of the gang were eventually apprehended and appeared in court they received some of the longest sentences ever passed at that time; seven of them were sent to prison for thirty years apiece. Three members of the gang, one of whom masterminded the robbery, were never tracked down.

But the story was only just beginning. Charlie Wilson was 'sprung' from Winson Green prison in Birmingham after serving only a year of his sentence and escaped to Canada (where he was recaptured and returned to Britain). Ronnie Biggs broke out of Wandsworth jail in London the following year, fleeing first to France where plastic surgery altered his face, and then to Australia where he was joined by his wife and two sons. Another son was born while they were living there, Biggs working as a carpenter.

When the police traced the fugitives to Australia, Biggs was again able to evade justice, this time leaving minutes before the police arrived at his hideout and fleeing to Brazil where he dodged the extradition agreement with Britain by fathering a child by a local girl; Brazilian law allowed him to stay at liberty to bring up the child. Biggs set up court in Rio de Janeiro, where he has become a local celebrity, and where journalists, pop stars and anyone else with the price of a drink in his pocket is welcomed into his entourage.

The *News of the World* led the rest of the Fleet Street pack with its Great Train Robbery exclusives. The story of Charlie Wilson's escape was exposed by the *News of the World* and the details of Ronnie Biggs's escape were also revealed with the help of one of the men who was involved in the £10,000 paid to spring Biggs.

When Biggs was tracked down in Australia the *News of the World* carried the exclusive story of the woman with whom he lived before his wife joined him; when he turned up in Brazil the paper secured the rights to the story of Raimunda de Castro, his mistress and mother of his son, Mike.

This is what happened to the rest of the Great Train Robbery gang:

Charlie Wilson, who was sentenced to thirty years, was brought back from Quebec to finish his sentence. After release he was charged with a massive VAT fraud but the case was abandoned because the jury could not agree on a verdict. He was murdered in Marbella in 1990, and the police suspect the killing was triggered by his part in a cocaine-smuggling racket.

Gordon Goody, given thirty years, was released in the mid seventies and set up a beach bar in Spain.

Ronald 'Buster' Edwards, given fifteen years, now runs a flower stall. He was the subject of a film, *Buster*, starring Phil Collins.

Roger Cordrey was given twenty years but this was reduced on appeal. He now lives in the west country.

James Hussey and Thomas Wisbey, both given thirty years, were subsequently given seven-year sentences for trafficking in cocaine.

Roy James, given thirty years, was charged with Charlie Wilson on the VAT fraud. He now lives in Spain.

James White was given eighteen years. After release he went back to his original trade, painting and decorating.

Bruce Reynolds was given fifteen years. Since then he has had a three-year sentence for supplying drugs.

Robert Welch, was given thirty years. After release he helped with a voluntary prisoner-support group.

18. 'What Sort of Beast . . . ?'

Winifred Shannon received the telegram with mixed feelings – was it going to be good news, or bad news? When she opened it she was filled with happiness:

'Permission for leave granted Graham for one week, please confirm if convenient,' it said. It was signed by the psychiatrist at Broadmoor who was in charge of Winifred's brother, Graham Young. Graham had been sent to Broadmoor, the secure hospital for the criminally insane, when he was a fourteen-year-old schoolboy. He had admitted poisoning his father, his sister and a schoolfriend. He was never charged with murdering his stepmother Molly who died a month before he was arrested; the police could not prove anything because her body had already been cremated. But Graham later admitted he had been dosing her with antimony for over a year, and the night before she died he gave her enough thallium to kill twenty people.

It could have been the perfect crime, but the persistent illness of other members of his family eventually led to his father going into hospital where he was found to be suffering from arsenic poisoning. Graham's school, suspecting him but unwilling to believe that a schoolboy could be systematically poisoning his entire family, called in a psychiatrist. The psychiatrist posed as a careers officer for an individual interview with Graham, and was so alarmed by his knowledge of – and fascination with – poisons that the police were called in immediately.

The following day Graham confessed and led the police to his secret caches of poison hidden in sheds and in tins under hedges. He had been able to buy poison from local chemists' shops in north London simply by signing the poisons register which he did under the assumed name of Evans. Nobody queried his age.

Graham Young was sent to Broadmoor; the judge at his trial suggested that he be detained for 'not less than fifteen years'. But after eight years he was freed, after first spending 'leave' with his sister Winifred, by then a housewife and mother, living in Hemel Hempstead in Hertfordshire.

Winifred, like the rest of the family, was very nervous about Graham's release. But after he spent his week's leave with her and her husband Denis she believed he was fit for release. She was reassured by his doctors at Broadmoor that he would not try to poison her or her family again, and she and Denis were prepared to give him the benefit of the doubt.

Graham Young did not poison any of his family. Instead, he found a job at a nearby photographic laboratory and set about systematically poisoning the work force. Two men died, horrible, painful deaths. Four other people were treated for side-effects of thallium poisoning, and two of them spent several weeks in hospital in great pain. Graham Young was again not suspected – the staff at the laboratory knew nothing about his previous conviction. But eventually, when his past was revealed, he was arrested and, after a trial at St Albans Crown Court,

15 January 1971

Medical Certificate
Graham Frederick YOUNG

This man has suffered a deep going personality disorder
which necessitated his hospitalization throughout the whole
of his adolescence. He has, however, made an extremely
full recovery and is now entirely fit for discharge, his
sole disability now being the need to catch up on his lost
time.

He is capable of undertaking any sort of work
without any restrictions as to residence, travel or
environment. His natural bent is towards the non-
manual and clerical and in the first instance he would
do extremely well training as a store keeper. He is
of above average intelligence and capable of sustained
effort. He would fit in well and not draw any attention
to himself in any community.

(E.L Unwin)
Consultant Psychiatrist

he was sentenced to life imprisonment. He returned,
once again, to Broadmoor, where he died in 1990, aged
forty-two. Despite threats that he was going to commit
suicide, and despite his encyclopaedic knowledge of
poisons and how to obtain them from normal domestic
products, the inquest recorded a verdict of death by
natural causes.

The bizarre story of Young's mission to poison the
world was revealed after his trial when his sister Winifred
told her story to the *News of the World*, under the headline, My Brother the Poisoner.

Graham Young came from a solid, respectable middle-
class background. His mother died when he was just

three months old, and for the next two years he was looked after by his Auntie Win and Uncle Jack who both adored him. When his father remarried Graham moved home to be with his stepmother Molly, his father Fred and his older sister Winifred. He was a lonely, studious child, obviously bright. By the age of twelve it was clear that he was fascinated by chemicals, but his father and stepmother assumed he was simply following a natural inclination and would probably go to university or find a job involving scientific knowledge.

There were a few clues to his coldness: when Molly banned him from bringing chemicals into the house (after he burned a hole in his school-uniform pocket) he left a drawing of a tombstone with 'RIP Molly Young' written on it lying around in a place where she was bound to see it. At school he monopolized the laboratories for his own bizarre experiments on live mice. But he did not seem to his family significantly different from other boys.

'The first hint of what we now know was poisoning was in the winter of 1961 when Molly, our stepmother, began being sick,' Winifred told *News of the World* reporters John Lisners and Alan Shadrake.

It was usually after she'd eaten. The first couple of times she thought it was just a bilious attack and did not call the doctor. Then my father was sick a couple of times and so was Graham. It seemed he had poisoned himself by mistake. He'd put it in a cup he thought was Molly's and then it had been given to him.

Molly was eventually kept in hospital for ten days; during this time the sickness stopped. Her illness continued for over a year; her neighbours noticed that she lost a lot of weight and seemed to age before their eyes. Fred and Winifred were also taken ill. When Molly died, her death was put down to a prolapse of the spine caused by a road accident she had been involved in the previous year. She was cremated. At the funeral tea one of Graham's uncles was taken violently sick after eating a sandwich.

Winifred was the first to accuse Graham of poisoning the family. She was given a cup of tea by him one morning, but drank very little because of the bitter taste. She was dizzy and ill on her way to work and, in hospital later that day, she was diagnosed as suffering from belladonna poisoning. Back home she accused Graham who went to his room sobbing bitterly. He appeared to be so distressed that Winifred apologized to him.

At his trial it was suggested that Broadmoor was not a suitable place for a fourteen-year-old, but a psychiatrist who interviewed him told the court that he was too dangerous for a normal mental hospital. In Broadmoor his fascination with poisons continued, and there were instances of him putting Harpic in the nurses' tea, growing deadly nightshade (for belladonna) in the grounds and being under suspicion when, only a month after his arrival, another patient died from cyanide poisoning. Graham knew all about extracting cyanide from the laurel bushes that grew in profusion in the grounds.

But in many ways he was a model patient and the psychiatrists who monitored him were impressed. Graham told his sister that one of their theories was that he had been subconsciously trying to get back to his first mother- substitute, Auntie Win, and that to do so he was poisoning those in the way: his stepmother, his father and his sister. The explanation didn't take in the school friend who Young had systematically dosed with poison in his lunch sandwiches.

Young was of well above average intelligence, and he spent his time in the Broadmoor library studying classical history and the history of war (he was refused permission to study drugs, but there would have been little he could have been taught; the nurses soon realized that he understood the nature and side-effects of every medicine administered to every patient). The nurses were less impressed with him than the doctors; they had more contact with him and were aware of his threat that, when he got out, he would poison one person for every year that he had been in Broadmoor.

Eventually, and against the better judgment of the nurses and some members of his family, he was recommended for release. He was sent on a storekeeping course at a government training centre and he then found a job at Hadland's photographic laboratory at Bovingdon, near his sister's home in Hemel Hempstead. He moved into a bedsitter and started work on 10 May 1971. The walls of his room, like the walls of his room at Broadmoor, were decorated with pictures of Nazi leaders and the music he played was that of death marches. By his bed, he kept a collection of books on poisons and forensic medicines.

When he got the job his lack of work record was explained by letters from his psychiatrist saying that he had been mentally ill, but was now completely recovered and capable of holding down a job. His employer, knowing nothing of the nature of his 'illness', was happy to give him a chance. His workmates found him quiet, although he could talk animatedly about politics or chemicals if anyone was prepared to listen. He seemed to be inept with money and his colleagues, feeling sorry for him, would often lend him cigarettes or change for bus fares. He repaid kindnesses by being more than willing to make tea for everyone.

Less than a month after he joined the first of his work-mates was taken ill. Bob Egle, who was fifty-nine, would suffer tremendous dizziness, diarrhoea, vomiting and nervous paralysis over the next few weeks until he died, just less than two months after Graham Young joined the firm. During this time another of Young's workmates was ill on and off, and retired shortly afterwards; from that point onwards his health improved. In retrospect, he remembered how he frequently left the tea that Young served him because of its bitter taste, and how Bob Egle had frequently finished it for him. Ironically, Graham Young was chosen to represent the staff at Bob Egle's funeral as the older man seemed to have been protective and fond of the young man.

For two months life at Hadland's laboratory was normal, and Bob Egle's strange and unexplained illness ceased to be the main topic of conversation. But then a part-time worker, Fred Biggs, became violently ill with stomach pains and vomiting. Several other members of staff developed the same and other symptoms. Hair fell out, men became impotent, leg joints were stiff and one man suffered from severe suicidal tendencies. The staff were so worried that the local doctor called in the Medical Officer of Health for the area, and staff meetings were called to try to allay their fears. One theory that was explored – and then rejected – was that the staff were suffering from heavy metal poisoning, such as thallium poisoning. Thallium is used in some photographic processes but was not used at the Bovingdon laboratory. What nobody realized was that Graham Young was making regular pilgrimages to London to buy thallium and that he was, once again, signing the poisons register in the name of Evans.

After twenty days of agony Fred Biggs died. When the staff were told, Graham Young turned to a woman with whom he worked (and who was also being poisoned) and remarked, 'I wonder what went wrong. He shouldn't have died. I was very fond of old Fred.'

The workforce was near to panic – so many were being taken ill with symptoms similar to those of the men who had died. The local doctor came to talk to them and his suspicions were aroused when the earnest, dark-haired young storekeeper questioned him about the effects of poisons and demonstrated that he knew more than the doctor. He spoke to the owner of the company who, although he had to fight his own incredulity, contacted the local police. They had never been informed that Graham Young was living in their midst but, when they ran checks with Scotland Yard, they came up with his criminal record. An alert went out immediately; Graham Young was to be arrested.

He was visiting his father in Sheerness, in Kent, when they found him. His father, though devastated by his son's earlier experiments with poisons and not happy about his release from Broadmoor, did maintain contact with him. Graham Young was in the kitchen making himself a sandwich when the police car drew up. Fred Young knew without being told that something serious had happened, and simply stood aside and pointed to his son. He couldn't bring himself to speak to Graham as he was led away, but he heard Graham say:

'Which one are you doing me for?'

Young pleaded not guilty to six charges of murder and attempted murder. He wanted his name in the history books and he knew from his experience of pleading guilty, when he was fourteen, that a 'guilty' case would be over very quickly. He wanted the chance to take the witness stand himself. His trial involved seventy-five witnesses. The most chilling moments came when his diary was read out in court. He had chronicled in detail the various side-effects that his victims had suffered.

In the cells he remained as calm and unemotional as ever. He had one question for the officers who were assigned to look after him. He wanted to know whether Madame Tussaud's had applied for details about him to include in their Chamber of Horrors display of famous murderers. They had.

It is a peaceful summer scene – children playing on the swings and slides, families picnicking, old folk sitting on the benches enjoying the fresh air, young couples strolling hand in hand.

It is hard to believe that seventeen years ago beautiful Bathpool Park in the centre of Kidsgrove, Staffordshire, was the scene of one of the most chilling murders in the annals of British crime.

It was in a shaft leading from the park to a network of drainage tunnels that the body of pretty, seventeen-year-old Lesley Whittle was found, hanging naked from a wire noose.

Police did not know at the time that Lesley was the

fourth victim of a notorious multiple killer whose black clothes earned him the nickname of the Black Panther. He was a clever criminal who challenged the detective powers of five different police forces.

The discovery of Lesley's body led to one of the biggest manhunts ever mounted in Britain, with a £25,000 reward on the head of the killer.

Lesley Whittle and her mother Dorothy lived in Highley, Shropshire, in a comfortable detached house. Lesley's father, George, had built a successful coach business from scratch and, when he died, he left £300,000.

After his death the business was run by his son, Ronald. Seventeen-year-old Lesley was at college studying for her A levels, and hoping to go to university – a happy and popular girl.

It was four o'clock in the morning of 14 January 1975 when the killer broke into her bedroom and forced her, at gunpoint, to leave the house with him. She was wearing only her nightdress, dressing-gown and slippers.

Her kidnapper left behind three pieces of Dymo printed tape which he stuck to a vase in the living-room. They gave instructions that £50,000 in used notes was to be taken in a white suitcase to the Swann shopping centre, Kidderminster, between 6pm and 1am that evening, and then the carrier was to wait for a call at one of the three telephone boxes in the centre.

The printed message said '. . . if police or tricks – death'.

Lesley's distraught mother discovered her daughter was missing at breakfast time and immediately contacted her son, Ronald, who was married and lived a few miles away. Ronald decided that their only course of action was to call in the police.

The immediate reaction of some of the officers on the case was that it was a hoax and that Lesley would arrive back home at any moment. Kidnapping was an even rarer crime in Britain at that time than it is now. But one man took it seriously: Detective Chief Superintendent Robert Booth of West Mercia Police.

Ron Whittle, whose story was told exclusively in the *News of the World* after the case was over, rapidly arranged with his bank manager to mortage his own house, his mother's house and part of the family firm to raise the money which the police then marked. Unfortunately, there was a news leak about the kidnapping and an item was carried on the television news that evening (one lesson the police learnt for future kidnapping cases was to take the media into their confidence and ask for a news blackout).

While Superintendent Booth was at the Whittle family home that evening, and Ronald was waiting for the phone call at the Kidderminster shopping centre, another officer called off the operation – believing it had been blown by the news broadcast. There was nobody at the phone kiosk at one minute past midnight when the phone call came (a telephone operator, specially briefed to log all calls to the three boxes at the shopping centre, recorded a call to one of the boxes followed, a few seconds later, by a call to a second one. Neither call was answered.)

The news release prompted a flood of hoax calls which made life for the police extremely difficult. Ronald Whittle was sent on a couple of wild goose chases as other criminals tried to pick up the ransom money. The next night brought no further contact from the kidnapper because he was thwarted by a brave security guard who died for his trouble.

The kidnapper parked a stolen car at Dudley, in Worcestershire, and made his way towards Dudley Zoo where he was going to leave another kidnap message for Ronald Whittle. It appeared that he also planned to hand over Lesley in exchange for the money.

But at 10.30pm Gerald Smith, who was working at a transport depot opposite the zoo, saw a man bending over by a lamp post. When he challenged him, the man drew a gun and shot Mr Smith six times in the back. With enormous courage, Mr Smith was able to crawl to a phone box and call the police.

Gerald Smith eventually died of his injuries fourteen months later; this meant that his killer could not be charged with his murder. British law says that there can be no charge of murder if the victim survives for more than one year and one day after the attack.

Mr Smith was able to give the police a good description of the man who shot him. Ballistics experts confirmed that the gun was the same as one used in two raids on sub-post offices where victims had died – crimes committed by a notorious criminal dubbed the Black Panther. There had been three post office murders, all committed by the same man, who dressed in black and moved quickly and silently.

But the shooting of Mr Smith did not appear to have any connection with the kidnap of Lesley Whittle, and the police did not know at this stage that the two criminals they were hunting, the kidnapper and the Black Panther, were the same man. Because of the shooting, the Panther was forced to abandon the car, a green Morris

1100 saloon which he had stolen six weeks earlier.

The night after Gerald Smith was shot, the kidnapper made contact with the Whittle family again. He phoned the home number of Len Rudd, depot manager of the family firm, and played a tape-recording of Lesley's voice to Mr Rudd. Her voice said:

'Go to Kidsgrove Post Office telephone box. Behind the board at the back of the door there will be further instructions. I'm all right, Mum. No police please.'

By this time, Superintendent Booth was being helped by Scotland Yard, and it was the Yard team which took over responsibility for the operation that night.

When Ronald Whittle got to the phone box he eventually found another piece of Dymo tape, very well hidden, at the back of the notice panel. The tape instructed him to drive into Bathpool Park and flash his headlights. He would then see a torch beam and he was to run towards it.

It had taken Ronald Whittle a long time to find the phone booth, and even longer to find the concealed tape. It was very late, 3.30 in the morning, by the time he reached the park. In the meantime a courting couple, a local disc jockey and his girlfriend, drove into the park at about 3am and parked for a cuddle. They used the same entry route that the ransom message had told Ron Whittle to use, and they saw a torch being flashed at them. Perhaps because they did not respond, and perhaps because it was now so very late, the Panther panicked.

For seventy-two hours Lesley had been held in a shaft under the park. She was bound and gagged, and had a wire noose around her neck – the kidnapper had padded it with tape to avoid it cutting into her. She was kept on a ledge, with a mattress and a sleeping bag. When his plans to pick up the white suitcase full of money appeared to go wrong again, the Panther pushed Lesley off the ledge. According to medical evidence she died of fright – her heart literally stopped beating – before the noose strangled her.

By the time Ron Whittle arrived in the park half an hour later, his sister was probably already dead. Ron flashed his lights many times, and even climbed out of the car and shouted his own name, but there was no response. The kidnapper had made his escape through the network of tunnels leading from the shaft where Lesley died.

It was when the car, abandoned after the shooting of Gerald Smith, was found a week later that the police knew for the first time that Lesley's kidnapper was the Black Panther who had shot the three sub-postmasters. In the car they found half a foam mattress, a tape-recorder, paper, envelopes, forty feet of strong rope, a petrol can, blankets, a puncture-repair outfit, a black anorak, a torch, a bottle of Lucozade, and some barley sugar. But the trail seemed to have gone cold, with no more contact from the kidnapper.

In an effort to persuade him to get in touch, Superintendent Booth appeared on television with Ron Whittle. Booth feared that the police involvement had frightened off the kidnapper, so he and Ron Whittle staged a row in front of the cameras.

'There was no real row – it was all a charade to get the kidnapper to contact me,' Ron later told the *News of the World*.

Booth hoped that the kidnapper, seeing them falling

out publicly, would have the confidence to reapproach Lesley's brother. The plan was doomed to fail, because, by then, Lesley was already dead.

But the broadcast brought some more clues. A head teacher remembered one of his pupils handing him a piece of Dymo tape, found in Bathpool Park, with the words 'Drop suitcase into hole' punched on it. Another schoolboy told of finding a torch down a shaft in the park. The police mounted a huge search of the park. They found a shaft cover that had obviously been recently moved, and it was there they found Lesley's naked body hanging from the noose. Near her was a sleeping bag and a pair of binoculars, and, at the bottom of the shaft, a pair of men's shoes, size seven.

A massive and painstaking inquiry was underway. In the course of the investigation 28,000 statements were taken, 32,000 telephone calls were recorded, two and a half million index cards were filed and more than 60,000 people were interviewed. The pair of men's shoes discovered near Lesley's body were found to be from a batch of 30,000 made by Bata – and all but forty-two pairs were traced by the police.

The binoculars were traced back to the shop in Cheshire where they were bought nearly three years before; the sleeping bag near the body had been bought in Stafford two years earlier. It was this kind of meticulous detective work that would, ultimately, catch the Black Panther.

Scotland Yard detectives are confident that hours and hours of patient checking and cross-checking would have paid off eventually. As an example of their work, a search of more than half a million driving-licence application forms would have found a match with the Panther's distinctive handwriting, samples of which were found in the abandoned car. But it was hard, slow graft. In those days police files were not computerized and everything had to be checked by hand. Everyone on the murder team, headed by Commander John Morrison from Scotland Yard, worked at least fourteen hours a day.

One major handicap for the police was that, although the Panther had been a criminal for some years before turning to murder and kidnapping, he had no police record.

A fingerprint found at the scene of Lesley's death was of no help to the police in finding her killer: a team of Scotland Yard officers compared it manually with ten million fingerprints that they had on file, without results.

The Panther was a loner with no contacts with other criminals – there was nobody who could give information about him.

In the end it was a chance stroke of luck – and the incredible bravery of two young police constables – that landed him in the dock and hastened the end of the investigation.

It was eleven months after Lesley was kidnapped that two police constables, Stuart McKenzie and Anthony White, were driving through Mansfield, Nottinghamshire, at 11pm when they spotted a man carrying a holdall. There was a sub-post office nearby. When they stopped to question the man he told them he was a lorry driver on his way home. When they asked to see inside the bag he bent down to open it – and snatched a shotgun which he turned on them.

He ordered the two constables back to the car and sat

in the front, next to PC McKenzie, with the gun pointing into the policeman's ribs; PC White was ordered to crouch in the back. He told McKenzie to drive to Blidworth, a village eight miles away.

For five and a half miles the two constables tried to keep their captor talking while signalling to each other with their eyes in the mirror. Suddenly, McKenzie slammed on the brakes and White made a grab for the gun. He was shot in the hand but managed to hold on to the man while McKenzie ran round to the passenger side, calling for help from bystanders who were queuing at a fish-and-chip shop.

The public were quick to respond: they pulled the gunman from the car, the gun was wrested from him and one man felled him with a karate chop. He was handcuffed to railings and the two police constables had to hold back the angry crowd who were trying to beat him.

The gunman's true identity was discovered at the police station and he admitted that he was the Black Panther, although he pleaded that his wife and daughter should not be told. His name was Donald Neilson and he was an outwardly respectable thirty-eight-year-old family man, with a wife Irene and a teenage daughter Kathy.

Police raided his home in Bradford that night and, in a locked attic room, they found eight hoods, several dark-coloured track suits, wire identical to that used to hang Lesley Whittle, a Dymo tape dispenser, a professional burglar's kit, and a selection of books on crime, the SAS and the Commandos. Underneath the floorboards were two shotguns and hundreds of rounds of ammunition.

Neilson turned to crime after a succession of business ventures went wrong; he ran a carpentry business, a taxi business, a firm making greenhouses. When they failed he took to robbing post offices, telling his victims that he 'only wanted government money' which, to his distorted morality, was better than stealing from individuals.

Although he never escaped with large amounts of money, the robberies were carried out carefully. Neilson would leave his wife Irene and teenage daughter Kathy, saying that he was going out on a carpentry job. He would wear normal clothes and carry a bag that they assumed contained his tools.

In fact, the bag contained his 'uniform' of a black hood with slits for the eyes, black tracksuit, white gloves. It also contained a hand drill that he used to open windows and a sawn-off shotgun.

Neilson had acquired a whole armoury of guns and ammunition by breaking into the home of an arms dealer whose name and address he had found in a magazine about guns.

The Panther's crimes were meticulously planned. Whenever he was out on the prowl he wore clothes that had been washed in disinfectant, to throw tracker dogs off his scent. He carried survival rations so that, if necessary, he could live rough. And he used trains for getaways, knowing that the police would expect him to have a vehicle.

Although he was probably raiding post offices from 1969, it was 1974 when he first killed. He broke into the sub-post office at New Park, Harrogate in Yorkshire, and woke the postmaster's eighteen-year-old son Richard. He demanded to know where the keys to the safe were kept.

When he failed to find them he tied up Richard and taped his mouth, then went to his parents' bedroom. He woke fifty-four-year-old Donald Skepper by shining a pencil torch, that was strapped to the barrel of the shotgun, in his face.

Mr Skepper shouted, 'Let's get him', and was instantly gunned down, dying shortly afterwards in his wife's arms. The Panther escaped empty-handed.

Seven months later another sub-post office was broken into, this time at Higher Baxenden, Accrington, Lancashire. Neilson climbed in through the bedroom window of fourteen-year-old Susan Astin who screamed when she saw him. Her forty-four-year-old father rushed to her aid and was shot first in the shoulder and then in the back. Although dying from his wounds Derek Astin managed to push the raider downstairs. The gunman sprang to his feet and shot again, this time using a .22 automatic pistol that hung from a cord around his neck.

Both these raids took place at 4 am and, in both cases, the gunman had drilled holes in the window frame to release the window catch.

The third murder happened in the early evening, at the sub-post office in Langley, Worcestershire. Postmaster Sidney Grayland and his wife Peggy were stocktaking when there was a knock at the door.

When Sidney opened it he was shot at pointblank range with a pistol. His wife ran out and was pistol-whipped around her head, tied up and dumped in a corner. Her injuries were so great that she nearly died. But, in the attack, the gunman's mask had been dislodged and Peggy was able to give the police a description of him: he was small in height, medium build, in his forties, clean shaven and with dark hair.

Detectives hunting the Panther built up more details

about him. He spoke in monosyllables, probably to disguise a strong northern accent (on one of his early raids he put on a West Indian accent). Although he killed ruthlessly, he was sometimes strangely compassionate and loosened his captives' bonds. He was always dressed in black, and his victims described him as walking agilely on the balls of his feet, like a PE instructor.

One detective said, 'I know everything about this man except his name, address and telephone number.'

But it was the kidnapping and murder of Lesley Whittle that turned the Panther from a vicious murderer and thief into the most wanted and hated man in Britain, – and brought Scotland Yard into the case.

Neilson read a newspaper report about the money left in George Whittle's will and planned a crime that he thought would finally end his financial problems. At his trial Neilson, whose real name was Nappey (he changed it after being teased at school and during national service), pleaded not guilty to four murders, claiming that, in the shootings, his gun had gone off accidentally and that Lesley Whittle had fallen from the ledge.

He was found guilty on all counts and was given four life sentences, and sixty-one years for the kidnapping.

After the case, Ronald Whittle praised Bob Booth:

'That man gave us 120% effort to try and get Lesley back,' he told the *News of the World.* He described how he and his mother felt when they saw Neilson on trial for the murder of his sister.

What sort of beast would do that to a quiet, innocent 17 year old with everything to live for and who had never done any harm to him or anyone else? My mother and I felt a cold rage when we heard him trying to deceive the jury with talk of 'goodies' and 'comforts' he gave to her while she was in captivity. There were many times when I could happily have leaped out of my seat and taken him by the throat.

The Panther was not the only person with whom Ron Whittle felt angry.

His exclusive story in the *News of the World* was headlined, 'I Accuse,' and told how he believed the police could have handled the case better and saved his sister's life. He also told how he believed that Neilson had no intention of letting him leave alive, if he had been able to pass on the ransom money. Most of all, he told of his family's anguish at losing Lesley. It was twelve months after Lesley's death that her murderer came to trial but, as Ron Whittle said,

The passage of time doesn't help. You just can't help thinking about it. I have become less efficient in business, and there is nothing I can do about it. I am not an emotional person . . . I didn't cry when I went to identify Lesley's body. But this doesn't mean I feel her death any the less.

19. *Brought to Justice by the* News of the World

It was an exciting time for twenty-four-year-old Alison Manwaring. She was setting up home with her boyfriend, Gordon Healis, and they were going to marry as soon as his divorce came through. They'd found a house they wanted to buy and that evening Alison had been measuring the windows for curtains. She was as happy as she had ever been as she hugged and kissed Gordon goodbye, and drove home to the house in Barking, Essex, where she lived with her sixty-two-year-old father Matthew.

The Manwarings were a contented, ordinary family. They had lived through the deep grief of Alison's mother's death from cancer, and there had been slight family friction when Alison first went out with Gordon, because he was black. But her father had quickly warmed to him and was delighted when the couple had announced their engagement.

Gordon expected to see Alison again the next morning; she picked him up every day to give him a lift to work. When she didn't turn up, he called around at the house. There was no reply. He went round several times that evening. Alison's car was not there and neither was the red Ford Escort Cabriolet that Alison's twenty-six-year-old brother Mark had left there. Mark, an RAF jet navigator serving in Cyprus, had asked his father to sell the car for him while he was away. Gordon contacted Barclays Bank where Alison worked. She had not been into work, nor had she called in to say why she was absent.

By the following day, a Saturday, Gordon was very alarmed. It was totally out of character for Alison to disappear without contacting him, and there was also no sign of her father, Matt, a retired bank messenger. With Matt's brother, Derek, he broke into the house.

'I found a letter to me from Alison. It didn't make sense when I read it,' said Gordon. 'We also noticed that the door frame had been damaged. I didn't sleep that night.'

The note, which Gordon desperately hoped was true, said, 'Gordon, Daddy and I have had to go away for a couple of days. Can't explain now. It's very important. See you soon. Love Alison.' Gordon hoped against hope that they would be home by Sunday evening for Alison to go to work on Monday. But, by Sunday afternoon, he and another of Matt's brothers were so worried that they collected together photographs of Alison and her father and went to the police. The next day, with the couple still missing, Gordon found something at the house which changed the case from one of missing persons to something much more serious – he found bloodstains on the carpet. There were more bloodstains on an armchair and in the washing-machine where somebody had tried to wash an armchair cover; some items, including a collection of china, were missing.

Mark flew back from Cyprus and he and Gordon, numb with shock and bewilderment, spent the rest of the week desperately hoping that Matt and Alison had only been kidnapped and would be returned to them safe and well. In those horrific days Mark and Gordon both turned to the *News of the World* for help. The newspaper offered a £25,000 reward, printed 10,000 posters that Mark and Gordon distributed, and two reporters, David Rigby and Gary Jones, spent hours with the two men, helping them deal with the added trauma of finding themselves in the media spotlight. It was the determination of the paper to do something practical to help – under the slogan, 'Don't Let the Bad Guys Win' – that impressed Mark and Gordon. In the words of Detective Superintendent Mike Morgan, who was heading the case, '£25,000 can loosen a lot of tongues.'

On the Thursday a letter arrived, addressed to Mark; it was typewritten and pretended to be from Alison. It claimed that she had had to go away, and revealed details of her private life (including an abortion, which her brother did not know). It also claimed that their father, a gentle and well-loved man who was blind in one eye, had been drinking heavily. The intention was to make Mark and the rest of the family believe that Alison and Matt had disappeared because of their problems. Mark later said he believed that there would have been more letters, building up a picture of a desperately unhappy pair, who, ultimately, would have decided to commit suicide.

But before any more were delivered, the tongues started to loosen, the police received phone calls, and on the Saturday evening the bodies of Alison and Matthew Manwaring were found. They had been savagely murdered: Matt had been blasted with a shotgun and Alison had been tortured, sexually assaulted and strangled; their bodies had been dismembered and buried in black dustbin bags in a garden in Abbey Wood, south-east London. Benjamin Laing, a twenty-four-year-old driver, was under arrest (he admitted selling Mark's car) and it was in his girlfriend's garden that the bodies were found.

For Gordon Healis, who had survived the week on desperate hope, it was 'the day my life ended'.

'It was to have been the happiest day of my life, Alison and I were moving into our new house. It was her 25th birthday. We should have been having a quiet drink together to celebrate. Instead, I was told she was dead.'

It was just as traumatic for Mark. After Laing was sentenced at the Old Bailey in April 1993 to a minimum twenty-five years jail for murdering his father and sister, Mark told the *News of the World*:

It may be a small thing, but I remember seeing my father's driving licence, ripped into eight pieces and thrown into a bin bag. I thought 'That was a clean licence my father had kept for forty years. And it was ripped up and put in a black plastic bag, just like my father's body.'

Laing walked into the lives of the Manwaring family when he answered an advert for the sale of Mark's car. He is a keep-fit enthusiast, half-Ghanaian and half-Scottish, and was brought up in Africa from early childhood until he was thirteen. His father, Kojo Laing, is a respected novelist and was a well-paid civil servant in the years that Laing and his mother, and five brothers and sisters lived in Ghana. Because of his father's job as a district commissioner, the family lived in isolated outposts of the country and young Benjamin was schooled in the laws of the jungle. He was taught to hunt game with a Winchester shotgun and butcher it for the larder and he could casually wring the neck of a chicken for the family table. He showed the same dispassionate disregard for life when, years later, he gunned down Matt Manwaring and strangled Alison.

When his parents separated Laing came to live in Britain. He was bright: he passed ten GCSEs and four A levels, but turned down the chance to go to university. He was already planning a life of crime. In 1987, disguised in a shaggy black wig and armed with an air pistol, he mugged a series of taxi drivers, threatening to blow their brains out if they did not hand over their takings. But he blundered by keeping the pistol and the wig in the boot of his car, and when he was stopped for speeding the police found the evidence. He was given six years' youth custody, but continued to protest his innocence.

On his release in 1991 he worked as a delivery driver for Selfridges but, before long, he turned back to crime. He needed money. He was living with twenty-eight-year-old Sharon Thompson and her two children, but he was a womanizer. He continued to need money for women and when he killed the Manwarings he had a date to take another girlfriend to Alton Towers two days later. He had no car and only £8 in the bank at the time – yet he coolly drove to the fun park in Mark Manwaring's £7750 red Cabriolet as though he had no cares in the world. Security video cameras showed him having a whale of a time on the fun-fair rides.

The crime was premeditated: he had approached three other people advertising cars for sale but had pulled out when, in each case, they turned out to be fit young men. He waited until he hit on 5′ 5″ tall, half-blind Matt Manwaring before putting his murder plan into operation. He had not expected Alison to arrive home but, when she did, he killed her, too, and then cleaned up the house, drove away and dumped her car. His brother, best friend, and girlfriend were later given conditional discharges for helping dispose of the gun.

Laing had researched the incidence of suicides in preparation for faking clues about his victims' disappearance. He had also written out a shopping list of disguises he would need, including a wig, specs, hair gel and contact lenses to change the colour of his eyes. He planned to use two different disguises, one when he appeared as the purchaser of the car and another when he sold it. His research was neatly handwritten in a blue exercise book found in his bedroom after his arrest, along with a magazine article about a death that had been put down to suicide, but might have been murder.

According to Mark Manwaring, Laing also made inquiries about hiring a mechanical digger for the day after he committed the crime, probably to help him bury the bodies. After killing the Manwarings he took Alison's diary and used the private information from it to write the letter to Mark. But Laing made major mistakes. He was recorded on security cameras trying to get money out of Mark Manwaring's building-society account, and he left his fingerprints on a bag containing personal property he stole from the Manwaring house. He was arrested after going to the police to admit that he had bought the car from the Manwarings and he concocted an amazing story that the killing had been carried out by Fijian terrorists. He claimed to have been gunrunning for the 'Fijian Freedom Fighters' whom, he said, must have followed him to the house in Barking. He said the terrorist group later showed him plastic bags containing the dismembered bodies which were then taken to his girlfriend's house for burial.

Mark Manwaring and Gordon Healis were both in court to see Laing sentenced to life imprisonment with a recommendation that he serve at least twenty-five years. With the help of a £20,000 donation from the *News of the World* they have set up the Manwaring Trust to help other victims of violent crime. Speaking of Laing, Mark said:

Laing committed the ultimate crime by taking my family from me. Then he continued with the ultimate insult in covering up what he'd done . . . Laing had an arrangement to go to Alton Towers but he had no car and no money. My father and sister were not even murdered for the price of a car. They were murdered because he needed a car to impress the girls and his mates and he robbed Alison's account to give his friends a good weekend. That so much was destroyed for so little is an insult to human life . . . He chose my car because it was easy to pick on a frail old man. I can't describe what it's like to be the victim of a crime like this. It eats you up.

In one of Benjamin Laing's father's novels, *Search Sweet Country*, there is a sentence, 'The God of your shrine asks you: Would you like a perfect soul or a brand new super-duper Mercedes Benz 450 automatic?' Benjamin Laing answered the question; he was prepared to trade two lives for a Ford Escort Cabriolet and a trip to Alton Towers.

It was nine o'clock on a Friday evening at the *News of the World* office, and crime reporter Gary Jones was thinking of finishing work for the day. He answered the telephone on his desk without much enthusiasm. The man's voice on the other end sounded like one of the crank callers who occasionally ring the newspaper. He told Gary that he had been offered money to kill someone and that, if the paper didn't pay him for his story, he might go ahead and do it.

'It's Friday night, mate, and I'm still in the office – I think I might just shoot somebody myself,' said Gary, wearily. But the man kept him talking and, after a few minutes, Gary found himself wondering if there was some truth in the story. But the caller refused to give his name or any details. Gary told him to ring back in half an hour if he was prepared to give his name.

'When he came back on he said he was sorry he had messed me about first time, but he really had been approached to kill someone, a woman. He told me he didn't believe in killing women. I was still very doubtful, but I arranged to meet him the next day,' said Gary. As he heard more details of the murder plot the following day, the crime reporter began to take the man more seriously. He checked him out: Ron Farebrother, a cousin of Barbara Windsor's ex-husband, Ronnie Knight, was everything he claimed to be. He had the contacts to make anyone believe he was a gangland contract killer, but he was genuinely horrified at the idea of being asked to murder a woman.

'You may hate your wife as much as you like – but you don't murder the mother of your kids,' he said.

At this first meeting Gary heard an outline of the plot. A previously wealthy businessman, whose property companies had been hit by the recession, wanted his wife 'accidentally' killed so that he could claim £560,000 insurance money. He had planned the hit; he wanted her knocked down by a lorry.

'I still thought this might be the wind-up of the century,' said Gary. 'Hitmen don't use cars. Contract killers don't stage road accidents. It also sounded implausible, but there was enough in it to make me want to carry on checking it out.'

The next step was for the 'hitman' to be wired up with a tape-recorder and sent to meet the businessman. Gary Jones and a photographer, Ed Henty (who was later to die in an IRA bomb attack on the City of London), followed and watched the meeting at East Croydon railway station on Saturday, 28 September 1991. The businessman, balding fifty-two-year-old Malcolm Stanfield, turned up driving a Jaguar XJS and took Farebrother to the plush Selsdon Park Hotel, about three miles away. There, over coffee and biscuits, he told Farebrother why and how he wanted his wife killed. Every word he said was recorded on the *News of the World* tape-recorder hidden under Farebrother's jacket.

'I want my wife taken out', said Stanfield.

'What do you mean, taken out for a meal or something?' said Farebrother.

'What I mean is taken out permanently – dead,' said Stanfield.

Five times Farebrother tried to persuade Stanfield to drop the plan, telling him that, even if his wife had been unfaithful, it wasn't sufficient reason to 'bump her off'. Stanfield explained that she had not been unfaithful, but that there was another woman in his life.

'But that's got nothing to do with it. I want it done for the insurance. The premiums are costing me a fortune so the sooner you do it, the better,' said Stanfield who had lost £110,000 in property deals and was being sued by a builder for £127,000. He picked up a sheet of the hotel's headed notepaper and sketched a map of how his wife, Lorraine, was to be killed in a hit-and-run accident.

'It's got to be done like an accident so that I get the insurance premium straightaway,' he said. The plan was for Lorraine to be mowed down outside the Bell pub in Outwood, Surrey.

'I'll get my wife to park some distance away so she has to cross this narrow country lane. Make sure it's a big truck, the bigger the better. Make sure you hit her full on – I don't want her knocked off the road.'

He put his wife's name and address – misspelling her first name as Lorrian – on the sketch plan and handed it to Farebrother. He also gave the 'hitman' a photograph of himself and his wife taken at a recent wedding reception, and a cheque for £30,000, to be cashed after the insurance payout. He then drove Farebrother back to the station where they had met.

Armed with evidence, Gary Jones contacted Scotland Yard's Regional Crime Squad.

I was still doubtful. I thought the two men could be in it together, trying to make money out of the *News of the World*. The detective who came to meet us at the Croydon Moat House Hotel was also inclined to be cynical. 'What's this load of bollocks?' were his first words to me. But, after hearing Ron Farebrother's story, he, too, felt there might be something in it, so it was arranged that Farebrother should take an undercover cop, known as George, to meet Stanfield.

'George' was introduced as the driver of the hit-and-run lorry and, after listening to Stanfield, he realized that it was a deadly serious murder plot. The plans were laid. Stanfield arranged for George to get a sighting of his wife when he took her to Drury Lane Theatre to see the musical, *Miss Saigon*; unknown to him, he was being watched by detectives who took photographs of him. Then the date for the murder bid was set for Saturday, 5 October.

Stanfield arranged to play golf on the Royal Ashdown Forest course, to give himself a cast-iron alibi. But he persuaded Lorraine, his wife for twenty-eight years, to meet him at the pub at 12.30pm so he could give her some cash to pay some bills. He persuaded her to park about half a mile away by telling her that he would be with a business acquaintance and he did not want the man to see his expensive car. This arrangement ensured that Lorraine would walk along the lane, which had no pavements, at the time the lorry was approaching.

It was while Stanfield was playing the fourteenth hole that his wife, and the mother of his three grown-up children, was to be killed. He hit a decent shot to the green and showed no flicker of emotion as he played out the hole. Unknown to him, a 'player' searching for a lost ball nearby was a detective, watching his movements. More detectives photographed Lorraine parking at the spot where her husband had told her to leave the car, and walking in pouring rain towards the pub. The lorry, a hired Leyland truck, drove towards her and she stepped out of the way. In the cab, detectives filmed her within a couple of feet of the wheels of the truck. There were no witnesses in the lane; if the hit had been real, Lorraine would have been killed.

After his game, Stanfield drove back to his £250,000 home. When, shortly afterwards, he opened the door to the police he played the worried husband.

'Is it Lorraine?' he asked. 'Is everything alright?'

The police asked him to go the station with them, without telling him any more. On the way Stanfield was the concerned, worried husband.

'Is it something awful?' he asked when he was taken into the police station.

'Well, if you think being arrested on a murder charge is awful, then yes,' he was told.

Lorraine Stanfield waited at the pub for her husband but, when he failed to show up, she left to return home. As she walked outside she was met by two detectives who told her of her lucky escape. She did not believe them. It was not until she met her husband in the police cells, and he admitted that he had tried to have her killed, that she accepted it.

Seven months later, Malcolm Stanfield came up at the Old Bailey and was sentenced to nine years in prison.

After the case, the police publicly thanked the *News of the World*. Detective Inspector Des Cook said:

'When we were first informed about this murder plot we believed it was almost too bizarre to be true. I'd like to thank the paper for its assistance in bringing Stanfield to justice. Your evidence was presented in a most professional manner.'

Lorraine Stanfield was still in a state of shock but she, too, thanked the *News of the World* and Ron Farebrother for saving her life:

I wouldn't be here if it wasn't for you. I am now changing my birthday to October 6th, the day after my husband intended me to die. I can't think why, after 28 years of marriage, he should think these awful things – and callously plan to kill me. I'm so relieved to think I'm alive when I wake up in the morning. I could so easily have been killed and lost the love of my children and grandchildren. To have lived with someone for so long then to discover he wanted you murdered is like having lived a farce of a marriage. I want to put this behind me, but I don't think life will ever be the same.

Ironically, from his cell Stanfield told his wife that he still loved her and did not want her to divorce him. For Gary Jones, meeting Lorraine Stanfield was the hardest part of the story:

'She is a lovely woman with a lovely family. I find it hard to believe that anyone can have wanted to have her killed. I'm very glad I listened to the "crank" caller.'

20. Victim in a Box

It was the biggest reward ever paid out by a British newspaper, and the *News of the World* was proud to hand it over to Susan Oake, the woman who shopped her former husband, kidnapper and murderer Michael Sams. When estate agent Stephanie Slater was abducted at knifepoint and a ransom of £175,000 demanded for her release, the newspaper put up a reward of the same sum for the capture of the evil criminal behind her ordeal.

It was a phone call from Susan, the mother of Sams's two grown-up sons, that put the police on to the man who had held Stephanie and who had also murdered eighteen-year-old prostitute Julie Dart. It was a phone call that took courage, and which Susan made without any thought of financial reward: when she dialled the number, she knew nothing of the *News of the World* offer. It was her courage that the paper was determined to reward.

The story of the ordeal of twenty-five-year-old estate agent Stephanie Slater at the hands of her kidnapper shocked the nation. It was on 22 January, 1992 that, as a routine part of her job for Shipways estate agents, she went to show a 'client' around an empty house in the Great Barr area of Birmingham, not far from her own home. Once inside the house the 'client', fifty-year-old Sams, disguised behind thick-rimmed glasses and with false warts glued to his face, turned nasty. Stephanie was bundled, blindfolded, into the passenger seat of his car, covered with a blanket and driven to his hideout, a workshop in Newark. To kill time, and make sure he arrived at the workshop under cover of darkness, Sams coolly spent a couple of hours trainspotting, with his terrified victim in the car next to him.

Stephanie was held for eight days, never setting eyes on her captor after her meeting with him at the Great Barr property. She was forced to sleep in a coffin-like box, which was made of chipboard and was wedged inside a large wheelie-bin, tipped onto its side: a 'box-in-a-box' as she later described it to police. Bricks on top of the bin weighted it down. There was just enough room for Stephanie to slide in, but she could not raise her head or turn over, and chains around her hands were threaded through a hole and secured outside the box with a heavy bar. Her ankles were also tied, and Sams told her that if she struggled she would bring rocks crashing down onto the box and be killed.

During her captivity he fed her on soup, porridge and Kit Kat chocolate bars, and she was forced to use a makeshift lavatory that he had constructed of a plank of wood over a bucket. She was allowed out of the box and could sit on a chair while Sams was at the workshop, but always wore a blindfold. Her astonishing stoicism saved her life: she remained calm and even managed to establish a relationship with her kidnapper. He kept her updated on the events of Coronation Street, her favourite TV soap, rubbed her hands to warm them up, and on one occasion gave her a comforting hug.

While holding Stephanie prisoner, Sams negotiated

with her bosses at Shipways for the payment of the ransom he demanded. Eventually, on 29 January, Stephanie's immediate boss Kevin Watts embarked on a nightmare journey to deliver the money. He drove in thick fog from phone box to phone box, picking up instructions and messages left for him on road cones as to where to take the money. His radio link with police failed, and yet despite the weather and the appalling risks he was running he left the money, as directed, on a disused railway viaduct near Barnsley. Unknown to him, Sams was waiting below to haul the cash, placed on a tray, to the ground, and to make his getaway on a scooter. Kevin Watts shared with Stephanie Slater a quiet, unemotional courage which enabled both of them to survive when many others would have cracked up.

For Stephanie, the final day of her captivity was the worst. Knowing that she was going to be confined in her coffin-prison the whole of the day while he was carrying out the ransom run, Sams allowed her to sleep the night before on a mattress on the floor of the workshop. He stayed with her that night, and the following morning locked her into the box again. Because of the appalling weather and the hold-ups, she was confined for so long that she was convinced that she would be left in there to die: that her abductor had deliberately abandoned her, or that his plans had gone wrong and he had either been arrested or forced to flee. She was relieved when he finally returned, made her change into her own clothing (he had given her men's trousers and sweaters to wear during her captivity) and drove her, still blindfolded, to within a few hundred yards of her own home. Stephanie had extracted a promise from him that he would take her as close to home as he could, a promise which Sams later said had made him change his original plans for her release, and which meant that he obviously ran a much greater risk of being caught.

It was three weeks after Stephanie's release that Sams, who was dubbed The Ransom Ripper, was trapped. His first wife Susan asked one of her sons to video the BBC Crimewatch programme, which she knew would include a taped recording of the kidnapper's voice, made when he was negotiating the ransom. She knew instantly, when she heard it, that it was the husband she had split from in 1975.

'I couldn't believe my ears,' Sue, who was forty-eight at the time, told the *News of the World*. 'I expected to hear a stranger's voice. I remember screaming "It's him! It's him! Oh God! It's him!" . . . The more I could hear the more I knew it was him. I just knew I had to ring the police. Loyalty doesn't come into it. I couldn't have lived with myself if I hadn't rung.'

Despite that conviction, Sue Oake worried as she made the call that she was betraying her two sons, Robert and Charles, both in their early twenties. But both of them agreed with what she did: 'Wrong is wrong. It doesn't make any difference that he's my dad,' said Charles.

Even before his arrest, police had connected the kidnapper of Stephanie with the murderer of Leeds vice girl Julie Dart, whose body was found near a disused railway line in Lincolnshire. After Sams was in custody, a full picture of his criminal ambitions emerged – he wanted to be more famous than the Black Panther (Donald Neilson – see Chapter 17) and to pull off the 'perfect' crime.

Sams was born in Keighley, Yorkshire, in 1941, the product of a wartime affair his mother had while her husband, Ted Sams, was abroad. His natural father was George Benniman, and after his mother's marriage to Ted Sams broke up ten years later, 'Benniman' was added to his name. Although it was not explained, Sams and his younger brother John knew they had different fathers. His mother remarried and he acquired another step-father. He was a bright boy, sailing through his eleven-plus and doing well at grammar school, where he passed eleven 'O' levels and one 'A' level GCEs despite the dyslexia which made reading, spelling and punctuation difficult for him. (This was a noticeable feature of his ransom demands. The police believed they had been deliberately misspelled to confuse them.)

After leaving school at eighteen, Sams set up a success-ful central-heating and double-glazing company, running the business well enough to be able at one time to employ six other people. He met his first wife Sue when he worked on the installation of a lift at the mill where she worked as a laboratory assistant. They married in 1964, and Sue gave birth to Robert four years later and Charles two years after that. To friends and neighbours they appeared a happy family: Sams was prosperous, they lived in a five-bedroomed house, and had foreign holidays every year.

But ten years after their wedding Sams's personality changed, and Sue found herself married to a cruel and obsessive man. He was occasionally violent towards her, blacking her eye and making her nose bleed, but the cruelty was more consistently mental.

'He pulled everything I did to bits – my clothes, my telephone manner, the way I brought up the kids. He once told me that it was his intention to deliberately make me have a breakdown.'

He threatened to kill her, and he appeared to get his greatest sexual kicks when he simulated raping her – attacking her unexpectedly and pinning her to the floor. He also, chillingly, talked constantly about committing 'the perfect crime', although he never specified what it would be. As his marriage foundered, so did his business. Sams became convinced that his wife had had an affair with a policeman, and this was the first fuel for the hatred he would develop for the police.

By the mid-seventies he was involved on the fringes of crime, enjoying mixing with criminals who were in a bigger league than he was. When he was arrested for his part in a car-ringing operation – stealing cars and changing all their identification marks – he cooperated with the police and named his accomplices. While he was awaiting trial his house was firebombed, probably as a revenge attack, and Sams blamed the police for not protecting him better. It was while he was carrying out repairs to the building that he fell from a ladder and damaged his right leg. In prison, where he was serving a nine-month sentence, a malignant tumour was discovered in his knee, and his right leg was amputated. Sams's hatred of authority increased, because he believed that his leg could have been saved if the tumour had been diagnosed earlier.

It was in prison that he began seriously to plan his perfect crime, which had now taken shape in his head as a kidnapping. He had noted the awe in which the Black Panther was held by fellow inmates, and started to harbour plans of carrying out a similar – but successful –

abduction. He met his second wife Jane through a lonely hearts advertisement before he went to jail for the car crime, and she stood by him during his sentence and during his convalescence from the leg amputation. They married four months after the operation, Sams on crutches. But the marriage was unhappy from the start, and within three years they were living apart.

During the marriage the couple moved to Leeds, and Sams worked for Black and Decker, the power tool company. He was eventually given a redundancy payment, and used the money to set up his own tool repair company in Peterborough. He married for a third time, again finding his bride from a lonely hearts advertisement. Teena, his wife, had also been married twice before, and was reeling emotionally from the death of her teenage son.

It was in mid-1990 that Sams moved into the Newark workshop. He and Teena lived in a nearby village, in an attractive whitewashed cottage next to a railway line: Sams has had a lifelong interest in trains and train-spotting, and wherever he has lived has kept a large model train layout. By April 1991 he was in financial difficulties, falling behind with his mortgage payments and illegally claiming state benefits. Against this background his third marriage was falling apart, with Teena threatening to pack her bags and go.

It was at this time that the vaguely-formed plans for a perfect kidnap began to crystallize. In his gloomy workshop he started to log his plans onto his computer, working out ways to disguise his looks and change the appearance of his car. He fashioned wooden panels to block out the rear windows and make it look like a van, and on these he painted 'Cracked and Broken Drains', with a mobile phone number. He added a roof rack and drain rods to complete the transformation.

At this stage he was still not clear whether he would kidnap a prostitute or an estate agent, although he may have regarded the prostitute as a trial run for the 'real' thing with the estate agent. He built the coffin-box in which he planned to hold his victim captive, and then attempted to abduct a Leeds prostitute called Mary. She managed to escape.

His next victim was to be an estate agent from Crewe, and he went to considerable lengths to research the woman and her movements. However, when he turned up at the empty property where he had arranged to meet her she was late, and he was approached by a builder working nearby, who spoke to him about his 'plumbing' company. Afraid that the builder would be able to identify him, Sams aborted his plans.

He returned to the idea of kidnapping a prostitute, and on 9 July, 1991 he picked up Julie Dart, a pretty eighteen-year-old who was new to the 'game' and was doing it to pay off her debts. Police believe that she was imprisoned in the same box that was later to be Stephanie Slater's home for eight days. Sams had an infra-red sensor in his workshop to detect movement, and it was connected so that its pulse would trigger the phone at his cottage. Some time during her first night of captivity Julie, who was known to be claustrophobic, must have tried to escape, triggered the alarm, and sent Sams racing on the twenty-minute drive to his workshop. He killed Julie, and put her naked body into a wheelie-bin.

The summer heat caused her to decompose rapidly, and Sams dumped her, trussed in a pink-and-white sheet, in a field. It was ten days before she was discovered. In the meantime, Sams had demanded £145,000 from the police for her release. He continued to send letters to Leeds police for the following three months, always careful to leave no clues on the paper or envelope (he wore rubber gloves and stuck the envelopes down with tap water).

In October 1991, frustrated by his lack of success, he made a new set of ransom demands, this time from British Rail. He threatened to derail a train if they did not pay him £200,000, and went so far as to suspend a concrete block from an isolated bridge over a busy main-line track, with trains passing below every ten minutes. But this plan, like the others, failed and he did not collect any money. The perfect crime was not working out perfectly, but Sams was not prepared to quit.

Stephanie Slater became his next victim. With his hair coloured and his complexion changed with makeup, he went into the Shipways branch where she worked, and arranged to meet her at the empty house he had already researched. This time, his plan appeared to have worked: he escaped with the £175,000, which he hid near to the site where Julie Dart's body had been found, and Stephanie was released physically unhurt.

But despite the care that he took, the Ransom Ripper had left behind him a vital clue, the sound of his own voice on tape. Perhaps he had reckoned without the courage of Sue Oake, his first wife, who was willing to contact police with her suspicions the minute she heard the broadcast.

Police who arrested the small, one-legged criminal were astonished: they had expected a strong, fit man. The ransom trail, laid with such care and precision, had left them believing that they were dealing with a rugged SAS-type. When the original tip-off came in, and Sue told them that her ex-husband only had one leg, they feared they were going after the wrong man.

'I went to get Britain's public enemy Number One, and found a shambling one-legged trainspotter' said Detective Sergeant Tim Grogan, who made the arrest. Yet when he and other officers arrived at Sams's cottage they found so many things that fitted; they knew the man they were looking for was a trainspotter, they knew he had a computer, they knew that a fish-food container had been used in one of his ransom demands, and Sams had an aquarium. When they drove to his workshop, the route matched the description that Stephanie had been able to give them, despite the fact that she was blind-folded at the time. And when they arrived at the work-shop Sams had his radio tuned to Radio Two, just as Stephanie had said it had been during her captivity.

After Sams's arrest he admitted kidnapping Stephanie, but denied murdering Julie Dart. Careful detective work provided the court with evidence linking him to Julie's death: the dog hairs on the sheet used to wrap her body matched his two pet dogs; fibres on the sheet matched an old carpet from his workshop; envelopes used in the ransom demands were found to have a tiny defect, and others with the same defect were found at his home; two hairs found at the workshop matched Julie's, and bloodstains in the workshop matched Julie's rare blood group. Crucially, computer disks that Sams had wiped were able to be treated by experts to bring up the deleted files, revealing Sams's plans for kidnapping Julie and Stephanie, as well as his British Rail ransom plot.

Despite his defence that a 'friend' of his had abducted and murdered Julie, using his computer and his workshop for the crime, the jury found Sams guilty on 8 July, 1993, almost two years to the day from Julie's disappearance. He was given four life sentences: one for each kidnapping, one for murdering Julie and one for imprisoning Stephanie. He was also given ten years for the British Rail ransom demand.

Three days later he confessed to the murder of Julie Dart.

In prison while on remand, Sams wrote his own 182-page account of his crimes, extracts from which were published exclusively in the *News of the World*, by reporter Greg Miskiw. Sams told how he had tested whether Stephanie trusted him by telling her he was going to have sex with her.

'Stephanie's face did not change. She just said "No, I don't think I'd like that, thanks." I held her hands and kissed them. "Thanks," I said. "Anything other than that reply and I would have known that you were frightened of me and therefore didn't trust me." '

It was a terrifying torture game he was playing with his young victim, and there is no doubt in the minds of any of the police who have since had dealings with him that he would have killed her as easily as he killed Julie Dart had she not instinctively known the rules by which to play. She answered him truthfully when he asked her to describe what she had seen of him when they first met at the empty property, even telling him that she had noticed his limp. He had been desperate to find out if she knew he had only one leg – whenever he had any physical contact with her he was at pains to make sure she did not touch it, but he was afraid she might have noticed, when he guided her about the place with her hands on his shoulders, that he wore a shoulder strap which was securing his artificial limb.

He also tested her obedience by telling her that he was leaving the workshop, closing the door, but standing inside silently watching her. When she did not attempt to remove the blindfold he believed he could trust her.

He wrote about a terrible dream which he claimed turned him from a cold, calculating potential killer into a loving, caring father figure for Stephanie:

'It was in the early hours of the morning that I woke crying after a dream. I dreamed I had killed her accidentally. It was from then on that I knew I could never have harmed her. My tone, manner and actions must have shown a marked difference to Stephanie, my first being to alter the hide to make her warm and comfortable . . . She became my daughter and her actions were those of a young child thrust into an unknown world and desperately needing reassurance from her kidnapper dad. As the week wore on my dreams increased. All physical contact with my wife stopped, generally going to bed at different times . . . Whatever had gone wrong would not have mattered, she would have gone home.'

Sams's obvious affection for his victim will fascinate forensic psychiatrists for years to come. In court he was keen to make the most of his gentle treatment of her, and to put as much distance as possible between the cold-hearted, callous murder of Julie Dart and the sympathy and kindness he showed Stephanie. Experts are used to the syndrome in which victims become emotionally dependent on their captors, and Sams himself had been watching for this to happen in Stephanie's case. He even persuaded himself that it had done so. But it was he, the aggressor, who was in fact being subsumed by the gentle, unemotional personality of the victim. Stephanie Slater was clear from the moment of her release that she felt no affection or liking for the man who had held her.

Since her ordeal she has been unable to return to work – she tried, briefly, but could not stand the pressure of the job. She has become reclusive, but friends and family hope that, with the ordeal of the court case, at which she had to give lengthy evidence, over, and Sams imprisoned indefinitely, she will be able to rebuild her life.

Sams himself has stayed in contact with his third wife, Teena. Her original plan to divorce him has not been dropped.